COURTS, LITIGANTS, AND THE DIGITAL AGE

COURTS, LITIGANTS, AND THE DIGITAL AGE

LAW, ETHICS, AND PRACTICE

Second edition

Karen Eltis
University of Ottawa
Columbia Law School

IRWIN LAW

Courts, Litigants, and the Digital Age: Law, Ethics, and Practice

Published in 2016 by

Irwin Law Inc.
14 Duncan Street
Suite 206
Toronto, ON
M5H 3G8

www.irwinlaw.com

ISBN: 978-1-55221-420-6
e-book ISBN: 978-1-55221-421-3

Library and Archives Canada Cataloguing in Publication

Eltis, Karen, author
Courts, litigants, and the digital age : law, ethics, and practice / Karen Eltis, University of Ottawa, Columbia Law School. — Second edition.

Includes bibliographical references and index.
Issued in print and electronic formats.
ISBN 978-1-55221-420-6 (paperback).—ISBN 978-1-55221-421-3 (pdf)

1. Judicial ethics. 2. Judicial process. 3. Privacy, Right of. 4. Technology and law. 5. Court records—Access control. I. Title.

K2146.E48 2016 347'.014 C2016-901445-2
C2016-901446-0

Canada
Ontario
Ontario Media Development Corporation
Société de développement de l'industrie des médias de l'Ontario

Printed and bound by CPI Group (UK) Ltd, Croydon, CR0 4YY

1 2 3 4 5 20 19 18 17 16

Contents

Acknowledgements

I would like to thank my husband, Rony Greenberg, for his encouragement, illumination, and very important insight leading up to this book and beyond. Our son, Daniel, and daughter, Tali-Myriam, bring me immeasurable joy and inspire me anew every day as no one else can. I thank them for the most precious gift of all.

I express my deepest gratitude to the Honourable Professor Irwin Cotler and to Dean Nathalie DesRosiers for their valuable guidance and encouragement early on and throughout the years, which has meant more to me than I can begin to say here, and without which this book (and much else) would not have been possible.

Special thanks to Brandon Silver and Laura Crestohl for their excellent research assistance, and to Gail Deutchman for her boundless energy, friendship, and much appreciated help. Sincere thanks to Alisa Posesorski and the Irwin Law team who worked tirelessly to bring this book to fruition.

Preface

A. RECENT AND IMMINENT NORMATIVE CHANGE IN THE PRIVACY SPHERE SINCE 2012

To speak of Internet law (or cyber law) generally, and privacy law more particularly, is to speak of a changing normative landscape, shifting under our feet.

While still in its relative infancy, privacy law, or "Internet law" more broadly, has been steadily and rapidly developing since the first edition's publication in 2012. Where there was little definitive judicial resolution — or even discussion — of issues such as the recognition of (often intangible) privacy harm, freedom of digital speech (let alone computer code as speech), or the question of litigant anonymity when the first edition of this book was published, much has changed since, perhaps mirroring heightened social sensitivity to privacy breaches.

Whereas less than four years ago one was at pains to find examples of courts acknowledging losses arising from privacy breaches, the environment in the United States, and even more so in Canada, has changed dramatically. In the words of one commentator, "litigation and individual actions relating to privacy breaches in Canada are no longer just hypothetical, they are a new reality. The actions tend to involve disclosure of personal information through insecure disposal of records, theft and loss of unencrypted data on mobile devices, and unauthorized access to records."[1] This sentiment is equally true in the United States, as we breathlessly await

1 See more, online: http://greyswanadvisory.com/uncategorized/litigation-and-losses-mount-over-canadian-privacy-breaches/#sthash.nUOE9h6B.dpuf.

the Supreme Court's decision in *Spokeo, Inc v Robbins*[2] on privacy harm and perhaps, eventually, we will hear a judicial resolution of the Apple/FBI standoff.

B. PRIVACY AS AN ALLY OF ACCESS TO JUSTICE

Most notable for our purposes is the seminal case of *AB v Bragg Communications Inc*,[3] which signalled a retreat from the long-standing default — an unquestioned preference for the open court principle, notwithstanding the vicissitudes and peculiarities of the cyber-context. Instead, cognizant of the nuance that the digital age imports, the Supreme Court of Canada allowed an adolescent to proceed anonymously with a request that an Internet Service Provider (ISP) release the identity of the creator of a fake Facebook account, which included various explicit and disturbing sexual references. Importantly, and with broad ramifications, the Supreme Court presumed harm based on the circumstances, recognizing intangible privacy harms to vulnerable groups in particular and using these as a basis for allowing AB to procede anonymously in her legal action.

This landmark recognition of the relationship between protecting litigant privacy and access to justice is an important starting point. Accordingly, in Chapter 3, this book investigates the next steps to be considered as a logical outgrowth of the *Bragg* decision, inspired by comparative inquiry. It argues that a contextualized understanding of privacy, which recreates some of the "brick and mortar" safeguards historically associated with court documents, is desirable. Thus, for instance, only "meaningful data" is unleashed online following a qualitative triage aimed at holding back superfluous (however potentially harmful) sensitive information that is not reasonably connected to the underlying rationale of the open court principle. This demonstrates that there is finally cognizance of the vicissitudes of the networked environment. For if we rethink privacy within the cyber context, it can be considered an ally of access to justice.

The courts' tendency to protect litigant confidentiality in the digital age has continued since. Thus, for instance, the Federal Court of Canada has seen fit to certify a medical marijuana class action against Health Canada (the first in Canada to certify under the novel tort of "public disclosure of private facts"), notably allowing the plaintiffs to file under pseudonyms.[4]

---

2 Argued 2 November 2015.

3 2012 SCC 46.

4 *John Doe v Canada*, 2015 FC 916.

So too again in *Jane Doe 464533 v ND*,[5] where the Ontario Superior Court of Justice issued its decision (recognizing a new privacy tort) bearing a public restriction notice, redacting and anonymizing its decision to protect the confidentiality of the parties.

C. PROPORTIONALITY

The obvious overlap between personal and professional data (as in the now-infamous Ashley Madison scandal), encryption, and quasi-ubiquitous surveillance (as in the Apple/FBI dispute) render the classic "reasonable expectation" standard somewhat obsolete, or at least unhelpful in articulating and enforcing privacy rights and duties. Assessing an individual's right to privacy by reference to society's conception of the measure of privacy that one is entitled to reasonably expect is particularly awkward when such expectations are rapidly eroding, precisely by reason of eventual social habituation to recurring intrusions.

Despite the apparent distinctiveness of these cases (and many others), revisited in unison, they herald the emergence of a far more robust and nuanced conception of privacy. It is a conception predicated on proportionality, as the Ontario Superior Court of Justice wisely opined in *R v Rogers Communications*,[6] rather than the essentially tautological reasonable expectations standard.

This very principle of proportionality and balancing of competing interests should in turn be harnessed with an eye towards resolving the current Apple/FBI privacy impasse, and others like it that are sure to follow.

---

5 2016 ONSC 541.

6 2016 ONSC 70.

Introduction

The one thing [the victorious plaintiff] Costeja did not want us to know about him is now the only thing the entire world knows about him.
— Comedian John Oliver regarding the unintended consequences of Costeja's win before the European Court of Justice in 2014

A. INTRODUCTION

Technology plays an incontrovertibly central role in contemporary judicial work and lives, both on and off the bench. Along with tremendous benefits, it imports substantial new challenges that increasingly have an impact on courts, litigants, and professional ethics in the broader sense. And yet, notwithstanding its growing relevance, the question of technology's ramifications for the courts more generally and for judges in particular has thus far evaded scholarly inquiry almost entirely, leaving courts (for the most part) with little choice but to attempt to fit new technologies into outdated regimes and practices, devised for outdated tools.[1] So, too, has technology left judges perplexed regarding expected conduct,

1 As will be demonstrated in the following chapters. In a different context, see Daniel J Solove, "Panel VI: The Coexistence of Privacy and Security: Fourth Amendment Codification and Professor Kerr's Misguided Call for Judicial Deference" (2005) 74 *Fordham Law Review* 747 at 773, observing that "many judicial misunderstandings stem from courts trying to fit new technologies into old statutory regimes built around old technologies. The problem with the statutes is that, when they try to track existing technology too closely, they become too rule-like and lose the flexibility of a standard. Basic principles get lost or forgotten in the shuffle of technicalities."

as rule makers, judicial conferences, and ethics councils struggle to keep pace with innovation and technology's staggering advances.[2] As the Supreme Court of Canada remarked in the recent decision in *R v Spencer*, "relevant provisions [of the existing normative framework] provide little assistance in evaluating the reasonableness of [the accused's] expectation of privacy."[3] Although decided in a criminal context, the Court's observations are indeed telling not only with respect to the dearth of guidance emanating from the normative framework now in place but perhaps even more so with a simple, albeit powerful recognition regarding the notion of a "reasonable expectation of privacy." Privacy, the Court opined, "also includes the related but wider notion of *control* over, access to and use of information."[4] The latter view of privacy in the digital age significantly focuses on self-actualization and individual evolution, which anonymity is said — but not without controversy — to facilitate.[5]

More often than not, efforts at elucidating the nature of privacy and its affiliation to the governing framework in the justice setting specifically give rise to nebulous or conflicting guidelines at best, or silence at worse. In turn, ad hoc responses are prompted in an area where predictability and stability are key.

What then must we do? The first step is for courts (and justice system actors more generally) to *identify* the issues that technology — and particularly the Internet — raise for privacy and beyond, in order to increase understanding and allow for informed decision making. Second, we must revisit and, in some cases, rethink conventional paradigms that, at times, fail to satisfactorily address the intricate issues raised by technological advances, in the judicial context.

The underlying premise of what follows, it must be emphasized, is not to *exclude* judges from the Internet revolution, but rather to harness technology, cautiously and thoughtfully, towards the administration of justice. Justice must be not only efficient as the impulse or end-goal tends to be whenever technology is involved, but also mindful of the intricate competing interests that must be carefully exposed, balanced, and taken into

2 In an area where dearth of guidance is characteristic. See, for example, Adam Dodek, "Help Wanted: A Judicial Code of Conduct" *Law Times* (25 February 2008).

3 2014 SCC 43 at para 55 [*Spencer*].

4 *Ibid* at para 40 [emphasis added]. Reminiscent of the German approach discussed below.

5 As Cromwell J remarks in *Spencer*, above note 3 at para 48, citing Doherty JA's reasoning in *R v Ward*, 2012 ONCA 660 at paras 71 and 75.

sober account. Most important, justice needs to be achieved (at least in part) by taking what are often simple, yet attentive precautions aimed at avoiding the sort of inadvertent glitches that risk its being brought into disrepute. A particularly regrettable example is how the Internet, broadly speaking, increasingly chills access to justice — at times prompting premature or even extorted settlement, for fear of permanent exposure of intimate or misleading personal details.

In truth, fear of the courts' inability to protect the privacy of litigants or witnesses can surely dissuade participation in the justice system for society's most vulnerable. It can ultimately frustrate access to justice in an era of infinite cyber memory, where mistakes are less easily remedied, as the Supreme Court of Canada has now recognized in the landmark case of *AB v Bragg Communications Inc*[6] (discussed in Chapter 3).

B. WHY SHOULD COURTS CARE?

A recurring question in this context is this: How might the Internet differ from past or sister mediums, and why might this prompt revisiting or even reinterpreting existing rules? In the broader context, and to better situate the discussion, consider the following example incarnating what the UK newspaper *The Guardian* labelled the Internet's "law of unintended consequences" or "a memorable fight over the right to be forgotten."[7] It involves a Spanish attorney's battle with Google over his reputation and the arguably changing meaning of accuracy of information and freedom of expression in the digital age.

Mario Costeja González, the man in question, was alarmed upon finding that a piece published in 1998 recounted the repossession of his home to pay off certain debts: facts that he did not want exposed. The piece, featuring what he considered to be embarrassing financial woes, prominently surfaced among the Google results associated with his name. In effect, the mere mention of his name online, he argued, became synonymous with debt, by reason of the debt-related story appearing first and dramatically overshadowing (even overwhelming) any other presumably relevant — and more recent — information relating to him. Accordingly, his professional persona — and, indeed, identity (online and therefore offline) — he

6 2012 SCC 46.

7 James Ball, "Costeja González and a Memorable Fight for the 'Right to Be Forgotten'" *The Guardian* (14 May 2014), online: www.theguardian.com/world/blog/2014/may/14/mario-costeja-gonzalez-fight-right-forgotten.

submitted, had been tainted and possibly reduced to what he contends is an isolated incident.

This story is reminiscent of an earlier such incident involving another Spaniard, a physician named Hugo Guidotti Russo, who more than twenty-five years ago had a widely covered dispute with one of his patients over an allegedly botched breast surgery.[8] The physician has since, the argument goes, practised successfully. Still and again, the mere mention of his name in cyberspace (the first "go to" destination for many patients and potential employers) produces graphic reporting of his supposedly botched work, thus presumably dissuading all but the (rare) most dedicated and meticulous searchers, who would take pains to go beyond these headlines, from associating with the good doctor. Even if that is not the case and we concede for the purpose of argument that Dr. Russo was negligent at the time, what the cyber search provides is a *decontextualized and fragmented* version of his career and professional identity, something due to the hierarchical nature of search engine results, where the searches are not listed chronologically and otherwise pertinent factors are not heavily weighted.

For our purposes and somewhat surprisingly, it was Costeja's case (rather than Dr. Russo's)[9] that was eventually decided by the European Court of Justice, leading to a significant and much-debated European ruling on online personal data — and on the so-called right to be forgotten on the Internet.[10]

---

8 Paul Sonne, Max Colchester, & David Roman, "Plastic Surgeon and Net's Memory Figure in Google Face-off in Spain" *The Wall Street Journal* (7 March 2011), online: www.wsj.com/articles/SB100014240527487039215045760941307 93996412 [Sonne et al].

9 See, for example, Josh Halliday, "Europe's Highest Court to Rule on Google Privacy Battle in Spain" *The Guardian* (1 March 2011), online: www.theguardian.com/technology/2011/mar/01/google-spain-privacy-court-case.

10 *Google Spain SL, Google Inc v Agencia Española de Protección de Datos, Mario Costeja González* (13 May 2014), C-131/12 (ECJ Grand Chamber), online: Info Curia http://curia.europa.eu/juris/document/document.jsf?text=&docid=152065&pageIndex=0&doclang=EN&mode=req&dir=&occ=first&part=1&cid=129070 [*Costeja*]. In *Costeja*, the European Court of Justice held that by virtue of the "right to be forgotten" (as set out under art 12 of ECJ Directive), a search engine is under a duty to remove links to irrelevant and outdated information that is not in the public interest, upon individual request. On the "right to be forgotten" more generally, see, for example, Nathalie Mallet-Poujol, "Le droit à l'oubli numérique" (Paper delivered at an online conference, Université de Montréal, Montréal, Que, 8 February 2011) [Mallet-Poujol]. See also Karen Eltis, "Breaking Through the 'Tower of Babel': A 'Right to Be Forgotten' and

The ruling, subsequently confirmed and possibly extended by a French court in the Shefet case,[11] appears to compel search engines (most notably Google, which it deems a "data controller")[12] to remove links to certain impugned search results at the request of individual Europeans (and potentially by others beyond Europe's borders).[13] It so held by virtue of the contentious above-mentioned "right to be forgotten," recently enshrined in article 12 of the revised 1995 European Data Protection *Directive* 95/46/EC.[14] This provision was long impugned by American companies and jurists alike as signalling the "biggest threat to freedom of expression on the Internet in the coming decade."[15] Further complicating an already thorny situation which places the American construction of free expression (and US Internet giants that echo that view) at odds with the predominant continental vision of privacy is the European Court of Justice's failure to impart much-needed practical guidance for online erasure in *Costeja*. The decision therefore underscores the divisive character of "the right to be

---

How Trans-systemic Thinking Can Help Re-conceptualize Privacy Harm in the Age of Analytics" (2011) 22 *Fordham Intellectual Property, Media & Entertainment Law Journal* 69 [Eltis, "Breaking Through the 'Tower of Babel'"].

11 Dan Shefet sued Google in France to remove links to URLs relating to a "defamation campaign" against his law firm. Owen Bowcott & Kim Willsher, "Google's French Arm Faces Daily €1,000 Fines over Links to Defamatory Article" *The Guardian* (13 November 2014), online: www.theguardian.com/media/2014/nov/13/google-french-arm-fines-right-to-be-forgotten.

12 *Ibid.*

13 *Ibid.* As Bernal explains, only search results arising from a search under a particular name are removed. Neither the underlying source material nor the same (contentious) search results obtained when searched for in any other way are required to be removed. See, for example, Paul Bernal, "Is Google Undermining the 'Right to Be Forgotten'?" *CNN Opinion* (7 July 2014), online: www.cnn.com/2014/07/07/opinion/bernal-google-undermining-privacy-ruling/.

14 EC, *Directive 95/46/EC of the European Parliament and of the Council of 24 October 1995 on the protection of individuals with regard to the processing of personal data and on the free movement of such data*, [1995] OJ, L 281/31. See generally the address of Mallet-Poujol, above note 10 (arguing the need for "a right to be forgotten" in the context of the age of blogging and social networking, and ways of ensuring such a right); see also Natasha Singer, "Just Give Me the Right to Be Forgotten" *The New York Times* (21 August 2011) BU3, online: http://nyti.ms/1TD4yII.

15 See Jeffrey Rosen, "The Right to Be Forgotten" (2012) 64 *Stanford Law Review* 88, online: www.stanfordlawreview.org/online/privacy-paradox/right-to-be-forgotten. Many American scholars view this topic as the biggest threat to free speech on the Internet in the coming decade.

forgotten" across common law[16] and civilian lines, which now extends beyond the United States.[17] Thus, for instance, UK justice minister Simon Hughes vociferously pledged to oppose the *Costeja* decision, which he considered tantamount to censorship[18] not to mention unenforceable.[19] These comments coincide with Google itself restoring a number of links that it had initially suppressed[20] at the request of individual Europeans.[21] It did so after first disapproving of[22] and subsequently attempting to comply with *Costeja*,[23] presumably in an effort to placate its many European detractors.

---

16 Primarily Anglo-Saxon.

17 Sonne et al, above note 8.

18 "We have criticized the government of China . . . for closing down people's right to information. There are other countries with strict information access. It is not a good position for the EU to be in to look as if it is countenancing restrictions in the access of the citizen to access to information because it could be a very bad precedent." Stuart Lauchlan, "Britain Pledges to Fight Europe's Right to Be Forgotten Bad Law" *diginomica* (10 July 2014), online: http://diginomica.com/2014/07/10/britain-pledges-fight-europes-forgotten-bad-law/.

19 Hughes said:

> If politicians think they can delete findings about their expenses, that's not going to happen. If people think they can delete their criminal history, it won't occur. It looks to me as if it may be an unmanageable task. It will be a phenomenal task. It's not technically possible to remove all traces of data loaded on to the internet from other sources. You can't exercise the right to be forgotten. The information system could not be made to do it.

Owen Bowcott, "EU 'Right to Be Forgotten' Law Unenforceable, Says Justice Minister" *The Guardian* (9 July 2014), online: www.theguardian.com/technology/2014/jul/09/eu-right-to-be-forgotten-law-unenforceable-justice-minister-simon-hughes.

20 See, for example, "Google Restores Links to Some Media Articles It Erased" *CBC News* (4 July 2014), online: www.cbc.ca/news/business/google-restores-links-to-some-media-articles-it-erased-1.2696245.

21 These may be as pedestrian as some unhappy with online reports of a couple having sex on a train, a soccer referee's dismissal, or French office workers making Post-it art.

22 Rhiannon Williams, "Eric Schmidt: ECJ Struck Wrong Balance over Right to Be Forgotten" *The Telegraph* (15 May 2014), online: www.telegraph.co.uk/technology/google/10833257/Eric-Schmidt-ECJ-struck-wrong-balance-over-right-to-be-forgotten.html.

23 Google did so by releasing a web form (available online: https://support.google.com/legal/contact/lr_eudpa?product=websearch) to be filled out by Europeans invoking said right. It promised it would "assess each individual request and attempt to balance the privacy rights of the individual with the public's right

Telling for our purposes are the comments of Google's Peter Barron to *BBC News* that the company is "learning as we go."[24] Google and other such private entities are incomprehensibly saddled with the gargantuan task of determining how to "balance the need for transparency with the need to protect people's identities"[25] — a highly delicate and divisive assignment normally exclusively reserved for courts (especially constitutional courts) or policy makers. But in the absence of much-needed interpretive guidelines, the said "data controller" seems to have understandably, however lamentably, resorted to an ad hoc approach. Cryptically, the court in *Costejo* instructed Google to suppress links that are "inadequate, irrelevant or no longer relevant" and said little else other than that Google was to take the "public interest" — a fluid concept subject to differential interpretation in the United States and Europe respectively — into account.[26] As one online reputation management (ORM) firm executive remarked in reference to Google's replies to individual requests "to be forgotten": "no one really knows what the criteria [are] . . . . So far, we're getting a lot of noes . . . . It's a complete no man's land."[27] This is the situation despite the diligent effort of Google's legal counsel to outline the company's underlying thinking on this point.[28] But transparency and accountability are notoriously

---

to know and distribute information." See "Google Responds Promptly to ECJ Ruling on 'Right to Be Forgotten'" *Future of Privacy Forum* (30 May 2014), online: www.futureofprivacy.org/2014/05/30/google-responds-promptly-to-ecj-ruling-on-right-to-be-forgotten/. Google further established a panel of experts to aid in the process.

24 David Lee, "Google Reinstates 'Forgotten' Links after Pressure" *BBC News* (4 July 2014), online: www.bbc.com/news/technology-28157607.

25 *Ibid.*

26 At least to our knowledge (which itself raises questions of transparency and accountability), beyond the much-cited criteria of "inadequate," "irrelevant," and "no longer relevant," nothing else was proffered by the court by way of guidance.

27 Simon Wadsworth of the UK ORM firm Igniyte, referring to the ECJ's recent decision. Mark Scott, "European Companies See Opportunity in the 'Right to Be Forgotten'" *The New York Times* (8 July 2014), online: http://nyti.ms/1zosEfP.

28 See, for example, *inter alia*: Brice Dickson, *Judicial Activism in Common Law Supreme Courts* (Oxford: Oxford University Press, 2007). Google's chief legal officer said to *The Guardian*:

> When it comes to determining what's in the public interest, we're taking into account a number of factors. These include whether the information relates to a politician, celebrity or other public figure; if the material comes from a reputable news source, and how recent it is; whether it involves political speech; questions of professional conduct that might be relevant to

difficult to cultivate when balancing between what are delicate constitutional values that judges themselves struggle with in most democracies. Indeed, such balancing draws passionate censure and denunciation when performed by seasoned high court judges[29] with constitutional authority, *a fortiori* when this highly sensitive exercise is performed or attempted by inexperienced and reticent corporate actors, who are presumably lacking the requisite experience and legitimacy for deciding such matters in lieu of courts.

In a word, therefore, *Costeja*, which Jonathan Zittrain aptly labels a "bad solution to a very real problem,"[30] may inadvertently and ironically have the *effect* of appointing (chiefly American) "data controllers" as unwitting private censors: arbiters of the European public interest. What is more, the decision may be deemed a culmination of the growing divergence between Anglo-Saxon and continental approaches to privacy,[31] significantly extending beyond the United States, to the United Kingdom. In effect, as previously noted, the United Kingdom appears to be joining ranks with the United States in rejecting the "right to be forgotten," at least as set out by the European Court of Justice.

> consumers; the involvement of criminal convictions that are not yet "spent"; and if the information is being published by a government. But these will always be difficult and debatable judgments.

David Drummond, "We Need to Talk about the Right to Be Forgotten" *The Guardian* (10 July 2014), online: www.theguardian.com/commentisfree/2014/jul/10/right-to-be-forgotten-european-ruling-google-debate.

29 That is, cries of judicial activism. See, for example, Kermit Roosevelt III, *The Myth of Judicial Activism* (New Haven, CT: Yale University Press, 2006). See also Mark Dawson et al, eds, *Judicial Activism at the European Court of Justice* (Cheltenham, UK: Edward Elgar, 2013).

30 Jonathan Zittrain, "Don't Force Google to Forget" *The New York Times* (15 May 2014) A29, online: http://nyti.ms/1jhgks0. See also David Streitfeld, "European Court Lets Users Erase Records on Web" *The New York Times* (13 May 2014) A1, online: http://nyti.ms/1iHQwPH.

31 This divergence is broader than the previously framed US/EU dichotomy. For a discussion of the narrower US/EU dichotomy, see Jeffrey Rosen, "Continental Divide" *Legal Affairs* (September/October 2004), online: www.legalaffairs.org/issues/September-October-2004/review_rosen_sepoct04.msp:

> When Europeans think about privacy, they are most concerned about personal dignity and the right to control one's public image, a right threatened primarily by the mass media, the Internet, and commercial data warehouses. By contrast, American conceptions of privacy are focused on personal liberty and the right to be free from state surveillance, a right threatened primarily by government intrusions into the home.

The decision further reflects internal normative contradictions *within* the continental tradition and emphasizes the urgency of reconceptualizing digital privacy in a more transsystemically[32] viable fashion in Europe and beyond.

As noted above, online, eternally enshrined falsehoods or inadvertent distortions, boasting the aura of accuracy, are not easily remedied by truths. The difficulty of proving an otherwise irrefutable fact online was somewhat amusingly illustrated by a piece in *The New York Times* by Zick Rubin. The article was aptly titled "How the Internet Tried to Kill Me."[33] Rubin chronicled his painful struggle with search engines and numerous fruitless attempts to prove that he was still alive, after a clerical error had him listed as deceased (rather than having merely changed professions!).[34]

---

32 Defined as the "ability to identify points of interface between [legal] systems" and harness them towards effective policy-making and the creation of interoperable definitions of foundational concepts. The McGill Faculty of Law in Montréal coined the term and articulated the concept "transsystemia" to explain its "transsystemic legal education." This unique model is based on the notion of the world of borderless human interactions in which we live today. For a further explanation of transsystemia and the need for a cosmopolitan understanding of the law, see Paul-André Crépeau Centre of Private and Comparative Law, "Transsystemic Legal Education," online: www.mcgill.ca/centre-crepeau/transsystemic. See also Lysanne Larose, "Transsystemic Legal Education," online: McGill Law: Quebec Research Centre of Private and Comparative Law http://archive.today/kPFRw.

33 Zick Rubin, "How the Internet Tried to Kill Me" *The New York Times* (12 March 2011) WK11, online: http://nyti.ms/1MhvITO [Rubin].

34 *Ibid.*

> When I Googled myself last month, I was alarmed to find the following item, from a Wikia.com site on psychology, ranked fourth among the results:
>
> "Zick Rubin (1944–1997) was an American social psychologist."
>
> This was a little disconcerting. I really was born in 1944 and I really was an American social psychologist. Before I entered law school in midlife, I was a professor of psychology at Harvard and Brandeis and had written books in the field. But, to the very best of my knowledge, I wasn't dead . . . . When I complained to Wikia.com, I got a prompt and friendly reply from its co-founder, Angela Beesley, sending me her "kind regards" and telling me that she had corrected the article. But when I checked a week later, the "1944–1997" had returned. So I e-mailed her again (subject line: "inaccurate report that I am dead"), and got the following explanation:
>
>> My change to the page was reverted on the grounds that the info included in this article was sourced from Reber and Reber's the Dictionary

Another man had to seek police protection after being chased by an angry mob following false accusations on Facebook, where he was labelled as a killer and rapist:[35]

> 23-year old Triz Jefferies is just a normal guy from Philadelphia, but he must have angered a pretty malevolent person, because someone decided to post his name and photo on a Facebook page dedicated to finding the so-called Kensington Strangler, a serial rapist and killer. As a direct result of that post, a large group of angry citizens began sending text messages and posting flyers up, reposting the claim that Jefferies was the perp behind at least three murders and several sexual assaults.
>
> Jefferies himself, though, didn't realize how serious the accusations had become until an angry mob gathered around his house, ready to lynch. Terrified, Jefferies called the police, who came over and submitted Jefferies to a DNA test, which found him innocent of any of the murders or rapes.
>
> Police Commissioner Charles Ramsey reiterated the man's innocence at a press conference. "He is not a suspect, he is not connected with this," Ramsey said.
>
> The whole ordeal is hardly over for Jefferies, though: Facebook messages and flyers are still flying about that continue to accuse Jefferies of the crimes. It's very possible another mob will gather around his house before this is all over.[36]

More concretely, an appeals court (District Court, as it is known) in Tel Aviv, Israel, has held that search engines (in that case, Google) are compelled to remove (de-index links to) search results that are "clearly defaming" when the third party posting the material refuses to or is unable

---

> of Psychology, third edition, 2001. Is it possible the page is talking about a different Zick Rubin? The article is about a social psychologist.

I didn't doubt that the Dictionary of Psychology was a highly authoritative source, and yet I persisted in wondering why Reber — or, for that matter, Reber — would know more than I would about whether I was alive or dead.

35 John Brownlee, "Innocent Man Dodges Facebook Mob after False Accusations of Being a Serial Murderer/Rapist" *Geek* (23 December 2010), online: www.geek.com/articles/news/innocent-man-dodges-facebook-mob-after-being-wrongly-accused-of-being-serial-murdererrapist-20101223/.

36 *Ibid*. See also Jessica Hopper, "Wrong Man Shown in Wanted Photo for Philadelphia 'Kensington Strangler'" *ABC News* (21 December 2010), online: http://abcnews.go.com/US/man-wrongly-accused-kensington-strangler-photo-address-facebook/story?id=12449507.

to do so.[37] Of course, as many jurists are painfully aware, courts tend to employ terms such as "clearly" when matters are anything but.

The decision arose in the context of an attorney, Ami Savir, defending another attorney against disciplinary proceedings before the bar association's disciplinary board. The court convicted the attorney of misconduct (on several counts) and published its decision on its website court.org.il. By some unfortunate algorithmic mishap, attorney Savir's own name — rather than that of his client — began to appear under the headline "is an attorney convicted in five different affairs" when Google searches were performed under his name.[38] Here, what is primarily involved is not a question of deletion (or, more accurately, de-indexing), although that may appear to be the case at first glance; instead, and as Chapter 3 discusses in detail, this incident as well as the court's noble but murky attempts to contain or mitigate the significant reputational damage that ensued (on the heels of the much-debated *Costeja* decision) speaks to the practical importance of re-creating some of the "bricks and mortar" safeguards historically associated with court documents, rather than indiscriminately posting online. If nothing else, and as outlined in Chapter 3, this practice can serve as a first line of defence against the ills subsequently requiring a somewhat messy cleanup in the Savir case *inter alia*.

Less dramatically, but no less significantly, businesses face similar difficulties, particularly in terms of the decontextualized and fragmented nature of information online. The fate of a popular restaurant on a commonly visited review site illustrates this. Although the first and most prominent review of New York City's Tapeo 29 is quite dreadful and might discourage future patrons from visiting this establishment, a closer look reveals all reviews appearing beneath the first — and therefore requiring greater effort on the part of future diners to check — to be excellent.[39]

Plainly put, in an Internet of infinite memory, where our "portraits" are amateurishly assembled in an online aggregator, many of us have

---

37 *Adv Savir v Bar Noi* (2014), CA 44711-11-14 (Tel Aviv District Court), online in Hebrew: www.nevo.co.il/psika_html/mechozi/ME-14-11-44711-4.htm.

38 See Haim Reviva, "Israeli District Court: Google Must Remove Defaming Search Results" (5 July 2015), *law.co.il* (blog), online: www.law.co.il/en/news/israeli_internet_law_update/2015/07/05/israel-court-forces-google-to-remove-defaming-search-results/?year=2014&month=8.

39 "Tapeo 29," *Yelp*, online: www.yelp.com/biz/tapeo-29-new-york. The negative review that appeared first has been removed or moved since the website was last visited. For additional examples, see Clair Cain Miller, "The Review Site Yelp Draws Some Outcries of Its Own" *The New York Times* (2 March 2009), online: http://nyti.ms/1QAyGB3.

quite possibly and irrefutably lost control over our identity and how we are perceived (and in one dramatic case, whether we are even understood to exist![40]).

That is particularly worrisome in the form of cyber intimidation (a broader phenomenon that is more narrowly referred to as "revenge porn.") Although beyond the scope of this endeavour, it is worthy of mention as an area which has garnered some degree of rare consensus as worthy of suppression. This consensus is perhaps due to cyber intimidation's particular gravity and vile impact on women, and perhaps even by reason of the American understanding of pornography as generally exceeding the bounds of otherwise robustly protected speech. It is illustrated by Google's recent policy on point.[41]

C. EVOLVING VISIONS OF PRIVACY

The problem of digital privacy as it concerns justice broadly speaking is foremost a conceptual one. Indeed, the very *notion* of privacy in the cyber age is routinely misconstrued and misunderstood.

In the context of the information age, the "reasonable expectation" standard, so prevalent in the Anglo-American conception of privacy, is falling into rapid desuetude. Not only does the standard appear to respond to contemporary circumstances inadequately, but it tends to reinforce social tolerance of intrusions once deemed unreasonable.

Paradoxically, the more we are watched, the less privacy we expect and the more we *expect to be watched*. The less we are bothered by being watched, the more we expect others to share in our complacency. Therefore, if privacy continues to be defined by reference to reasonable expectations and seclusion, technological imperatives necessarily dictate that the sphere in which one can reasonably claim solitude will contract.[42]

---

40 Rubin, above note 33.

41 Carrie Goldberg, "The IRL Impact of Google's New 'Revenge Porn' Policy" (23 June 2015), *Cyber Civil Rights Initiative* (blog), online: www.cybercivilrights.org/irl_google.

42 More generally on point, see Karen Eltis, "Can the Reasonable Person Still Be 'Highly Offended'? An Invitation to Consider the Civil Law Tradition's Personality Rights-Based Approach to Tort Privacy" (2008) 5:1 & 2 *University of Ottawa Law & Technology Journal* 199, online: www.uoltj.ca/articles/vol5.1-2/2008.5.1-2.uoltj.Eltis.199-220.pdf.

Perhaps this development is why civilian (continental) jurisdictions and other jurisdictions in Asia, for instance,[43] are shifting towards a "legitimate" rather than a "reasonable" expectation model. The focus is on the harm occasioned when legitimate expectations of privacy are infringed.[44]

Moreover, as I have argued elsewhere,[45] privacy today is not about wanting to be hidden from view. Many people, particularly of the younger generation, reject seclusion and take pains to be exposed (be it via social networking, YouTube videos, or Twitter). It is not that we do not wish to be known or seen but rather that we expect to be seen as we portray ourselves when we set out to bare our identities online.

Plainly put, where the idea is to share personal information in the cyber — as in the "real" — world, the intention is to expose what one considers an accurate rendering of oneself (whether it is in truth precise or not). Or if interpreted perhaps more cynically, the goal is to preserve and control our ability to (mis)represent ourselves to the world.[46]

In most cases, people do not fear revealing (even very) personal information, only its distortion and deformation, which is often irreparable.[47] It is not that individuals no longer desire privacy. They simply want a form of privacy that translates as dignity or "informational self determination" (to quote the German High Court) rather than spatial seclusion.[48] In other words, instead of isolation (or aloneness), people covet and, in fact, require what sociologist Erving Goffman labelled "impression management."[49]

According to Goffman, most people (litigants, judges, and future judges included) make significant effort to control or manage their identities (or the perceptions thereof) through what Goffman calls "presentation of self."

---

43 As evidenced by the progressive "APEC Privacy Framework" *Asia-Pacific Economic Cooperation* (2005), online: www.apec.org/Groups/Committee-on-Trade-and-Investment/~/media/Files/Groups/ECSG/05_ecsg_privacyframewk.ashx.

44 See "APEC Privacy Framework," *ibid.*

45 See Karen Eltis, "Breaking Through the 'Tower of Babel,'" above note 10.

46 Garrett Lynch, "Yoshikaze 'Up-in-the-Air' Second Life Residency" (12 February 2011), online: asquare www.asquare.org/works/yoshikaze-up-in-the-air-second-life-residency.

47 Sarah Lyall, "For $1,000, Site Lets Celebrities Say It Ain't So" *The New York Times* (27 March 2011), online: www.nytimes.com/2011/03/28/world/europe/28icorrect.html?_r=2 [Lyall].

48 1 BvR 209, 269, 362, 420, 440, 484/83.

49 Erving Goffman, *Stigma: Notes on the Management of Spoiled Identity* (New York: Simon & Schuster, 1963) at 130 [Goffman].

Offline, people rely on personal style, dress, body language, and "the revealing and withholding of personal information to convey to the world who they are, or who they want to be taken to be."[50] As Goffman explains: "The physicality of the offline world provides built-in protections. When people talk to a group of friends, they can look around to see who is listening. When they buy a book or rent a video, if they pay in cash, no record is made connecting them to the transaction."[51]

Not so in cyberspace. Accuracy, especially that relating to identity, is significantly *contextual* in a fragmented, inherently decontextualized networked environment. There, even otherwise exact information can easily convey a misleading impression, depending on algorithm results (take, for instance, the above-mentioned supposedly defunct psychologist). Or, otherwise "accurate" data can be maliciously stage-managed. So, too, can time-tested truths be presented alongside and on par with blatant falsehoods to the point of indistinguishability.[52]

The end result might well be to bring individuals into disrepute, and given the Internet's infinite memory, not for a finite period or in a manner that might be corrected with reasonable effort. Worse yet, an unassailable version of one's identity, entirely incompatible with one's one truth (or perhaps even "*the* truth"), might emerge and become entrenched as public record, upon which future thought is built. Goffman would describe this as "virtual versus actual identity."[53] An individual might thus, in Goffman's words (discussing stigma more generally), be "reduced in our minds from a whole and usual person to a tainted discounted one."[54]

What is more, identity, which Michel Foucault presented as a flexible construct, is no longer malleable or is certainly less so as we become trapped in our deeds or even self-presentation of years past (what *The New York Times Magazine* labelled "the end of forgetting").[55] The capacity to re-

---

50 Adam Cohen, "One Friend Facebook Hasn't Made Yet: Privacy Rights" *The New York Times* (18 February 2008), online: http://nyti.ms/1nRnqbg: ". . . It's more complicated online. Social networking sites like Facebook and MySpace create identities for people and disseminate information about them to large numbers of people."

51 *Ibid.*

52 See, for example, Anthony Lewis, "Digital Age: When Should the First Amendment Lose?" (18 May 2008) (video), online: Youtube www.youtube.com/watch?v=RxHExkcWKFo.

53 Goffman, above note 49 at 2.

54 *Ibid.*

55 Jeffrey Rosen, "The Web Means the End of Forgetting" *The New York Times Magazine* (21 July 2010), online: http://nyti.ms/w2wBvf.

invent oneself is therefore presumably either lost or severely compromised. Identity and its potential evolution is frozen in time, decontextualized, or, in Goffman's parlance, "spoiled."[56]

How, for our purposes, does this affect the courts?

D. THE PERCEPTION OF JUSTICE AND INDIVIDUAL FEARS

As these pages endeavour to illustrate, the above-exposed difficulty is germane to the justice system as a whole.

First, justice rests on perception. The power and legitimacy of judges are anchored both in the public's trust and in the public's reading of and faith in judges' ability to decide impartially and independently. Institutional independence, too, is a function of the perception of a reasonable and informed person. In the Internet age, that perception, in turn, depends, increasingly and at least in part, on the product of cyber searches concerning the courts generally and the judges individually, as shall be discussed.

Second, in systems based on the rule of *stare decisis*, such as the common law,[57] the precision of information upon which caselaw — and ultimately the law itself in a broader sense — is predicated finds itself challenged by a myriad of cyber information of questionable accuracy, tendered as evidence or reaped online by the judges themselves.

Third, the authority of the court and its very integrity risks being compromised, foremost by the *loss of control* over its records and even by jurors defying its orders with regard to outside communication.

Fourth, but far from finally, the cardinal value of access to the courts is similarly at issue and potentially jeopardized, with potential litigants, witnesses, and other participants in the justice system fearing both undue and everlasting exposure of their most intimate details or even threats with offline ramifications. Yes, these preoccupations preceded the Internet, but they are significantly exacerbated as Internet usage increases and expands to the Internet of things.

The fear of having personal details exposed via court records online is particularly salient — although not limited to — the immigration context. There, an increasing number of refugees are deterred from applying, fearing retribution in their country of origin should their claim be rejected

56 Goffman, above note 49.

57 Primarily common law systems, but increasingly hybrid systems such as Québec or Israel, and even the purely civilian.

and the underlying reason for their application (such as political persecution or sexual orientation) be revealed.[58] This concern is especially active in the United States, where the *E-Government Act of 2002* requires courts to make available all written opinions on their websites.[59]

The Canadian site CanLII, which publishes court decisions, fell prey to a Romanian blackmailing site, notwithstanding the precaution it takes to de-index said decisions. The Romanian site, as documented by *The Globe and Mail* and discussed in Chapter 3, would expose litigants' personal information, offering to scrub out these often delicate details in exchange for CDN$200 per litigant.[60]

What must we do?

Mindful of the above, and in an effort to provide some much-needed guidance to judges, litigants, and their attorneys, the following pages draw attention to the relevant practical, legal, and ethical issues. This book further endeavours to extract lessons from the developing issues surveyed. It does so with an eye towards ultimately fostering a more "principled application" of new technologies, in a manner that allows innovation to advance litigant privacy, promote judicial dignity, and strengthen the public's respect for the court system and its integrity. In particular, it dwells on issues such as proper judicial use of Internet sources, judicial ethics and social networking, electronic court records and anonymization techniques, control of the courtroom and jurors' use of new technologies, and the Internet's impact on judicial appointments and the diversity of the judiciary.

---

58 Lyall, above note 47. See also Adam Wagner, "Gay Refugees Cannot Be Sent Home and Told to Hide Their Sexuality" (8 July 2010), *UK Human Rights Blog* (blog), online: http://wp.me/pJiO3-Pi.

59 Conversation with Professor Arthur Leonard regarding an attorney's request to redact the names of gay applicants for asylum who are subsequently "outed" and severely persecuted in their home countries.

60 See Christine Dobby, "Canadians Upset with Romanian Website That Exposes Court Case Details" *The Globe and Mail* (4 January 2014), online: http://fw.to/CxGJdIc.

CHAPTER 1

Framing the Issues

A. INTRODUCTION

Online judgment databases and the court's duty to respect litigant privacy, *ex parte* email communication,[1] inadvertently emailed draft decisions, and the issue of government-owned and -operated court servers, as it relates to judicial independence,[2] are but a few of the many issues arising with greater — indeed, disconcerting — frequency. The cumulative effect of these, it stands to reason, is to prompt courts to *revisit* the conventional construction of fundamental concepts such as disclosure, accountability, competence — even impartiality — and the balance to be struck between foundational values such as transparency and privacy in the modern age.[3]

In order to permit courts to stay current in a time of rapid, if not perpetual, change and with a view to bringing some clarity to judging in times of evolving technology, the following will endeavour to provide an *overview* of the issues arising from the interplay between technology and judging. In an effort to alert courts to up-and-coming matters deriving

1 Jeff Coen, "TV Pitchman Held in Contempt for E-mail Deluge on Judge" (11 February 2010), online: Chicago Breaking News http://articles.chicagobreakingnews.com/2010-02-11/news/28528888_1_kevin-trudeau-infomercial-pitchman-e-mail-attack.

2 In *R v Lippé*, [1991] 2 SCR 114 at para 45, Lamer CJ defined "judicial independence" as independence from government, but interpreted "government" broadly enough to include "any person or body, which can exert pressure on the judiciary through authority under the state."

3 See T David Marshall, *Judicial Conduct and Accountability* (Toronto: Carswell, 1995), and Martin L Friedland, *A Place Apart: Judicial Independence and Accountability in Canada* (Ottawa: Canadian Judicial Council, 1995).

from the use of technology, the book will concern itself first with identifying emerging issues deriving from technological change generally. It will then more specifically address each of the issues, including but not limited to the networked environment's ramifications for judicial ethics and the use of online resources by judges.

This matter will be examined, with an eye towards generating practical recommendations and apt policy in a crucial area previously unexplored in any depth in the legal literature. This book will address the significant jurisprudential developments that have emerged since its first edition was published in 2012.

B. JUDICIAL INDEPENDENCE AND THE PRESSURE TO PRODUCE

Terms such as "innovation" tend — however unconsciously — to be almost inextricably associated with efficiency and enhanced productivity. Although few would deny that these are generally and ostensibly sought-after objectives, their desirability in the courtroom, upon further reflection, might not be self-evident. Although justice must be swift, as guaranteed by the *Canadian Charter of Rights and Freedoms*, for example,[4] not unlike similar-minded constitutional and quasi-constitutional documents in sister democracies worldwide, it must also be deliberate, competent, and meticulous.

This, of course, is *inter alia* required by the "fair trial" component of constitutional guarantees worldwide.

For our purposes, I argue that the dash towards embracing new technologies is somewhat overeager and is being done unquestioningly. I argue that unquestioningly embracing new technologies in haste can be premature for the justice system and might, in some cases, inadvertently result in compromising other significant values such as fairness and even judicial independence among them, on the altar of purported efficiency.

Policy makers' general readiness to welcome new technologies into the courtroom context, in want of in-depth discussions, arguably speaks to the desire for expediency or quick fixes to multi-faceted issues. The long-term price of hurried, perfunctory solutions, as the examples below illustrate, however, may outweigh their immediate benefits. Although the use of technology to forward the legitimate objectives of promoting judicial productivity, ostensible transparency, and the wise saving of costs should be encouraged, such encouragement should be given only after

4 Part I of the *Constitution Act, 1982*, being Schedule B to the *Canada Act 1982* (UK), 1982, c 11 [*Charter*].

solemn reflection and profound cost–benefit analysis (with the words *cost* and *benefit* moving beyond financial cost).

Let us now take a closer look.

C. MONITORING JUDGES: AN AFFRONT TO INDEPENDENCE, A THREAT TO DILIGENCE

In what is now said to appear like the distant past, before the day now known as 9/11 became forever etched in the world's collective memory, a meeting of the Judicial Conference of the United States, headed by then Chief Justice Rehnquist, was scheduled for 11 September 2001.[5] The gathering in question was to address a much-decried US government proposal to monitor federal judges' electronic communications and Internet use.[6] In the midst of vocal protest,[7] monitoring software was installed in order to surveil judicial Internet use.[8] The proposal, touted by Congress as a

5 The Judicial Conference of the United States is the principal policy-making body for the federal court system. The Chief Justice serves as the presiding officer of the Conference.

6 See *Report of the Proceedings of the Judicial Conference of the United States* (September/October 2001), online: www.uscourts.gov/about-federal-courts/reports-proceedings-2000-2009: "Shortly after the Judicial Conference session began on September 11, 2001, members were informed of terrorist attacks in New York and Washington, D.C. The Conference adjourned promptly upon notification of the evacuation of the Supreme Court Building. No Conference business was conducted on that day . . . ."

I have argued elsewhere that email eavesdropping presents novel challenges that need to be addressed with the *Charter* in mind. See Karen Eltis, "La surveillance du courrier électronique en milieu du travail: le Québec succombera-t-il à l'approche permissive américaine?" (2006) 51 *McGill Law Journal* 475, and Karen Eltis, "The Emerging American Approach to Email Privacy in the Workplace: Its Influence on Developing Caselaw in Canada and Israel" (2004) 24 *Comparative Labor Law and Policy Journal* 487.

7 See Lisa Gill, "Judges Turn off Monitoring — on Their Own Computers" *Newsfactor* (9 August 2001). See also Stefanie Olsen, "Judges Oppose Monitoring of Internet Use" *ZDNet* (10 September 2001); and Electronic Privacy Information Center, "EPIC Urges Federal Judiciary to End Workplace Monitoring" (6 September 2001), online: www.epic.org/alert/EPIC_Alert_8.16.html.

8 See Gina Holland, "Panel Endorses Monitoring of Judges" *Washington Post* (13 August 2001), online: www.washingtonpost.com/wp-srv/aponline/20010813/aponline175849_000.htm. See also the report by the Electronic Frontier Foundation, News Release, "Federal Judges Issue Internet Use Policy for U.S. Courts" (13 August 2001), online: http://w2.eff.org/Privacy/Workplace/

push for efficiency,[9] was said to represent a significant threat to judicial independence and to manifestly violate the separation of powers.[10]

If the federal judiciary's experience in the United States is any indication, the idea of monitoring judges' Internet and email use for content is far from theoretical.[11] The installation of monitoring software on judges' computers has long been a fact and, therefore, must be seriously addressed.[12]

Judiciary/20010813_aousc_monitoring_pr.html; and Brian Krebs, "Judicial Policy Board Votes by Mail on Web Monitoring" *Government Technology* (18 September 2001), online: www.govtech.com/gt/5940?topic=117680.

9 See Hardeep Josan & Sapna Shah, "Internet Monitoring of Federal Judges: Striking a Balance between Independence and Accountability" (2002) 20 *Hofstra Labor & Employment Law Journal* 153. This position was eventually moderated: see "Judges Ease Surveillance of Web Use" *The New York Times* (20 September 2001), online: www.nytimes.com/2001/09/20/us/judges-ease-surveillance-of-web-use.html.

10 On the separation of powers and the judicial branch generally, see Cheryl Saunders, "Separation of Powers and the Judicial Branch" (2006) 11 *Judicial Review* 337, online: www.adminlaw.org.uk/docs/Professor%20Cheryl%20Saunders%20-%20July%202006.doc. More specifically, in the Canadian context, s 11(d) of the *Charter*, above note 4, seeking to guarantee a fair hearing by an impartial and independent tribunal, encompasses a constitutional protection against judicial bias. "Independence" refers to freedom from interference from the executive or legislative branch. This aspect does not concern us at present as it relates to the tribunal's institutional, administrative, and fiscal independence, rather than that of individual judges. See *Valente v The Queen*, [1985] 2 SCR 673. The impartiality component denotes a judicial state of mind, characterized by the absence of actual or perceived bias, as described by Lamer CJ in *R v RDS*, [1997] 3 SCR 484 at paras 104–5.

In the United States, guidelines were later adopted in this context. See Administrative Office of US Courts, News Release, "Judicial Conference Approves Recommendations on Electronic Case File Availability and Internet Use" (19 September 2001), online: www.uscourts.gov/News/NewsView/01-09-19/Judicial_Conference_Approves_Recommendations_on_Electronic_Case_File_Availability_and_Internet_Use.aspx. For a more detailed discussion of this, see Josan & Shah, above note 9.

11 See Philip Gordon, "Judge Leads Fight for Workplace Privacy" *Denver Post* (20 September 2001) B-07.

12 See Michael Geist, *Computer and E-mail Surveillance in Canada: The Shift from Reasonable Expectation of Privacy to Reasonable Surveillance* (March 2002), a report prepared for the Canadian Judicial Council, which cites the Judges Technology Advisory Committee's survey titled *Court Technology Security: A Report of the Judges Technology Advisory Committee to the Canadian Judicial Council* (30 November 2001) at Table 2-7. According to Geist: "62 percent of respondents indicated that log-in and account activity by judges or judicial staff

Moreover, since technology creates new criteria for measuring judicial *productivity*, judicial dockets can be monitored with great ease, and expectations of judges' workloads and performance can vary as a function of technological advances,[13] arguably doing violence to both independence and impartiality.[14]

Consider the following more extreme case. Although its direct relationship to the cyber world is questionable, its relevance to the probable impact of seemingly imminent cyber-monitoring of judicial efficiency is evident. The case involves an Israeli judge who committed suicide in his home, due to what had become an unbearable workload and extreme pressure to perform in an ever more timely fashion.[15]

---

was monitored[;] 29 percent of respondents indicated that dial-in and e-mail usage by judges or judicial staff was monitored[;] 33 percent of respondents indicated that Internet usage by judges or judicial staff was monitored" (at 41). And at 42:

> The data was particularly troubling in light of responses regarding the adequacy of notice and implementation of computer and e-mail monitoring. Only 50 percent of respondents indicated that they had been informed that their computer activities may be monitored, only 33 percent of users were required to sign an Appropriate Use Agreement before receiving access to the computer system, and a paltry 5 percent of respondents indicated that their opening log-on screen clarified the expected use of the computing equipment by judges and judicial staff. Furthermore, with only 14 percent indicating that the judges or judicial staff are involved in the monitoring activity, it became apparent that the judiciary was not involved in the implementation aspect of the monitoring activities.

13 See "Computer Monitoring Guidelines," recommended by the Judges Technology Advisory Committee, July 2002, approved by the Canadian Judicial Council, September 2002, online: www.cjc-ccm.gc.ca/cmslib/general/news_pub_techissues_GuidelinesCM_2002_en.pdf. See principles 3 and 4:

> [3] As an overriding principle, any computer monitoring of judges, and judicial staff who report directly to judges, must have a well defined and justifiable purpose that does not encroach on deliberative secrecy, confidentiality, privacy rights or judicial independence.
>
> [4] Content-based monitoring of judges and judicial staff is not permissible under any circumstances. Prohibited activities include keystroke monitoring, monitoring e-mail, word processing documents or other computer files, and tracking legal research, Internet sites accessed, and files downloaded by individual users.

14 See Geist, above note 12.

15 See, for example, Aviad Glickman, "Judge Commits Suicide 'Due to Workload'" *Ynetnews* (12 February 2010), online: www.ynetnews.com/

As one local newspaper aptly summarized the dilemma: "We cannot ignore the burden of responsibility laid on a conscientious judge, who is torn between his duty to do justice with the litigants appearing before him and the system's expectation that he work faster, increase his output and produce ever more verdicts."[16]

Technology's capability for heightened monitoring of judicial productivity naturally places often-overworked judges under even greater pressure to perform. In this scenario, output or yield risks come at the expense of due care and well-thought-out decisions.[17] Speed is a poor substitute for craft, conscientious, and meticulous judging. As Israeli Supreme Court President Dorit Beinish observed on the heels of Benatar J's suicide: "Judges aren't factory workers and their work cannot be measured by their output."[18] Together with Benatar J's death, that fact must be borne in mind as the temptation to electronically monitor judicial productivity becomes irresistible.

D. SEPARATION OF POWERS AND INSTITUTIONAL INDEPENDENCE

Far less dramatically — but arguably no less significantly — the fact that court servers are *government owned* might foster a perception of infringement upon the separation of powers, thus prompting some Canadian courts to take active measures towards electronically distinct servers and tech support.[19]

---

articles/0,7340,L-4025875,00.html. According to *Haaretz*: "A source familiar with the court system said this was essentially equivalent to an order to either resign or face a complaint to the judicial ombudsman about his backlog. [Judge Maurice] Benatar was supposed to have given his answer in the coming days." Tomer Zarchin, Nir Hasson, & Yaniv Kubovich, "Jerusalem Judge Commits Suicide Due to Workload" *Haaretz* (9 February 2011), online: www.haaretz.com/print-edition/news/jerusalem-judge-commits-suicide-due-to-workload-1.342103.

16 See the *Haaretz* editorial, "The Law Decided His Fate" *Haaretz* (11 February 2011), online: www.haaretz.com/print-edition/opinion/the-law-decided-his-fate-1.342643.

17 *Ibid.*

18 Ron Friedman, "Panel Holds Meeting on Judges' Workload following Suicide" *The Jerusalem Post* (15 February 2011), online: www.jpost.com/NationalNews/Article.aspx?id=208247&R=R2.

19 See guidelines set out by the Canadian Judicial Council, including the Canadian Judicial Council's *Blueprint for the Security of Judicial Information*, 2d ed

As regards the cardinal principle of competence, a judge's deliberation and decision-making process can, in principle, be tracked by documenting his or her Internet research pertaining to a given case (what sources and with whom the judge may have consulted). It stands to reason that parties will eventually take opposing this practice as *ex parte* or as offending the (disputed) bar on independent factual research, as explored in greater detail below.[20] In the alternative, they might demand access to such information as a matter of transparency respecting the decision-making process. Did the judge allot sufficient time to the matter (an element of productivity)? Was the judge's LexisNexis Quicklaw query flawed? Did the judge google the litigant or consult with an outside party, such as an academic?

Where there is trepidation, there is also hope, as the Internet and its resources can serve to attenuate judicial unfamiliarity with new science and technology. It is to such issues that we now turn.

(2006), online: www.cjc-ccm.gc.ca/cmslib/general/news_pub_techissues_SecurityBlueprint_2006_en.pdf.

20 See David H Tennant & Laurie M Seal, "Judicial Ethics and the Internet: May Judges Search the Internet in Evaluating and Deciding a Case?" (2005) 16:2 *The Professional Lawyer*.

CHAPTER 2

A "Body of Precedent Written on the Wind?"[1]

Wiki Courts, "Link Rot," and Independent Judicial Internet Research

A. COMPETENCE AND ACCESS TO TECHNOLOGY

Competence is a vital ethical principle,[2] thus rendering judicial comfort with basic precepts of technology essential in this web-dependent society.[3] According to the Canadian Judicial Council's *Ethical Principles for Judges*, "Judges should take reasonable steps to maintain and enhance the knowledge, skills and personal qualities necessary for judicial office."[4] Likewise, the *ABA Model Code of Judicial Conduct* rules provide that "[a] judge shall

1 Judicial Conference of the United States.

2 *Jura novit curia — la cour connaît le droit* ("the court knows the law," sometimes translated as "the court knows the lay"). For an in-depth discussion, see Douglas Brooker, "Va Savoir! — The Adage '*Jura Novit Curia*' in Contemporary France" *bepress Legal Series*, Paper 845 (30 October 2005), online: http://law.bepress.com/cgi/viewcontent.cgi?article=4295&context=expresso. Of course, as Mashaw cautions: "Many arguments about judicial competence are vague about their normative foundations because 'competence' can convey a concern for either 'authority' or 'capacity.' Because 'capacity' is also a functionalist argument for allocating 'authority,' this conceptual confusion seems almost inherent in the interpretive debate." See Jerry Mashaw, "Between Facts and Norms: Agency Statutory Interpretation" (2005) 55 *University of Toronto Law Journal* 497 at 502.

3 See David H Tennant & Laurie M Seal, "Judicial Ethics and the Internet: May Judges Search the Internet in Evaluating and Deciding a Case?" (2005) 16:2 *The Professional Lawyer*, online: www.abanet.org/judicialethics/resources/TPL_jethics_internet.pdf.

4 Canadian Judicial Council, *Ethical Principles for Judges* (Ottawa: Canadian Judicial Council, 1998) Principle 4(2): Diligence.

perform judicial and administrative duties competently and diligently,"[5] noting that "[c]ompetence in the performance of judicial duties requires the legal knowledge, skill, thoroughness, and preparation reasonably necessary to perform a judge's responsibilities of judicial office."[6] In effect, a court is presumed to know the law and expected to be cognizant of and sensitive to social context.[7] In today's reality, that includes often-intricate concepts that the "experts" themselves have yet to address, let alone resolve.

As Elizabeth Thornburg correctly notes in her enlightening article on this point:

> [J]udges in the twenty-first century find themselves in a world where litigation — both civil and criminal — involves a vast array of complex and technical factual disputes. These lawsuits, in turn, may cause judges to seek a greater level of expertise in order to deal competently with the evidence that will be relevant to those disputes . . . . Courts are asked to decide questions such as: whether medicine can eliminate the risk of dying in severe pain; whether psychologists can predict future dangerousness; whether punishments deter crime; whether building projects threaten wildlife; and whether exposure to various chemicals creates a risk of public injuries or death. An appellate court, ordinarily bound by a case's trial court record, might want information outside the record because an issue is very difficult, or because the record is inadequate, especially if one party had far superior resources leading to a lopsided presentation, or because technical knowledge has evolved since the time of trial.
>
> At the same time, advances in communication technology have brought the world's library to the courthouse, requiring no onerous trips across town or index searches but only the click of a mouse. When judges feel the need for additional information, the easy availability of the Internet is a powerful temptation.[8] This combination of felt need and ready access has turned a once-marginal concern into a dilemma

---

5 American Bar Association, *ABA Model Code of Judicial Conduct*, 2011 ed (Chicago: American Bar Association, Center for Professional Responsibility, 2010) Rule 2.5(A) [*ABA Model Code*].

6 *Ibid*, comments to Rule 2.5.

7 "Lawyers and academics can help the judiciary along this path with their legal arguments and writings, but in the end the judges have to make the decisions. They must be enlightened decisions, aware of the social fabric of our time, with our finger on the pulse of humanity." See Constance R Glube, former chief justice of Nova Scotia, in her essay "The Role of the Judge" in Rosalie Abella & Melvin Rothman, eds, *Justice beyond Orwell* (Montréal: Yvon Blais, 1985) at 486.

8 Take, for example, the (social security benefits denial) case of *Purvis v Commissioner of Social Security*, 2011 US Dist LEXIS 18175 (DNJ), where the presiding

that affects courts and litigants daily. The problem of judicial research has always been with us, lurking in the margins, and yet we do not have a workable framework for discerning when it is and is not permissible. We can no longer comprehensively fail to engage this question, because it is now taking on a central importance to proper judicial decision-making in an increasing number of cases.[9]

Indeed, although directly salient to inmates' constitutionally protected right to a full answer and defence — rather than to judges' own preparedness — a recent Canadian decision proclaiming Internet legal research central to the above-said right is telling. Reflecting the essential nature and enhanced stature of Internet research to mounting a defence, but arguably telling far more broadly, the judge in that case opined that he was "hard pressed" to see how one can mount an effective defence without the Internet generally and the CanLII website (housing Canadian jurisprudence), in particular.[10]

Although the exact degree of requisite expertise remains to be determined, judges for certain must possess some understanding of the fundamental notions of science and technology in order to grasp the related issues permeating cases and to adequately filter and assess evidence.[11] Further, as online communication increasingly forms the subject of legal dispute, judges must develop the aptitude for understanding both (fundamental)

---

judge visited the plaintiff's Facebook page on her own initiative to discover what appeared to be the plaintiff smoking. Said the judge:

> [A]lthough the Court remands the ALJ's decision for a more detailed finding, it notes that in the course of its own research, it discovered one profile picture on what is believed to be Plaintiff's Facebook page where she appears to be smoking. Profile Pictures by Theresa Purvis, Facebook [link omitted] (last visited Feb. 16, 2011). If accurately depicted, Plaintiff's credibility is justifiably suspect.

9 Elizabeth G Thornburg, "The Curious Appellate Judge: Ethical Limits on Independent Research" (2008) 28:1 *Litigation Review* 131 (Lexis).

10 *R v Biever*, 2015 ABQB 301 at paras 92 and 126. See also Sarah Burton, "Life, Liberty, and the Right to CanLII: Legal Research behind Bars" (3 June 2015), *ABlawg.ca* (blog), online: http://ablawg.ca/2015/06/03/life-liberty-and-the-right-to-canlii-legal-research-behind-bars.

11 See, for example, Scalia J's mischaracterization of HBO as "cable" in *American Broadcasting Companies, Inc v Aereo, Inc*, 573 US ___ (2014), discussed in Brett LoGiurato, "Justice Scalia Did Not Know You Can't Get HBO for Free" *Business Insider* (22 April 2014), online: www.businessinsider.com/scalia-hbo-aereo-case-supreme-court-2014-4.

technical aspects of the digital revolution and also Internet culture.[12] They must at the same time avoid excessive reliance on and disclosure to support staff or even expert testimony, which can be problematic and threaten their independence to a certain degree.[13]

Despite these requirements, judges' participation in online culture has attracted controversy. Notwithstanding the above-stated need for judicial familiarity with the digital environment, judges' participation in online culture in the broader sense has (to some, paradoxically) met with disapproval and scorn. For example, Canada's most recent Supreme Court appointee, Russell Brown, was denounced by critics for his "prolific" blogging as a law professor. Some argued that his blogging took on a political flavour and could, therefore, be demonstrative of perceived bias.[14] That said, it is submitted in light of recent developments[15] that expecting abstinence from participation in online culture *prior to* appointment, for fear of candidates leaving a "digital trail" may ultimately be detrimental to the justice system. This expectation might deprive the public of other-

12 See, for example, Richard K Sherwin, Neal Feigenson, & Christina Spiesel, "Law in the Digital Age: How Visual Communication Technologies Are Transforming the Practice, Theory and Teaching of Law" (2006) 12 *Boston University Journal of Science and Technology Law* 227; *Elonis v US*, 13-983, 575 US ___ (2015); The Canadian Press, "Jennifer Pawluck, Convicted in Police Graffiti Case, Gets Suspended Sentence" *CBC News* (14 May 2015), online: www.cbc.ca/news/canada/montreal/jennifer-pawluck-convicted-in-police-graffiti-case-gets-suspended-sentence-1.3075207; Eli Hager, "Is an Emoji Worth 1,000 Words?" *The Marshall Project* (2 February 2015), online: www.themarshallproject.org/2015/02/02/is-an-emoji-worth-1-000-words; Julia Greenberg, "That ;) Can and Will Be Used against You in a Court of Law" *Wired* (2 February 2015), online: www.wired.com/2015/02/emoji-in-court-cases.

13 And in order to avoid situations such as that of an English judge who informed the parties before him that he did not know what a website was. See Lewis Page, "Judge in Tech Trial Says He Doesn't Know What Website Is" *The Register* (17 May 2007), online: www.theregister.co.uk/2007/05/17/judge_website_shocker.

14 Adam Dodek, "Accountability Needed: Why Was Justice Russell Brown Appointed to the Top Court?" *The Globe and Mail* (5 August 2015), online: http://fw.to/o6hsOSi. Here is an example of a quotation by Professor Brown (as he then was): "Current events remind us that the notion of limited government — particularly as it pertains to freedom of conscience and freedom of expression — can never be taken for granted in Canada." Jason Markusoff, "How Conservative Is New Supreme Court Judge Russell Brown?" *Maclean's* (28 July 2015), online: www.macleans.ca/news/canada/how-conservative-is-new-supreme-court-judge-russell-brown/.

15 Discussed in Chapter 7.

wise competent, fair-minded magistrates who were simply involved in community life (which now includes the Internet) — within the bounds of propriety — as is naturally expected of prominent practitioners and academics. (This matter is further discussed in Chapter 7.)

In this vein, and as I have written elsewhere,[16] Lysianne Gagnon warned of potential candidates for judicial office who were cautious of maintaining a "dossier vierge de polémiques" — a "virgin dossier, free of debate" — until the long-awaited day of their appointment.[17]

Chief Justice Beverley McLachlin seems to echo this point, stating the following:

> I think the Canadian public understands that intelligent, engaged lawyers and judges think about problems and may on occasion express [their thoughts], particularly in their prior roles . . . . Justice Brown was an academic and part of being an academic is engaging in a vigorous debate on legal issues and the functioning of the court.[18]

Although judges, particularly in the United States,[19] can perhaps more freely share their views subsequent to their appointment, the concern, as discussed in Chapter 7, is that expressing their opinions online (and therefore publicly) might cause them to appear to be "more pundit than professor."[20]

In short, to reach elusive equipoise — or at the very least mediate intelligently — between the right to free expression and professional restraint, we must be mindful of whether the views impugned for their political overtones were made prior to or post appointment; we must also assess their flagrancy. Views expressed prior to — in contradistinction to post appointment (and, of course, depending on the flagrancy) — may simply be evocative of digital competence and a temperament that favours

---

16 "L'impact des nouvelles technologies sur les tribunaux et sur le processus de nominations des juges : un premier survol" (2011) 41 *Revue générale de droit* 267.

17 *Ibid* [translation].

18 Yves Faguy, "McLachlin on the Past Year at SCC" *The National* (15 August 2015), online: www.nationalmagazine.ca/Articles/August-2015/McLachlin-on-the-past-year-at-the-SCC.aspx?lang=EN.

19 See *SCOTUSblog*'s list of 353 books published by US Supreme Court Justices: Ronald Collins, "353 Books by Supreme Court Justices" (12 March 2012), *SCOTUSblog* (blog), online: www.scotusblog.com/2012/03/351-books-by-supreme-court-justices.

20 Sean Fine, "Law School Blog Sheds Light on Supreme Court's Newest Judge" *The Globe and Mail* (31 July 2015), online: http://fw.to/EYJ5INJ.

active participation in cultural and community life.[21] They need not be considered as indicative of bias.

What is more, the advent of the networked environment inevitably raises questions regarding "instant judicial expertise" due to the availability of practically infinite, albeit admittedly superficial, knowledge or information. Therefore, as Thomas Moyer J correctly observed: "courts have . . . been forced to *react*, often without the requisite scientific training or education; forced to make an informed decision regarding whether scientific evidence is a cutting-edge breakthrough or what has been called 'junk science,' oftentimes even prior to the expert community itself."[22]

A well-known example coming to us from the United States is that of the childhood vaccine controversy. An American judge was unenviably forced to rule in a case where parents alleged that an ingredient in a childhood vaccine caused (or precipitated) their daughter's autism. In a landmark decision, the court ruled in favour of the parents on the specific set of facts,[23] despite the fact that "scientists don't know if a vaccination — independent of fever or infection — can cause such a stress."[24] As this case illustrates, the judge — although not proficient in science or medi-

21 A cherished trait on the continent, as discussed in Chapter 7.

22 US Supreme Court Justice Steven Breyer once observed: "A judge is not a scientist, and a courtroom is not a scientific laboratory, . . . but to do our legal job properly, we [need] to develop an informed, although necessarily approximate, understanding of the state of that relevant scientific art," cited in Thomas J Moyer & Stephen P Anway, "Biotechnology and the Bar: A Response to the Growing Divide between Science and the Legal Environment" (2007) 22 *Berkeley Technology Law Journal* 671 at 673.

23 The girl is said not to be "typically autistic." See Mike Stobbe & Marilynn Marchione, "Analysis: Vaccine-Autism Link Unproven" *USA Today* (7 March 2008), online: http://usatoday30.usatoday.com/news/health/2008-03-07-3676631517_x.htm; a federal court reached a different conclusion. See Matt Cherry et al, "Vaccine Court Finds No Link to Autism" *CNN* (12 March 2010), online: www.cnn.com/2010/HEALTH/03/12/vaccine.court.ruling.autism.

24 "'There are no scientific studies documenting that childhood vaccinations cause or worsen mitochondrial diseases, but there is very little scientific research in this area,' said Chuck Mohan, executive director the United Mitochondrial Disease Foundation, a Pittsburgh-based group that raises money for research." See "Vaccine Settlement No Landmark, Officials Say: Government Maintains Georgia Girl's Case No Proof of Autism Link" *Associated Press* (3 July 2008), online: www.msnbc.msn.com/id/23519029/ns/health-mental_health/t/vaccine-settlement-no-landmark-officials-say.

cine — is nonetheless said to have "made a decision about science before scientists."[25]

Canadian judges may find themselves in a somewhat similar situation. Unlike "the United States, which has installed a specialized network of patent courts to resolve disputes, Canada has shifted the burden to Federal Court judges who have little or no scientific expertise to bring to the drug litigation."[26]

A cautionary tale relating to judges making science-related decisions hails from Italy. There, in a 2012 case, a court found a link between autism and vaccinations. Incredulously and speaking to the importance of proper judicial training on the use of medical or scientific expertise and digital sources, in particular, the judgment, which went viral, relied on a fraudulent paper and the testimony of a single witness.[27]

In light of the complexity of matters increasingly begging judicial attention — indeed, resolution — coupled with rising expectations of broadly defined competence and a deluge of "expert" evidence, judges are turning to the Internet generally and search engines (such as Google) or even Wikipedia for much-needed guidance: "to check facts, to look up information about companies embroiled in litigation, and to challenge statistics presented by attorneys in court."[28] This trend holds true for

---

25 Interview with Dr William Schaffner, ABC's *Good Morning America* (6 March 2008), online: http://abcnews.go.com/Health/MindMoodNews/story?id=4402930&page=1.

26 See Jacqui McNish, "As Patent Cases Clog Courts, Drugs Are a Lawyer's Best Friend" *The Globe and Mail*, Special Report on Business (12 March 2008): "In a widely quoted drug patent decision in 1993, former Federal Court judge Francis Muldoon complained that an 'unschooled judge cannot perceive the truth among all the chemical or other scientific baffle-gab.'"

27 Emily Willingham, "Court Rulings Don't Confirm Autism-Vaccine Link" *Forbes* (9 August 2013), online: www.forbes.com/sites/emilywillingham/2013/08/09/court-rulings-dont-confirm-autism-vaccine-link.

28 Declan McCullagh, "Search Engines Take the Stand" *CNET News* (13 May 2004), online: www.news.com/Search-engines-take-the-stand/2100-1032_3-5211658.html.

> Dozens of judges have penned opinions describing Google as a valuable — and sometimes crucial — source of knowledge . . . . "If a judge is taking as proof facts that are reported in any public medium that pertain to individual actions by persons involved in a case, that is troubling," said George Fisher, a Stanford University law professor. "Those are the sorts of facts that are supposed to be proved in the courtroom under the rules of evidence."

See William Wilkerson, "The Emergence of Internet Citations in Judicial Opinions: Examining the Supreme Court of the US and the US Courts of Appeals"

scientifically or technically complex cases,[29] which may require specialized knowledge, as well as for ordinary matters.[30]

In the United States, for instance, "[f]our hundred and one cases referenced a Wikipedia article and six cases referenced a wiki other than Wikipedia."[31] The same of course holds true for Internet search engines

---

(Paper delivered at the AGM of the American Political Science Association, Washington, DC, 1 September 2005).

29 See Edward K Cheng, "Independent Judicial Research in the *Daubert* Age" (2005) 56 *Duke Law Journal* 1263 at 1266 [Cheng, "Independent Legal Research"]. As Cheng argues: "The adversary system is particularly ill suited at handling specialized knowledge procedural safeguards: One safeguard would be to restrict independent research only to sources that are citable and publicly available."

30 As judges progressively assume the function of gatekeepers of expert evidence. Regarding Québec, see Denis Ferland discussing changes to the *Code of Civil Procedure* in his report "La révision de la procédure civile: Une nouvelle culture judiciaire," online: www.justice.gouv.qc.ca/francais/publications/rapports/crpc-rap2.htm. In the US context, see Adam J Siegel, "Setting Limits on Judicial, Scientific, Technical, and Other Specialized Fact-Finding in the New Millennium" (2000) 86 *Cornell Law Review* 167 at 202–3:

> In *Kumho Tire Co. v. Carmichael*, the Supreme Court significantly broadened the scope of the judicial gatekeeping role previously set forth in *Daubert v. Merrell Dow Pharmaceuticals, Inc.*, holding that federal district judges must ensure that all admitted scientific, technical, and other specialized expert testimony is both relevant and reliable. Faced with the challenge of making scientifically, technically, and legally sound admissibility determinations, many generalist trial judges will inevitably be tempted to educate themselves on the nature and substance of the complex matters requiring their attention. While some judges may rely on court-appointed technical advisors, scientific reference manuals, or privately sponsored judicial seminars for assistance, other judges may venture into cyberspace, review scientific journal articles not presented by the parties, or consult colleagues off the record. However, the extent to which judges can properly engage in such practices has become a matter of great debate and uncertainty due to the divergent teachings of *Kumho*, the *Code of Conduct for United States Judges*, 28 U.S.C. §§ 144 and 455 (the federal judicial disqualification statutes), and the *Federal Rules of Evidence*.

31 Lee F Peoples, "The Citation of Wikipedia in Judicial Opinions" (2009) 12 *Yale Journal of Law and Technology* 1 at 6 [emphasis added]. See also Noam Cohen, "Courts Turn to Wikipedia — But Selectively" *The New York Times* (29 January 2007), online: www.nytimes.com/2007/01/29/technology/29wikipedia.html: "More than 100 judicial rulings have relied on Wikipedia, beginning in 2004, including 13 from circuit courts of appeal, one step below the Supreme Court." For example, *US v Bazaldua*, No 06-4094, 2007 US App LEXIS 23917 at *3. n

such as Google, which, in turn, often refer to Wikipedia and like-minded sources, as an enlightening CNET news article recounts.[32] Among the colourful anecdotes is one about "an enterprising federal judge in New York [who] did his own Google search to demonstrate that a watch, jeans and handbag retailer named Alfredo Versace was infringing the trademarks of the famous Gianni Versace design house."[33] In effect, the European Court of Human Rights, the World Intellectual Property Office (WIPO), the Swiss Federal Council, the High Court of England and Wales, US federal courts, and a number of Australian courts *inter alia*[34] apparently resort to search engines such as Google and to Wikipedia itself.[35]

---

2 (8th Cir 12 October 2007); *Lennon v Metro Life Ins Co*, No 06-2234, 2007 US App LEXIS 23721 at *16 (6th Cir 10 October 2007); *Zeiler v Deitsch*, 2007 US App LEXIS 20065 at *9, n 5 (2d Cir 23 August 2007); *Boim v Fulton County Sch Dist*, 494 F3d 978 at 983 (11th Cir 2007); *US v Calabrese*, 490 F3d 575 at 577 (7th Cir 2007); *Phillips v Pembroke Real Estate, Inc*, 459 F3d 128 at 133, n 3, 140 n 9 (1st Cir 2006); *United States v Yazzen*, No 05-2156, 2006 US App LEXIS 16648 at *6, n 1 (10th Cir 29 June 2006); *Raymond v Ameritech Corp*, 442 F3d 600 at 602, n 1 (7th Cir 2006); *N'Diom v Gonzales*, 442 F3d 494 at 496 (6th Cir 2006); *United States v Zajanckauskas*, 441 F3d 32 at 34, n 1 (1st Cir 2006); *Allegheny Def Project, Inc v US Forest Serv*, 423 F3d 215 at 218, n 5 (3d Cir 2005); *Musarra v Digital Dish, Inc*, No C2-05-545, 2006 US Dist LEXIS 70442 at *42, n 30 (SD Ohio 28 September 2006); *MGM Studios, Inc v Grokster, Ltd*, 454 F Supp 2d 966 at 988, n 14 (CD Cal 2006); *Simpleville Music v Mizell*, 451 F Supp 2d 1293 at 1296, n 2 (MD Ala 2006); *Sacirbey v Guccione*, 2006 US Dist LEXIS 64577 at *2, n 2 (SD NY 7 September 2006); *Smith v Crose*, 2006 US Dist LEXIS 64250 at *2, n 1 (DNJ 7 September 2006).

32 McCullagh, above note 28.

33 *Ibid.*

34 See, for example, in the *Kay v Commissioner of Police of the Metropolis* case, [2008] UKHL 69; in the *Ždanoka v Latvia* case before the European Court of Human Rights (No 58278/00 2006) (ECHR); and in the *Media General Communications, Inc v Rarenames, WebReg* case decided by the WIPO Arbitration and Mediation Center, Administrative Panel Decision (Case No D2006-0964), among others. See also Martha L Arias, "Wikipedia: The Free Online Encyclopedia and Its Use as Court Source" *Internet Business Law Services* (6 March 2007), online: IBLS www.ibls.com/internet_law_news_portal_view.aspx?s=latestnews&id=1668. Also citing Wikipedia, see the Federal Magistrate Court of Australia cases of *Coolstar Holdings Pty Ltd v Cleary Ors*, [2006] FMCA 1442, and *Matheison v Hamilton*, [2006] FMCA 238; and from the Federal Court of Australia, the case of *Nine Films & Television Pty Ltd v Ninox Television Limited*, [2005] FCA 1404.

35 Jim Giles, "Special Report: Internet Encyclopaedias Go Head to Head" (15 December 2005) 438 *Nature*, 900.

A search on the above-mentioned CanLII for "Wikipedia" conducted on 4 February 2015 turned up 473 results. A similar search on LexisNexis Quicklaw revealed 175 cases. Examples include (but are not limited to) the following:

- the Appeals Commission for Alberta Workers' Compensation accepting definitions of medical terms from Wikipedia as evidence or supplemental submissions[36]
- the Municipal Court of Montréal citing Wikipedia for the definition of "Internet Trolls"[37]
- the Ontario Superior Court of Justice citing Wikipedia for a definition of "grandiosity" in an appeal from a decision of the Consent and Capacity Board[38]

B. "WIKIPEDIA JURISPRUDENCE"[39]

One example of many cited in a CNET article on "wikipedia jurisprudence" is that of an Australian federal court judge who denied a visa request from a Sri Lankan national claiming persecution. The court justified its rejection by remarking that "the claim was 'exaggerated,' since the man — claiming to be a well-known filmmaker in his homeland — did not turn up any hits on a Google search: 'His name does not appear when put into a search engine such as Google,' one member of the government tribunal observed. 'I would have expected — if he indeed has the notoriety and is as well-known as he claims — that his name would have appeared at least in some context.'"[40]

Beyond that, one must admit, with regard to intricate or obscure matters, in particular, the Internet and its search engines might be considered a helpful tool for improving judicial competence in the face of scientific and technological challenges.[41] Indeed, the lone recent scholarly writing

36 *Decision No: 2015-0040*, 2015 CanLII 3040 at para 8 (AB WCAC); *Decision No: 2014-1039*, 2015 CanLII 3359 at para 21 (AB WCAC).

37 *R c Lafortune*, 2015 QCCM 1 at para 5.

38 *Skeene v Cohen*, 2014 ONSC 7315 at para 18.

39 R Jason Richards, "Courting Wikipedia" (2008) 44 *Trial* 62 at 62 & 63.

40 See McCullagh, above note 28. See also Molly McDonough, "In Google We Trust? Critics Question How Much Judges, Lawyers Should Rely on Internet Search Results" (2004) 90 *ABA Journal* 30, online: ABA http://bgbg.blogspot.ca/pdf/InGoogle.pdf; Tennant & Seal, above note 3.

41 See Cheng, "Independent Legal Research," above note 29, cited in Karen Eltis, "The Impact of Technology on Courts and Judicial Ethics: An Overview"

on point argues[42] that judges facing unfamiliar and complex scientific admissibility decisions *can* and *should* engage in independent research to better educate themselves about the underlying principles and methods.[43] While doing so can aid judges in reassuming their rightful place of competence among a deluge of "expert" evidence, independent research or investigation by judges — cyber or otherwise — is not beyond criticism.

Perhaps no case better illustrates the confusion characterizing courts' view of the appropriateness of wiki and other Internet resources than *Platinum Links Entertainment v Atlantic City Surf Professional Baseball Club, Inc.*[44] In this case, the judge began by chastising the plaintiff's use of Wikipedia and then promptly proceeded to support his own reasoning using the cyber-encyclopedia he had just besmirched, as Peoples recounts:

> [O]ne court began a paragraph with a scathing critique of a party for citing Wikipedia. But a few sentences later, the court cited Wikipedia to support its own analysis or reasoning. In *Platinum Links Entertainment v Atlantic City Surf Professional Baseball Club, Inc.*, the plaintiff alleged that defendant's cancellation of a rap concert violated their civil rights. The plaintiff argued that the defendant was motivated by "racial animus" in cancelling the concert because it was a rap concert and the defendant perceived the potential for gang-related violence at the concert. The plaintiff cited the Wikipedia definition of rap music in support of this argument, and the court noted that it "does not necessarily consider Wikipedia an authoritative source." In the next sentence the court confessed, "Plaintiff's citation led this Court to look up, *sua sponte*, the term 'gangsta rap' on the same website, and this Court notes that the description does not make mention of race." Based on the Wikipedia definition and other factual evidence from the record, the court denied plaintiff's civil rights claim.[45]

A more recent Canadian example is that of *R v CDH*,[46] a sexual assault case in which the judge visited a dating website known as Match.com to

---

(Paper delivered at the 4th International Conference on the Training of the Judiciary, Sydney, Australia, 25–29 October 2009) at 34. See also Edward K Cheng, "Should Judges Do Independent Research on Scientific Issues?" (2006) 90 *Judicature* 58.

42 In the US context.

43 Notwithstanding the prohibition on *ex parte* or independent factual investigations, as discussed by Cheng, "Independent Legal Research," above note 29.

44 Slip Copy, 2006 WL 1459986 (NJ 23 May 2006).

45 Peoples, above note 31 at 10 [footnotes omitted].

46 2015 ONCA 102.

conduct independent research. The judge acquitted the accused of sexual assault, and while ruling on a sentence on the charge of simple assault, called the leading investigator into his office to inform him that information on the dating site could have been used to discredit the complainant. On appeal by the Crown, the Ontario Court of Appeal held that the conduct of the trial judge "created a reasonable apprehension of bias and lack of impartiality."[47] The Court of Appeal set aside the verdict of acquittal and ordered a new trial.

It is significant that the case elicited comments from jurists and organizations, such as the Canadian IT Law Association, calling on judges to refrain from online research.[48] This incident is especially egregious as the judge had created a fake profile in order to be able to search the site, which is open only to members.

C. INDEPENDENT JUDICIAL RESEARCH: IN AND OUT OF THE CONTEXT OF THE DIGITAL AGE

More concretely, as alluded to above, independent judicial searches are — to a certain extent — frowned upon at common law.[49] In traditional civilian/inquisitorial systems,[50] however, judges are *expected* to conduct their own investigations. Independent searches have traditionally been viewed with some degree of suspicion as an affront to the adversarial tradition[51]

---

47 *Ibid* at para 19.

48 "Judges Should Not Do Their Own Research on Match.com" *Canadian IT Law Association* (13 May 2015), online: www.it-can.ca/2015/05/13/judges-should-not-do-their-own-research-on-match-com.

49 See Patrick Glenn, *Droit québécois et droit français: communauté, autonomie, concordance* (Montréal: Yvon Blais, 1993); see Brooker, above note 2 at 44. As Brooker explains at 36: ". . . to Common Lawyers what Civilians take for granted: the judge is actively involved in examining all aspects of the parties case including arguments of law. This activity does not invariably involve intervention *jura novit curia* but speaks instead to the court's duty to decide correctly, a duty which may at times require intervention *jura novit curia*, particularly where party argument is not fully developed."

50 As distinguished from hybrid systems, such as the one in Québec. See *Lac d'Amiante du Quebec Ltee v 2858-0702 Quebec Inc*, 2001 SCC 51 at paras 28–29, discussing Québec's "mixed" system.

51 Brooker, above note 2 at 31, citing Damaška: "Mirijan Damaška captures the most extreme black-letter consequence of the adage, writing that *jura novit curia* authorises a judge to reach a decision based on, 'a legal theory that has not been subject to the arguments of counsel' for the parties":

or even the "principle of judicial unpreparedness."[52] As Wright and Miller observe: "Under our adversary system, the trial judge cannot behave like a French magistrate and embark on a personal fact-finding expedition, however deficient the efforts of counsel may appear."[53]

Indeed, Rule 2.9 of the *ABA Model Code of Judicial Conduct* provides that "[a] judge shall not investigate facts in a matter independently, and shall consider only the evidence presented and any facts that may properly be judicially noticed."[54] Commentary 6 explicitly adds: "[t]he prohibition against a judge investigating the facts in a matter extends to information available in all mediums, including electronic."[55] Thus, "unlike judicial

---

> Damaška's *jura novit curia* breaches *le principe de la contradiction* and *les droits de la défense* because the successful party receives judgements in her favour on legal grounds her opponent has been unable to challenge. *Le principe de la contradiction* and *les droits de la défense* do not, however, prohibit a court from intervening so as to decide according to its own point of law. In France, intervention *jura novit curia* may be required by *le principe d'égalité devant la justice* which is meant to guarantee that all citizens receive equal treatment from the courts and that no one should be treated either less favourably than anyone else. *Le principe d'égalité devant la justice* may impose a duty on the court duty to intervene with its own point of law because it is the courts' duty to decide according to the "applicable" law in all cases, regardless of the legal argument on which parties base their case.

Mirijan Damaška, *The Faces of Justice and State Authority* (New Haven: Yale University Press, 1986).

See France, NC proc civ, art 1015, Conseil d'État No 21-893, 5 July 1985, Gaz Pal 1985, 2, 742; see also Yves Brard, "La réparation du préjudice causé à un dirigeant de sociétiés par les procédures fiscales conduits envers ces sociétiés" (2000) 16:2 *RFDA* 365, outlining the decision of 16 June 1999 in which the Conseil overturned a decision of the Administrative Court of Appeal which decided on a point of law raised of its own motion without providing the parties with an opportunity to argue the point.

52 Neil H Andrews, "The Passive Court and Legal Argument" (1988) *Civil Justice Quarterly* 125 at 128–29. See Brooker, above note 2 at 31: "Spelled out, 'research' refers to a type of *jura novit curia* that permits a court to participate in the parties' adversarial proceeding without prompting from the parties themselves." And at 35: "Common Law notions of fair process and precedent assume each party has notice of all matters of fact and law that inform the decision, prior to judgement."

53 Charles A Wright & Arthur R Miller, *Federal Practice and Procedure*, 2d ed (St Paul: West, 1990) § 1357 at 340.

54 *ABA Model Code*, above note 5, Rule 2.9(C).

55 *Ibid*, comment 6. Notwithstanding, as Elizabeth Thornburg, above note 9, observes, this includes a significant loophole:

education programs, which have been largely uncontentious and well received, independent research is likely to be controversial, in part because the idea of judges unilaterally doing research conflicts with widely held adversary system values."[56]

Before the advent of the Internet age, judges were deterred from engaging in independent research for two principal reasons: first, and most important, the imperatives of the adversarial process; and second, the presumption of judicial knowledge of the law and all that is necessary for its interpretation. Consequently, in the extreme, independent judicial research has even been said to offend the principle of competence it is meant to bolster, for seemingly "a court that really knows the law would not have to undertake its own research."[57]

> By including the reference to judicial notice, however, the *Model Code* opens a loophole. If the ethics rules are meant to incorporate the totality of federal and state evidence rules' approach to what judges can "know" on their own, the research prohibition is a narrow one. Judges may not independently investigate adjudicative facts — the facts that are at issue in the particular case — unless they are generally known or "capable of accurate and ready determination by resort to sources whose accuracy cannot reasonably be questioned." But they may independently ascertain and use information that meets the requirements for judicial notice, and they may investigate "legislative facts" — those that inform the court's judgment when deciding questions of law or policy — to their hearts' content, bound by no rules about sources, reliability, or notice to the parties.

56 See Edward K Cheng, "Should Judges Do Independent Research on Scientific Issues?" (2006) 90 *Judicature* 58 at 61 [Cheng, "Should Judges Do Independent Research"]:

> Judges are deeply divided about the issue of independent research, which goes to the heart of their roles and responsibilities in the legal system. To many judges, doing independent research when confronted with new and unfamiliar material seems the most responsible and natural thing to do. To others, it represents the worst kind of overreaching and a threat to long-cherished adversarial values. But whether one supports the practice or not, one thing is clear. The issue of independent research deserves far greater attention than it has so far from jurists, academics, and practitioners alike.

See also Suzanne Goldenberg, "US Judges Use Wikipedia as a Courtroom Source" *The Guardian* (30 January 2007), online: www.guardian.co.uk/technology/2007/jan/30/wikipedia.news.

57 According to Brooker, above note 2 at 32: "The act of judicial research need not involve or imply a complete absence of knowledge. It does however imply partial knowledge, legal uncertainty, complexity or judicial dissatisfaction with the parties' legal argument."

Such was the criticism attracted by Lord Denning's infamous first decision as a Law Lord in *Rahimtoola v Nizam of Hyderabad*.[58] As Paterson recounts,[59] Denning "'spent the better part of the summer' undertaking independent research in to the law."[60] "The four other Law Lords participating in the decision however unanimously rebuked Denning's independent research and dissociated themselves from his judgement specifically on the grounds that the parties had not been heard on the points that formed the basis of Denning's judgement and also that now lower had passed on them."[61] Key decisions of Denning, based on his own research, were criticized or overturned on appeal because they violated the parties' rights to notice and a full defence.

Of course, this case is somewhat extreme, but examples of independent judicial research drawing disapproval are not hard to find. Closer to home, the Supreme Court of Canada's use of judicially secured social science evidence in *R v Askov*[62] elicited a certain degree of concern from scholars, including the researcher whose work was cited.[63] Manfredi and Kelly wrote: "According to Baar himself, the Court's use of legislative facts suffered from two fatal flaws. First, by relying on evidence obtained through its own efforts, the Court avoided even the minimal critical review provided by the adversary process."[64]

---

58 [1958] AC 379.

59 Alan Paterson, *The Law Lords* (Toronto: University of Toronto Press, 1982), as cited in Brooker, above note 2 at 32.

60 Brooker, *ibid* at 32–33, n 97. As per Paterson, cited by Brooker: "Denning joined a unanimous court as to the outcome of the case, but based his judgment on issues and points of law that had not been considered either by counsel or by the lower courts. Denning justified his action, stating (at 423–24) that, 'the law on this subject is of great consequence and, as applied at present, it is held by a great many to be unsatisfactory.'"

61 Brooker, above note 2 at 33. Noting, however, at 32–33, that unlike simple Internet searches, ". . . in Denning's case judicial research was motivated by a desire to change the result that would have followed from the application of the law that had been pleaded by the parties or to rewrite what he consisted to be 'bad' law." At 33, "judicial research, *à la* Lord Denning, was a radical departure from the Common Law adversarial tradition of judicial reliance on party argument, which F.A. Mann's [*sic*] described as the 'principle of judicial unpreparedness.'"

62 [1990] 2 SCR 1199 [*Askov*].

63 See Carl Baar, "Criminal Court Delay and the *Charter*: The Use and Misuse of Social Facts in Judicial Policy Making" (1993) 72 *Canadian Bar Review* 305.

64 See Christopher P Manfredi & James B Kelly, "Misrepresenting the Supreme Court's Record? A Comment on Choudhry and Hunter, 'Measuring Judicial

In reality, the permissibility of independent judicial research is far from clear.[65] However contradictory, firm evidence suggesting that judges are at liberty to engage in such pursuits is not lacking. As Brian Dickson CJ instructed: "The judge may also do further independent research if, in his or her opinion, the importance of the matter requires it, or if a point was inadequately researched by counsel. In the event that the case appears to turn on a point not raised by counsel in the factums or referred to in oral arguments, counsel will be recalled and given an opportunity to address the new concerns of the court."[66] This view was echoed at the trial level: "Judges can independently secure information. This may come from individual research, general reading or continuing education."[67]

And as Cheng observes in the American context, this issue is far from clearly defined, and the judges themselves are intensely divided on the tolerability of judicially secured data:

> One might expect that there would be clear and well-established rules governing independent research, but unfortunately there are not. Few cases have explicitly addressed the issue . . . . *[E]x parte* prohibitions only obliquely address the issue of library research, because their focus is arguably on informal communications that lack a citable or publicly available record . . . . In many ways, independent research is a natural extension of the recent trend toward judicial education programs in science. Those programs are built on the premise that if judges learn more about scientific principles and methods, they can more comfortably and competently handle scientific admissibility questions. The problem with judicial education programs is that they necessarily suffer the limitations of being broad in scope and separated in time. Independent

---

Activism on the Supreme Court of Canada'" (2004) 49 *McGill Law Journal* 741 at 756. See also Baar, above note 63.

65 George D Marlow, "From Black Robes to White Lab Coats: The Ethical Implications of a Judge's *Sua Sponte, Ex Parte* Acquisition of Social and Other Scientific Evidence during the Decision-Making Process" (1998) 72 *St John's Law Review* 291, and Jack B Weinstein, "Limits on Judges Learning, Speaking and Acting — Part I — Tentative First Thoughts: How May Judges Learn?" (1994) 36 *Arizona Law Review* 539.

66 The Rt Hon Brian Dickson, "A Life in the Law: The Process of Judging" (2000) 63 *Saskatchewan Law Review* 373 at 380.

67 Regarding judicially secured evidence, see Judge R James Williams, "Grasping a Thorny Baton . . . A Trial Judge Looks at Judicial Notice and Courts' Acquisition of Social Science" (1996) 14 *Canadian Family Law Quarterly* 179 at 13, also citing Peggy C Davis, "'There Is a Book Out . . .' An Analysis of the Judicial Absorption of Legislative Facts" (1987) 100 *Harvard Law Review* 1539 at 1541.

research enables judges to refresh their memories and plug gaps in their knowledge.[68]

In fact, just as independent judicial research attracted disapproval in *Askov*, so, too, did the Supreme Court of Canada's failure to vet evidence in *R v Morin* draw criticism.[69]

D. BEYOND THE COMMON LAW BAR: RELIABILITY OF INDEPENDENT CYBER SEARCHES

The Internet and its investigative tools, for obvious reasons chiefly relating to reliability and traceability, exacerbate the above-outlined concerns traditionally raised to caution against judicially secured information, *a fortiori*. Once again the problem of trustworthiness, perpetually haunting Internet sources,[70] resurfaces.

Judges, not unlike other people,[71] but more so by reason of their social role, must take tremendous precautions to ensure that the information

---

68 Cheng, "Should Judges Do Independent Research," above note 56 at 60–61.

69 [1992] 1 SCR 771 [*Morin*]. According to Baar, above note 63:

> An important element of the Supreme Court of Canada's recent constitutional judgments on criminal court delay was the use of quantitative data and social facts. However, use of this evidence was deficient in significant and diverse ways. In the *Askov* case, the court went beyond the evidence submitted by the parties, gathered its own data, but failed to test its conclusions against the earlier evidence. Later, in the *Morin* case, the court placed too much reliance on the adversary process, accepting invalid evidence that undermined its conclusions. In both *Askov* and *Morin*, court processes led to ineffective or incorrect use of material that, properly used, could have improved both the results and the reasons in these cases.

70 See, for example, John Broughton, *Wikipedia: The Missing Manual* (Sebastopol: Pogue Press/O'Reilly, 2008), and a review by Nicholson Baker, "The Charms of Wikipedia" *The New York Review of Books* (20 March 2008), online: www.nybooks.com/articles/archives/2008/mar/20/the-charms-of-wikipedia.

71 See, generally, Elie Margolies, "Surfin' Safari — Why Competent Lawyers Should Research on the Web" (2006) 10 *Yale Journal of Law and Technology* 82. See also Lynn Foster & Bruce Kennedy, "Technological Developments in Legal Research" (2000) 2 *Journal of Appellate Practice and Process* 275; Alvin M Podboy, "The Shifting Sands of Legal Research: Power to the People" (2000) 31 *Texas Technology Law Review* 1167; Patrick W Spangler, "The New World versus the Old World of Legal Research: Are Print Resources Completely a Thing of the Past?" (2006) 20 *CBA Record* 48; and Michael Whiteman, "The Impact of the Internet and Other Electronic Sources on an Attorney's Duty of

they obtain is reliable or risk undermining the ethical principle of equality and tainting judicial reasoning and, indeed, public confidence.[72] As Binnie J wrote with regard to the judicial obligation to provide reasons for judgment: "Reasons for judgment are the primary mechanism by which judges account to the parties and to the public for the decisions they render. The courts frequently say that justice must not only be done but must be seen to be done."[73]

Public access to the court's "thought processes" is an integral element of the much-cherished value of transparency and forms the basis for the public's confidence in the judiciary. These "thought processes," however,

---

Competence under the Rules of Professional Conduct" (2001) 11 *Alberta Law Journal of Science & Technology* 89.

72 In effect, judges are held to provide reasons for their decisions. This obligation to provide reasons was clarified by the Supreme Court of Canada in *R v Sheppard*, 2002 SCC 26 [*Sheppard*]. See also Hon Jamie WS Saunders, "The Morality of Judicial Reasoning" (2001) National Judicial Institute [on file with author]. According to Saunders J, at 2: "In a constitutional democracy there is an ethical obligation upon the judiciary to reason and to communicate that reasoning which is distinct from simply pronouncing a result." And at 15:

> Of the ten propositions advanced by Binnie J [in *Sheppard*] as an instructive but not exhaustive list to bear in mind when considering the duty of a judge to give reasons, the first in my opinion is perhaps the least remembered. "1. The delivery of reasoned decisions is inherent in the judge's role. It is part of his or her accountability for the discharge of the responsibilities of the office."

See also Justices Georgina Jackson & Adele Kent, "Teaching Judicial Ethics: The Canadian Methodology" (Paper delivered at the 2d International Conference on the Training of the Judiciary, Ottawa, 2 November 2004). Within one of his articles titled "The Open Court Principle Is a Hallmark of a Democratic Society. To What Extent Does That Inform a Judge's Ethical Obligation to Communicate and Reason," Saunders J cites the following passage from Piero Calamandrei, "The Crisis in the Reasoned Opinion" in Ephraim London, *The World of Law*, vol 2 (New York: Simon and Schuster, 1960) at 683:

> The most important and most typical indication of the rationality of the judicial function is the reasoned opinion. In all modern codes of procedure, whether civil or criminal, a reasoned opinion is prescribed as one of the requisites of the decision . . . . The requirement that there be a reasoned opinion is considered so important in Italy that it has been placed in the Constitution, where it is stated that "all judicial acts must be reasoned" (A.111).

73 As per the *Sheppard* decision, above note 72. For an excellent discussion on reasons for judgment and the judge's role, see Edward Berry, *Writing Reasons: A Handbook for Judges* (Victoria: E-M Press, 1998).

cannot be subject to proper scrutiny — be it public, academic, or appellate[74] — unless the sources that nourish them are clearly and verifiably identifiable.

Although scarce, the few cases that do deal with the issue of cyber searches from the bench are helpful in allowing us to gauge the issues that judges engaging in Internet research might face.

E. UNRELIABILITY OF CYBER SOURCES AND THE ADVERSARIAL PROCESS

Take, for instance, *Kourkounakis v Dello Russo*,[75] a medical malpractice case in which the presiding judge obligingly informed the parties that his clerk had conducted an Internet search on the plaintiff's expert. He nonetheless reassured them that he did not intend to use that information in his deliberations.[76]

Notwithstanding, and after the judge disparaged the expert witness in question and his credentials,[77] the plaintiff ultimately appealed, arguing that "the trial court erred by *sua sponte* 'googling' plaintiff's expert witness . . . ." Noteworthy is that he specifically invoked the "significant risk of misinformation [in using the Internet],"[78] rather than the common law discomfort with independent research.

74 On this last point, see the discussion in *Sheppard*, above note 72.

75 2005 US Dist LEXIS 8020 (SDNY 3 May 2005), 167 F App'x 255 (2d Cir 2006), *certiorari* denied, No 05-1669, 2006 US LEXIS 5913 (US 2 October 2006). See also *Stutzka v McCarville*, 420 F3d 757 at 761, n 2 (8th Cir 2005) (addressing the court's ability to take judicial notice of public records), and *Star v White*, 2006 US Dist LEXIS 71785 at *4, n 2 (ED Mich 29 September 2006).

76 Katrina Hall, "*Kourkounakis v. Dello Russo*: Should a Trial Judge Be Permitted to Independently Google an Expert Witness to Determine Credibility?" (2008) 112:3 *Penn State Law Review* 885, online: www.pennstatelawreview.org/articles/112%20Penn%20St.%20L.%20Rev.%20885.pdf.

77 Observing that he "does not appear to have practiced medicine since the mid-1990's, does not appear to have a valid medical license, never specialized or trained in ophthalmology, never performed or was accredited in LASIK, and never examined the plaintiff." See Hall, *ibid* at 887, citing *Kourkounakis v Dello Russo*, 2005 US Dist LEXIS 8020 (SD NY 3 May 2005) at *7. The United States Supreme Court denied *certiorari*, thus leaving the law in a state of uncertainty.

78 In any event, the trial court granted summary judgment in favour of the defendant, a decision affirmed by the Second Circuit, which did not address the issue of external research.

The problem, as one case comment observes, is not the "Googling *per se*, but in the websites that are returned by a Google search."[79] Sites suggested by even the most reputable search engines might not be as reputable due to the search engine's "understanding" of the user's search terms. What is worse, these unreliable sites are often virtually indistinguishable from their reliable counterparts, particularly to the untrained (however brilliant) cyber eye.

In the iconography, the argument goes, Justice is said to be blindfolded, with the blindfold representing a safeguard "against information that could corrupt her."[80] But increasingly online, the search engines that filter and order or rank the results that we obtain — not the information itself — are king. The algorithms used to select and order the information that judges would presumably use or even rely on are, in large part, protected by trade secret and therefore lack the requisite transparency.

As Professor James Grimmelmann correctly points out in the search neutrality context:

> Search is inherently subjective: it always involves guessing the diverse and unknown intentions of users . . . . Search engines are attention lenses; they bring the online world into focus. They can redirect, reveal, magnify, and distort. They have immense power to help and to hide. We use them, to some extent, always at our own peril. And out of the many ways that search engines can cause harm, the thorniest problems of all stem from their ranking decisions . . . .[81]

Further on that point, Scott Cleland observes that Google's "algorithm reportedly has over 1,000 variables/discrimination biases which decide which content gets surfaced."[82] And Lucas Introna and Helen Nissenbaum, for their part, caution that search engines will direct users to sites that are already popular and away from sites that are obscure.[83]

It is worth noting that the qualms in cases such as the above-cited malpractice case are primarily with the reliability and transparency prob-

---

79 See Hall, above note 76 at 890.

80 See Judith Resnick, "Managerial Judges" (1982) 96 *Harvard Law Review* 376 at 446.

81 James Grimmelmann, "Some Skepticism about Search Neutrality" (2010), online: http://james.grimmelmann.net/essays/SearchNeutrality.

82 Scott Cleland, "Why Google Is Not Neutral" (4 November 2009), *Precursor Blog* (blog), online: http://precursorblog.com/content/why-google-is-not-neutral.

83 Lucas D Introna & Helen Nissenbaum, "Shaping the Web: Why the Politics of Search Engines Matters" (2000) 16 *The Information Society* 169, online: www.nyu.edu/projects/nissenbaum/papers/searchengines.pdf.

lems plaguing cyber searches; they are not from the more general issues traditionally deriving from the historically controversial, judicially secured information offline. This emphasis is by no means insignificant. Although courts (at least in the United States, where most of the decisions on point originate) appear somewhat divided on the propriety of judicial cyber searches, there seems to be some degree of accord respecting the trustworthiness of sources as a crucial, if not determining, factor in assessing the permissibility of online judicial research.

For example, in a recent decision, the US Court of Appeals for the Second Circuit held that federal judges may use the Internet to "confirm their intuitions" about undisputed facts in cases before them.[84] In that instance, the defendant appealed the lower court's decision[85] in a supervised release revocation hearing, arguing that the judge's independent Google search, aimed merely at confirming certain otherwise uncontested facts (namely, that there are many different types of yellow hats for sale or in the judge's words "there are also lots of different rain hats . . . that one could buy"[86]) violated Rule 605 of the *Federal Rules of Evidence.*[87]

Although the ruling ostensibly permits independent judicial cyber searches, it is, in fact, significantly narrower. It pertains only to those facts

---

84 *United States v Bari*, 599 F3d 176 (2d Cir 2010), online: www.ca2.uscourts.gov/decisions/isysquery/47ec5646-9d82-47de-84ee-202c24791be5/1/doc/09-1074-cr_opn.pdf [*Bari*].

85 District Court for the Southern District of New York.

86 According to the Second Circuit in *Bari*, above note 84 at 178:

> Judge Chin considered evidence that the bank's surveillance footage showed that the robber wore a yellow rain hat and that a yellow rain hat was found in the garage of Bari's landlord. He stated as follows: "In addition, and I think this is the strongest piece of evidence frankly, we have the yellow hat. I am convinced from looking at the surveillance video [from the bank] of September 9 that [the hat found in the garage] is the same type of hat as appears in the video. It may not be precisely the actual hat, but it is the same type of hat. It is just too much of a coincidence that the bank robber would be wearing the same hat that we find in [his landlord's] garage."
>
> . . .
>
> Judge Chin then noted several similarities between the hat found in the landlord's garage and the hat worn by the robber. To emphasize the similarity between the hats, he stated that "there are clearly lots of yellow hats out there," and that "[o]ne can Google yellow rain hats and find lots of different yellow rain hats."

87 Rule 605 states that "[t]he judge presiding at the trial may not testify in that trial as a witness."

"not subject to reasonable dispute," in other words, what the court in this case deemed matters of "common knowledge." Opined the court:

> Twenty years ago, . . . a trial judge may have needed to travel to a local department store to survey the rain hats on offer . . . . Today, however, a judge need only take a few moments *to confirm his intuition* by conducting a basic Internet search . . . . As the cost of confirming one's intuition decreases, we would expect to see more judges doing just that . . . .[88]

The ruling's scope is further narrowed as the rules of evidence apply in their relaxed form in a case such as this, namely, a supervised release revocation hearing.

Although the decision does seem to suggest a certain leniency towards judicial cyber searches of uncontested or obvious matters, it is far from decisive. Instead, a safer conclusion is that the few courts that have ruled on point, in the United States and abroad, remain divided — if not entirely skeptical — regarding the permissibility of online searches by judges, even on somewhat obvious questions. Consider, too, how the New York Supreme Court addressed a more substantive question than this. The court scolded a lower court (Queens County) for conducting outside research online,[89] or what it described as "initiating its own investigation into the facts when, based upon the insufficient submissions of plaintiff, the court should have dismissed the complaint."[90] This case involved queries that went beyond "undisputed facts" and, unlike the previously cited decision, was not simply a supervised release revocation hearing, where the standard applied is somewhat more relaxed.

Notwithstanding and clearly reflecting the lack of consensus on the issue of independent judicial research that long *predates* the digital age, the dissent in *NYC Medical & Neurodiagnostic, PC v Republic Western Ins Co* opined as follows: "[I]t was a proper exercise of discretion for the court below to have *sua sponte* referred to a matter of public record, in order to ascertain the fact of defendant's status as an insurer. There is no logical reason not to include within the category of public records, such records when they are available from *reliable sources* on the Internet."[91]

---

88 *Bari*, above note 84 at 180 [emphasis added].

89 798 NYS2d 309 (2004) [*NYC Medical & Neurodiagnostic*].

90 *United States v Harris*, 271 F3d 690 (7th Cir 2001).

91 *NYC Medical & Neurodiagnostic*, above note 89 [emphasis added].

F. NOT ALL CYBER SEARCHES ARE CREATED EQUAL

Perhaps, and as pertains to the often decisive factor of reliability more directly, a distinction needs to be drawn between "cyber sources" more generally and Wikipedia searches, in particular. Although the former *may*, to a certain limited extent, be progressively tolerated provided that the cyber source is judged trustworthy,[92] the latter are, for the most part, greeted with opprobrium by higher courts.[93] The presumption is that they are inherently unreliable.

This assessment is not at all surprising. Wikipedia, the most popular "go-to" site for cyber research (or a Google search leading to Wikipedia),[94] "expressly makes no guarantee of the validity of the information it contains. [Instead] [t]he About page expressly warns users that not all articles are 'encyclopedic quality from the start' and 'may contain false or debatable information.'"[95]

Consider the US case of *Apple v Does*,[96] where a judge who made repeated references to Wikipedia attracted widespread criticism and scorn.

Likewise, in a later case, *Badasa v Mukasey*,[97] considered the leading US case on wiki-citing, the Eighth Circuit Court of Appeals chastised an immigration judge for the decision to deny asylum to a refugee, in part, based on Wikipedia findings. The court focused on Wikipedia's unreliability. Note that the disdain did not appear to be primarily elicited by fears of undermining the adversarial process but by the vicissitudes of cyber resources and unskilled, ad hoc use thereof. In that case, the

---

92 The concept of reliability is discussed further in this section.

93 As illustrated by the examples below. Needless to say, caselaw on point is scarce, given the emerging and, indeed, novel character of the issues discussed.

94 Cohen, above note 31; and Peoples, above note 31.

95 See Peoples, *ibid*, citing "Wikipedia About," online: http://en.wikipedia.org/w/index.php? title=Wikipedia:About&oldid=329127169. See *O'Grady v Superior Court*, 44 Cal Rptr 3d 72 [*O'Grady*], online: www.eff.org/files/filenode/Apple_v_Does/H028579.pdf, for an example of heavy reliance on Wikipedia. See also Arias, above note 34.

96 44 Cal Rptr 3d 72 (Ct App 2006). See also *O'Grady*, above note 95. See also Goldenberg, above note 56. In the United Kingdom, *The Register* said citing wiki is ample ground for overturning the *Apple v Does* case: Andrew Orlowski, "New Age Judge Blasts Apple" *The Register* (28 May 2006), online: www.theregister.co.uk/2006/05/28/apple_vs_does/; Evan Brown, "Apple v. Does It Mean Anything?" (26 May 2006), *Internet Cases* (blog), online: http://blog.internetcases.com/2006/05/26/apple-v-does-it-mean-anything/: "The court relied on Wikipedia as well in its opinion — no less than ten times!"

97 540 F3d 909 (8th Cir 2008).

wiki-citing judge unknowingly quoted a preliminary, or "in progress," Wikipedia entry without foundation, therefore bestowing authoritativeness and premising law on a baseless draft.

As Peoples points out, "[t]he Eighth Circuit failed to pick up on the fact that the Wikipedia entry at issue was a 'stub' not citing any references or sources. A stub is an 'article containing only a few sentences of text which is too short to provide encyclopedic coverage of a subject.'"[98] Many Wikipedia entries start out as stubs and are later developed into more complete entries. As one commentator put it, the incompetence of the DHS lawyer and immigration judge in citing Wikipedia "would almost be humorous if it weren't for the dire consequences of rejecting a valid asylum application and returning a refugee to a country in which they face torture and possibly death."[99]

Likewise, in the US tax case *English Mountain Spring Water Co v Chumley*,[100] the court questioned Wikipedia's reliability, even for purposes of a rudimentary and seemingly trivial or self-evident search for the meaning of the term "water." It said: "given the fact that this source is open to virtually anonymous editing by the general public, the expertise of its editors is always in question, and its reliability is indeterminable. Accordingly, we do not find that it constitutes persuasive authority."

Therefore, while "uncontested facts" *may* under certain circumstances be searchable online, at least according to the Second Circuit[101] and perhaps even the Superior Court of Québec (which used online sources to help determine the meaning of "shock-jock" in *Gillet c Arthur*[102]), Wikipedia might not be the best place to confirm "intuitions" on point, by reason of its untrustworthiness.

Thus, for instance, Mosely J of the Federal Court was not "impressed" by evidence brought forth from Wikipedia in *Bajraktaraj v Canada (Minister of Citizenship and Immigration).*[103]

As previously noted, when dealing with online sources, even the sharpest mind has manifest difficulty distinguishing between proper and

---

98 Peoples, above note 31 at 12.

99 *Ibid*, citing Jaya Ramji-Nogales, "Citing Wikipedia — Harmless Error?" *Concurring Opinions* (3 September 2008), online: www.concurringopinions.com/archives/2008/09/citing_wikipedi.html.

100 *English Mountain Spring Water Co v Chumley*, 196 SW3d 144 at 149 (Tenn Ct App 2005) [*English Mountain Spring Water*].

101 To confirm an intuition.

102 2005 CanLII 37500 (QC CS).

103 2005 FC 261.

rogue sources: truths and fabrication appear at par. Anthony Lewis, a First Amendment scholar and great proponent of the more absolutist American conception of freedom of expression, makes a suggestion about this in his most recent book. He writes that the marketplace of ideas model might require revisiting in light of the networked environment.

Consider that a simple search on US President Barack Obama's birthplace or religious identity can easily reveal the perils of inaccuracy plaguing cyber searches.[104] More important, it shows the disturbing intricacy related to distinguishing legitimate sources from their rogue counterparts or those without sufficient editorial oversight. This issue has been a source of significant concern, as Holocaust deniers (and other racist, white supremacists) unabashedly proffer their blatant lies, easily cloaked as legitimate truths, online, in a way that could never have been possible offline.

Deborah Lipstadt warns:

> What the Internet has done is put a lot of unfiltered information out there, and by so doing it makes it harder for people to differentiate what is legitimate information and what is not; what is fact and what is fiction. The Internet is a wonderful thing — it allows us to spread information in a way we never did before. But it puts out a lot of lies and it's easy access for people. Someone wrote to me that his son Googled "Jews, Soap and the Holocaust" and the first four sites were Holocaust denial sites. This is a myth. Jews were not made into soap. It never happened — there might have been experiments. Deniers say, "This is another lie that Jews made up." That's why I'm such a stickler and I get so upset and worried when you have people making up Holocaust memoirs like "Angel at the Fence." It's fodder for the deniers. The deniers then say, "Here's another example of a Jew being a denier. How can you believe 'Night' [by Elie Wiesel] or 'The Diary of Anne Frank' — it's all lies."[105]

Given this sobering difficulty, it stands to reason that, in the judicial context, availing oneself of cyber sources can be a dangerous practice. Most scholars and, indeed, judges, as many of the above-cited cases illustrate, do not yet have the ability to distinguish between unimpeachable and dubious sources with absolute confidence. (Few people do.) There

---

104 Karl Rove, "Political Campaigns Go Viral: The Impact of the Internet on Elections Has Only Begun to Be Felt" *The Wall Street Journal* (10 March 2011), online: http://online.wsj.com/article/SB10001424052748704132204576190472697049288.html.

105 See interview with Deborah Lipstadt, "Denying the Deniers: Q & A with Deborah Lipstadt" *JTA* (19 April 2009), online: www.jta.org/news/article/2009/04/19/1004269/denying-the-deniers-q-a-with-deborah-lipstadt.

may also be an absence of firm citation guidelines. In addition and most important perhaps, "citation of an inherently unstable source such as Wikipedia — or any other cybersource for that matter — can undermine the foundation not only of the judicial opinion in which Wikipedia (or perhaps even the Internet, broadly speaking) is cited, but of the future briefs and judicial opinions which in turn use that judicial opinion as authority."[106]

Of course, Wikipedia entries and the like can be modified by almost anyone, with little editorial control or oversight, thus augmenting the risk of unreliability and undermining judicial authoritativeness. Such fears are substantiated by various studies: one by Barger, for example, focused on the impermanence of cyber sources, finding that 75 percent of health information returned from a search engine expedition is inaccurate.[107]

---

106 See Cohen, above note 31. For example, according to Cohen's article, New York tax practitioner Kenneth H Ryesky "took exception to the practice." Stephen Gillers, a professor at New York University Law School, "saw this as crucial": "'The most critical fact is public acceptance, including the litigants,' he said. 'A judge should not use Wikipedia when the public is not prepared to accept it as authority.' For now, Professor Gillers said, "Wikipedia is best used for 'soft facts' that are not central to the reasoning of a decision. All of which leads to the question, if a fact isn't central to a judge's ruling, why include it?"

The Tennessee Court of Appeals agrees: "Given the fact that this source is open to virtually anonymous editing by the general public, the expertise of its editors is always in question, and its reliability is indeterminable. Accordingly, we do not find that it constitutes persuasive authority." See *English Mountain Spring Water*, above note 100.

107 Coleen M Barger, "On the Internet, Nobody Knows You're a Judge: Appellate Courts' Use of Internet Materials" (2002) 4 *Journal of Appellate Practice and Process* 417 at 438 (2002). See also Mark de Jong, "A Response to a 'Modest Proposal' Commentary" (2005) 97 *Law Library Journal* 193, online: www.aallnet.org/main-menu/Publications/llj/LLJ-Archives/Vol-97/pub_llj_v97n01/2005-11.pdf. See, for example, Cal Fussman, "But Can You Trust It?" (2003) 34:2 *American Libraries* 22; Health Improvement Institute & Consumer WebWatch, *A Report on the Evaluation of Criteria Sets for Assessing Health Web Sites* (30 September 2003), online: www.hii.org/eca.pdf; Joseph Turow et al, "Discussions of Health Web Sites in Medical and Popular Media" *Consumer WebWatch* (May 2003), online: http://works.bepress.com/joseph_turow/1. See also Wallace Koehler, "An Analysis of Web Page and Web Site Constancy and Permanence" (1999) 50:2 *Journal of the American Society for Information Science* 162; Susan Lyons, "Persistent Identification of Electronic Documents and the Future of Footnotes" (2005) 97 *Law Library Journal* 681 at 684; Helane E Davis, "Keeping Validity in Cite: Web Resources Cited in Select Washington Law Reviews 2001–03" (2006) 98 *Law Library Journal* 639 at 646.

G. LINK ROT: THE PARADOXICAL IMPERMANENCE OF INTERNET SOURCES

The risk of untraceable, "vanished," or migrated sources — often referred to as "link rot" — is all the more worrisome in the judicial context. It is especially problematic in the common law world, where caselaw is predicated upon prior decisions. The use of dubious or ephemeral sources by judges in drafting what is normally binding precedent not surprisingly amplifies the dangers not only to the parties but future litigants, courts, and the justice system as a whole. In other words, "the authority underlying the case law itself becomes authority, which makes it important for those researching the law to see why a court ruled as it did. If the authority upon which a court relies disappears, then a component of a court's decision disappears as well."[108]

In contrast, in the fictional movie *The Social Network*, Facebook founder Mark Zuckerberg's ex-girlfriend exclaims in frustration that the Internet "isn't written in pencil — it's written in ink."[109] Indeed, much ink has been proverbially spilled discussing the "end of forgetting" or lamenting the Internet's infinite memory in the context of litigant privacy.[110] In this case, the difficulty we are addressing is not the Internet's permanence, but rather the problem of unwanted deleting or erasure, notably of data integral to a court's decision and *a fortiori* precedent more broadly. Paradoxically, in the one instance where we might want the Internet to be more permanent or the information it proffers more durable, it is not.

In this vein, Meg Ambrose, who challenged the notion of Internet permanence in a different context,[111] may be entirely correct. In truth, memory in the digital age is not flawless, data are not always permanent,

---

108 Michael Whiteman, "The Death of Twentieth-Century Authority" (2010) 58 *UCLA Law Review Discourse* 27 at 33. "One of the stable aspects of traditional legal authority was the confidence that an attorney would be able to retrieve the authority upon which a judge relied in formulating her opinion. Not only could the researcher retrieve the authority, she also had the ability to retrieve the underlying sources of the authority. In other words, she could look behind the authority and lift the veil to see what sources the judge or legislators used to create the authority." *Ibid* at 32.

109 *The Social Network*, 2010, DVD (Culver City, CA: Columbia Pictures, 2011).

110 See, for example, the introduction to this book and Chapter 3 on litigant privacy.

111 Meg Leta Ambrose, "It's about Time: Privacy, Information Lifecycles, and the Right to Be Forgotten" (2013) 16 *Stanford Technology Law Review* 369, online: https://journals.law.stanford.edu/sites/default/files/stanford-technology-law-review/online/itsabouttime.pdf.

and although the Internet might be great at "remembering" those embarrassing views that we would rather not be associated with today, it tends to "forget" information that we cite, rely on, and need to remember. Court decisions are no exception to this. Needless to say, the seriousness of "forgotten" data is exacerbated when the information that needs to be located is evidence adduced by attorneys or cited by courts. That sort of data vanishing, as previously noted, does violence to the stability of precedent and transparency of justice, which, in the long run, can have an even more disturbing cumulative effect on *stare decisis* and the foreseeability of law.

Barger, whose study tangibly confirms the predicament, aptly summarizes the serious consequences related to improper use of online sources:

> When . . . a court purportedly bases its understanding of the law or the law's application to case facts upon a source that cannot subsequently be located or confirmed, the significance of the citation to that source becomes more ominous. If present readers of the opinion cannot determine how much persuasive weight was or should be accorded to the unavailable source, they have little reason to place much confidence in the opinion's authoritativeness.[112]

The lack of authoritativeness and durability of online sources effectively cripples the Internet's ability to tell courts anything of real substance about the reality it purports to depict. Even worse, it risks distorting future courts' understanding and creating a "body of precedent written on the wind," without textured characterization and in absence of any meaningful locatability.[113] For as Barger again points out, less than half of cyber sources cited by courts in her six-year study were still accessible at the time of writing, while the others had disappeared.

So the Internet appears to be what we describe in French as *un couteau à double tranchant* ("double-edged sword"): there is permanence where we do not want it and transience or precariousness where we require longevity. The Internet preserves where perhaps it should not and "forgets" where we need it to remember.

How does this unwanted "forgetting" play out in jurisprudence? An example is provided by someone who purchased a domain name cited by US Supreme Court Justice Samuel Alito in his concurring decision in

---

112 Above note 107.

113 Ken Strutin, "Written on the Wind: Be Cautious When Citing Internet Sites in Legal Documents" *New York Law Journal* (29 June 2004) at 5.

Brown v Entertainment Merchants Association.[114] The site provided the following 404 error message:

> Aren't you glad you didn't cite to this webpage in the Supreme Court Reporter at *Brown v. Entertainment Merchants Association*, 131 S.Ct. 2729, 2749 n.14 (2011). If you had, like Justice Alito did, the original content would have long since disappeared and someone else might have come along and purchased the domain in order to make a comment about the transience of linked information in the internet age.[115]

According to *New York Times* journalist Adam Liptak, the US Supreme Court has cited online resources 555 times since 1996, and nearly half of the cited websites (49 percent) no longer work.[116] Further, the American Bar Association cautions against "[a] subcategory of link rot — 'reference rot' — which occurs when the link (itself) exists, but the information referenced is no longer present." The original information is often replaced by unsavoury information.

There is also the matter of deliberately incorrect entries, planted on Wikipedia in order to purposefully manipulate evidence and courts. For example, there was a so-called "straw-man entry" in Israel. Ill-intentioned individuals calculatingly planted inaccuracies and disinformation on Wikipedia, with the intent to mislead and influence a particular outcome in a dispute.[117] Malicious litigants and unscrupulous or corrupt attorneys can presumably — and to a certain extent anonymously — manipulate online information relating to their case or connected issues in the hope that courts will naively look these up online and rely on their findings, if judges and their law clerks are not trained to be "Internet-savvy."

---

114 131 SCt 2729 at 2749, n 14 (2011).

115 See, online: http://ssnat.com/.

116 Adam Liptak, "In Supreme Court Opinions, Web Links to Nowhere" *The New York Times* (23 September 2013), online: http://nyti.ms/19e1Ne5.

117 See "25 Biggest Blunders in Wikipedia History" (10 February 2009), *Best Colleges Online.com* (blog), online: www.bestcollegesonline.com/blog/2009/02/10/25-biggest-blunders-in-wikipedia-history; Catherine Elsworth, "Fake Wikipedia Prof Altered 20,000 Entries" *The Telegraph* (6 March 2007), online: www.telegraph.co.uk/news/1544737/Fake-Wikipedia-prof-altered-20000-entries.html; John Seigenthaler, "A False Wikipedia 'Biography'" *USA Today* (29 November 2005), online: www.usatoday.com/news/opinion/editorials/2005-11-29-wikipedia-edit_x.htm; "Student's Wikipedia Hoax Quote Used Worldwide in Newspaper Obituaries" *The Irish Times* (5 May 2009), online: www.irishtimes.com/newspaper/ireland/2009/0506/1224245992919.html.

As for Tennant and Seal, they discuss how Wikipedia information changes over time:

> The impermanence of the internet, as content is modified and/or migrates to other locations, means that a citation to a URL today may not lead to the exact same information tomorrow. For example, if a judge cites a Wikipedia entry in an opinion by using the URL, and the entry is subsequently modified, the reader of the opinion who tries to access the entry will not get the same information the judge relied on. In addition, reliability, authoritativeness, and accuracy are all important concerns, since there is often no way to know anything about the author of internet content, or be assured that the information has not been tampered with.[118]

The *Bluebook*, for its part, also recognizes that "[m]any internet sources . . . do not consistently satisfy traditional criteria for cite-worthiness."[119] Unfortunately, though, the American citation guide has yet to provide much additional counsel as to proper use.

H. THE NEED TO ADOPT A BALANCED APPROACH TO CYBER MATERIAL USE

Yet cyber sources are not to be entirely discounted in this, the digital age. The Internet is omnipresent, and judges, subject to the ethical principles of competence and diligence, cannot reasonably blind themselves to innovation whose purpose is to enhance proficiency, iconic metaphors of blindfolded Justice notwithstanding. Further, attorneys are increasingly shifting to online authority,[120] and "the producers of primary legal information are increasingly turning to the web to deliver this information."[121]

---

118 Tennant & Seal, above note 3.

119 See Harvard Law Review Association et al, *The Bluebook: A Uniform System of Citation*, 20th ed (Cambridge, MA: Harvard Law Review Association, 2015) at 18.2.1. There are many guides to the *Bluebook* which provide commentary and instruction on how to use it. See, for example, Georgetown Law Library, "Bluebook Guide," online: www.law.georgetown.edu/library/research/bluebook.

120 Whiteman, above note 108 at 31. See, for example, McDonough, above note 40.

121 Whiteman, above note 108 at 31: "According to the US Government Printing Office (GPO) — the federal agency that publishes, prints, and distributes information from the three branches — primary legal sources will soon be available exclusively online. The GPO has stated that 'as many as 50% of all U.S. Government documents are now born digital, published to the Web and will never be printed by the Federal government,'" citing US Government Printing Office, *A*

Ultimately, and as indicated, the exceptionally intricate matters facing courts today frequently require specialized knowledge that the Internet can perhaps help demystify.[122] In its simplicity and ease, technology can arguably serve to impart a better ability to understand expert witnesses and sophisticated pleadings and to adeptly direct courtroom proceedings on point.

Faced with tremendous exigencies and held to what might easily be deemed unreasonable expectations of competence,[123] judges would presumably be remiss to confine their comprehension of progressively more intricate facts, let alone technical issues, to passive reliance on "experts" with all their jargon (or even on private consortiums teaching them science, as in the United States).[124] Doing so might to some minds be deemed an abdication of their basic duties, allowing outsiders to usurp the judicial role and, indeed, through their disproportionate influence supplant the judge's part and substitute her judgment with their own. So, in light of the above, judges can defer to a multitude of "experts" or google in fear, in uncertainty, or in an uninformed manner for clarification. Surely, though, they cannot be oblivious to the Internet revolution, which has touched us all. What is needed is the presence of clear guidelines on point.

The more reasonable direction, it would appear, is one firmly anchored in the principles of caution and *proportionality*. That is to say, judges should strive to strike the correct or finest balance between maintaining competence in light of innovation, on the one hand, and upholding reliability and authority, in a way that respects the adversarial process as well as public and appellate review, on the other.

Herein lies the importance of distinguishing "in progress" (stub), fly-by-night, or mendacious incarnations masking as legitimate sites offering serious information from their trustworthy and traceable counterparts.

Although the more general discomfort with "independent research" in the common law world *predates* the digital revolution and is arguably only exacerbated by it (the impulse to consult online sources being effortlessly

---

Strategic Vision for the 21st Century (1 December 2004), online: www.gpo.gov/pdfs/fdsys-info/04strategicplan.pdf.

122 Stobbe & Marchione, above note 23.

123 Potentially heightened by the push towards efficiency and technological surveillance, as noted in Section A, above in this chapter.

124 In addition to publications and seminars, that curriculum features a twofold "staple" event: the "National Judges' Science School" (an annual case-conference focusing on select issues, such as 2006's focus on evidence, expert witnesses, and causation), and the "National Judges' Medical School."

indulged), for courts' purposes, most of the flaws associated with cyber research can be attributed chiefly to its untrustworthiness.

For judges, the crux and immediacy of the problem, it bears repeating, seem to stem primarily from the unreliability and untraceability of Internet sources, thereby doing both transparency and authority violence. Undeniably, the "loosening of traditional notions of acceptable legal authority"[125] poses a particular problem for judges. They not only consult sources, but in so doing, also create authority upon which subsequent authority is premised.[126]

As Greer and colleagues observe:

> The Internet is a virtual library, consisting of an unlimited amount of information. Anyone is allowed to publish and access this information. Furthermore, the sites are created for a variety of purposes to inform, persuade, sell, and change an attitude or belief. The sites are not monitored, edited, regulated, or approved. All of these factors remind us of the fact that information that has been published on the Web, is no indication of its believability or accuracy . . . . Although the size of the Internet can be viewed as both a positive and negative factor, with such a vast amount of information available on the Web, it seems impossible that all of the sites can be considered credible. Therefore, it is important to differentiate between sites that are credible and those that are not.[127]

As Barger's study confirms, the impermanence of sources further exacerbates the substantive reliability problem (see Section G, above in this chapter). Consider the following example, tendered by Peoples in his insightful piece on the preponderant judicial use of Wikipedia:

> . . . [i]n *Fharmacy Records v. Nassar*, the court cited the Wikipedia entry for the hip hop artist DMX's album *Grand Champ* to establish the date of a fact at issue in the case, the date of the album's release, and to sup-

125 See Randy Diamond, "Advancing Public Interest Practitioner Research Skills in Legal Education" (2005) 7 *North Carolina Journal of Law and Technology* 67 at 90, discussing attorneys' use of electronic media.

126 See, for example, Kris Franklin, "The Rhetorics of Legal Authority Constructing Authoritativeness, the 'Ellen Effect,' and the Example of Sodomy Law" (2001) 33 *Rutgers Law Journal* 49 at 52: "Decisions about how authority can be used to support a particular position are not made lightly. But they are not inevitable either: legal arguments are *constructed* on a foundation of supporting authorities, and, like any construction; they can fail if their foundation is not secure."

127 Toni Greer et al, "An Educators' Guide to Credibility and Web Evaluation" (Spring 1999), University of Illinois/Urbana-Champaign, online: https://web.archive.org/web/20120602205122/http:/www.ed.uiuc.edu/wp/credibility.

> port the court's reasoning. The URL of the entry appears in the *Federal Supplement Second* as "http://en.wikipedia.org/wiki/Grand_Champ (last visited Aug. 11, 2008)." In the version of the opinion available on Westlaw, the URL appears as "http://en.wikipedia.org/wiki/Grand_ Champ (last visited Aug. 11, 2008)." The URL that appears on Westlaw includes several additional spaces — between "//" and "en"; between "en." and "wikipedia"; between ".org/" and "wiki"; and between "wiki/" and "Grand." A researcher examining this opinion on Westlaw who attempts to paste the URL into an open browser window will receive an "Address Not Found" message.[128]

So, how might courts proceed in order to benefit from the resources of the Internet while still maintaining the credibility of their decisions?

I. THE BEST EVIDENCE RULE ONLINE

In light of the above said, until improved guidelines emerge, judges would do well to avoid cyber sources altogether *when* more authoritative traditional sources exist. This approach comports with the US *Bluebook* Rule 18.2, which "requires the use and citation of traditional printed sources when available, unless there is a digital copy of the source available that is authenticated, official, or an exact copy of the printed source, as described in rule 18.2.1."[129]

---

128 Peoples, above note 31 at 37.

129 *The Bluebook: A Uniform System of Citation*, 19th ed (New York: Columbia Law Review Association, 2010) at 153:

> Rule 18 has changed considerably with the 19th edition, primarily to allow increased citation to Internet sources. Specific changes include: Rule 18.2.1(a) now provides guidance allowing citation to authenticated and official Internet sources as well as exact digital scans of print sources as if they were the original print source. These changes in rule 18 allowing citation to official, authenticated, or exact Internet copies of cited materials are also reflected in rules 10, 12, 15, 16, and 17. Guidance for citation to webpage titles of main pages and subheadings has been expanded in rule 18.2.2(b). Rule 18.2.2(a) now states that when no author of an Internet source is clearly announced, the author information should be omitted from the citation, unless there is a clear institutional owner of the domain. Additionally, institutional authors of Internet sources should be abbreviated according to rule 15.1(d). Rule 18.2.2(c) now states that citations to Internet sources should be dated as they appear on the Internet site, using only dates that refer clearly to the material cited. When material is undated, the date of the author's last visit to the website should be placed in a parenthetical after the URL. Rule 18.2.2(c) now also states that

Of course, judges may turn to a reliable cyber source as a preliminary *lead* and then substantiate that search with more authoritative print sources.[130]

> for blogs and other frequently updated websites, citations should include timestamps whenever possible. Rule 18.2.2(h) still encourages the archiving of Internet sources, but does not require the citation to indicate the location of an archival copy. Rules 18.6 and 18.7 now allow for the use of timestamps in citations to audio and video recordings. Rule 18.7.3 now provides citation guidance for podcasts and online recordings. Professor James Grimmelmann provided vital advice and assistance in revising rule 18.

From the preface to the 19th edition, online: www.legalbluebook.com/Public/Introduction.aspx.

For our purposes, the most significant changes respecting the Internet citation are between the 18th and 19th editions. The 20th edition (which has come out since) features comparatively only relatively minor modifications. Notable among these include:

> (18.2.1(d)) Encouraging the use of archival Internet sources when a reliable one is available (e.g. perma.cc or web.archive.org), (18.2.2(a)) Guidance on citing authors for social media,
>
> (18.2.2(b)(iii)) & (18.2.2(b)(v)) Guidance on citing titles for blogs and other social media.

The *Canadian Guide to Uniform Legal Citation* (also known as the McGill Guide, or the Red Book) has been updated to include a new section on citing online sources: See Svetlana Kochkina, "New Edition of the Red Book Is Here" (12 June 2014), *McGill Library Blog* (blog), online: https://blogs.library.mcgill.ca/lawlibrary/new-edition-of-the-red-book-is-here/. The 8th edition includes specific rules for citing blogs, Facebook posts, Reddit posts, tweets, and video aggregators. However, it does not address Wikipedia (or wikis in general). It states:

- "With the exception of online databases (section 6.22.1), this section provides guidance for sources found solely or primarily online. For general guidance in citing to online sources that supplement access to print publications, see section 1.6. For specific guidance with respect to certain sources available both online and in print, see the relevant section (e.g., jurisprudence (3.8), encyclopedic digests (6.5), newspapers (6.16))."
- "Where a source is only available online, exercise prudence in citing to potentially ephemeral content (e.g., personal webpages hosted by employing institutions, Facebook posts, Reddit threads)."
- "Do not cite to an electronic service that the majority of readers will not be able to access. For example, do not cite to Lawnet (Singapore) when writing for a Canadian audience."

130 As did the Seventh Circuit in *Nautilus Ins Co v Reuter*, 537 F3d 733 at 737 (7th Cir 2008).

In this context, uniform, verifiable guidelines for judicial use of Internet resources must soon be developed. As Williams J remarks: "It is often difficult to determine from reviewing a case what *the source* of the information the judge is using is, brief or some individual endeavour of the judge. Too often judges refer to material without identifying its source."[131] Therefore, some of the difficulties might, in part, be alleviated (although not fully resolved) by cultivating the ability to differentiate between proper and improper sources among judges and issuing firmer guiding principles for judicial research on the Internet, including proper citation.

Some courts have — albeit independently and in the context of evidence proffered — taken a first step in this direction by ruling on which websites might be acceptable for purposes of judicial notice, these featuring public records.[132] Thus, for instance, the court in *Polley v Allen*[133] held that judges can, and indeed must, appropriately take judicial notice of properly collected government statistics online if the URL in question allows for determining the content's accuracy. The underlying rationale, as elaborated in *Dingle v Bioport Corp*,[134] is that as "public records" these are not subject to "reasonable dispute."

More important perhaps, in order to workably apply this time-tested rule to the cyber context, the material in question must not only be undisputed in terms of its veracity, but must be capable of "accurate and ready" authentication and verification[135] by reference to materials whose "accuracy can not be reasonably questioned."[136]

J. KEEP A HARD COPY: THE PRESERVATION OF DIGITAL SOURCES

Although there is clearly a need to implant a common language for purposes of *citing* cyber sources, there appears to be an even greater need for developing a procedure for *preserving* referenced sources, thus subjecting

131 Williams, above note 67.

132 See dissent in *NYC Medical & Neurodiagnostic*, above note 89.

133 *Polley v Allen*, 2004 WL 690491 (Ky Ct App).

134 270 F Supp 2d 968 at 972 (WD Mich 2003). This decision and *Polley v Allen*, above note 133, are cited in Paul R Rice, *Electronic Evidence: Law and Practice*, 2d ed (Chicago: American Bar Association, 2008) at 333.

135 See *Victaulic Co v Tieman*, 499 F3d 227 at 236–37 (3d Cir 2007).

136 See Albert Shamash, "A Tangled Web? The Developing Law of Judicial Notice of Website Information" (Spring 2009) *New Hampshire Bar Journal* 38, online: www.nhbar.org/uploads/pdf/BJ-50-38.pdf.

them to public and appellate scrutiny if need be. Preservation guidelines specifically and explicitly relating to Internet sources must be put in place for both judges and attorneys. If these sources are absent, then the factual bases that serve as a foundation for the legal arguments built thereon risk being undermined, both by lack of uniformity and severe inaccuracy (all cyber sources not being created equal). Accordingly, ad hoc use of cyber sources must be strongly discouraged and replaced by digital information literacy and a good measure of critical thinking.[137] Preliminary guidelines (as noted above) are already available but must be built upon and forcefully applied in the courtroom, to both judges and litigants.

A promising development is that the US Judicial Conference has issued basic guidelines on critically appraising and preserving cyber sources.[138] The policy approved provides that "all Internet materials cited in final opinions be considered for preservation" and that "[e]ach judge . . . should retain the discretion to decide whether the specific cited resource should be captured and preserved." This measure is undoubtedly a constructive and important first step; however, the policy leaves the duty to preserve up to individual judges. The fact that the duty to preserve is merely discretionary tends to undermine much-needed clarity and uniformity in this context.

As previously noted, Internet searches give rise to serious misgivings in the judicial sources, if only by reason of their impermanence. As one judge observed, "Google is continually updating its search system, and results from an identical search can vary from day to day."[139] This observation is all the more true as search engines are going "social" with Google, for instance, planning to "allow users to recommend useful search results to friends and potentially reorder the way sites are ranked based on what they and their friends like or find useful."[140]

Perhaps surprisingly, avoiding the pitfalls occasioned by the transition from paper to Net is often quite simple to do. The measures are unfortunately not commonly taken, however, because digital information

---

137 Judicial Conference of the United States, *Guidelines on Citing to, Capturing, and Maintaining Internet Resources in Judicial Opinions/Using Hyperlinks in Judicial Opinions* (2009).

138 Judicial Conference of the United States, *Internet Materials in Judicial Opinions and Orders* (22 May 2009). For the full text of the policy, see Appendix.

139 See *Dorner v Commercial Trade Bureau of Cal*, 2008 US Dist LEXIS 70425 at 6 (E Dist Cal 2008).

140 Amir Efrati, "Google Wants to Be More Social" *The Wall Street Journal* (31 March 2011), online: http://on.wsj.com/1zkMTeR.

(unlike its paper counterpart) is, for the most part, naively assumed to be benign. Given these pitfalls, preserving a hard copy, in the form of a printout or a downloaded file, of all cyber sources cited or used should be made a priority; the sources should also be monitored cautiously to allow for public scrutiny, accountability, and effective appellate review.[141]

Otherwise, good intentions might, as Sartre would have it, lead us nowhere (or worse!). In an initial effort to respond to the issue of vanishing cyber sources, the US Supreme Court instructed the clerk's office to maintain a hard copy of all cyber sources invoked.[142] While the Supreme Court still retains a hard copy of web-based content included in Court opinions, all such content from the 2005 Term forward is now also being preserved and made available on the Court's website. Although the practice is important, even *sine qua non*, it still has, as one commentator has remarked, a good number of glitches to overcome.[143] When Michael Whiteman, author of "The Death of Twentieth-Century Authority," attempted to visit the Court's website specifically dealing with the problem of dead links, he found that the link itself was no longer active.[144]

K. SUMMARY OF WAYS TO PROTECT INTEGRITY OF ONLINE INFORMATION

Courts are duty-bound to protect and preserve electronic data, particularly data relied upon in the decision-making process. Publicity and transparency are — and must continue to be understood as — a bulwark against misuse or abuse of power and a means to promote confidence in the judicial system, without which no justice can be done, let alone seen to be done. Although the Internet can be said to assist in allowing justice to be done, great care must be taken to ensure that the availability of a deluge of data unscreened and oftentimes unreliable does not ultimately serve to undermine the very confidence on which the judicial system rests. As a New York State ethics opinion issued more than fifteen years ago asserted,

---

141 To paraphrase the Supreme Court of Canada setting out the importance of giving reasons in *R v REM*, 2008 SCC 51.

142 William R Wilkerson, "The Emergence of Internet Citations in U.S. Supreme Court Opinions" (2006) 27 *Justice System Journal* 323 at 334.

143 Whiteman, above note 108.

144 *Ibid*. In a 22 July 2010 visit to the US Supreme Court's website, Whiteman found that the link titled "Problem With Out of Date Information?" was a dead link, online: www.supremecourt.gov/problemwithoutofdateinfo.aspx.

attorneys relying on cyber research must "take care to assure that the information obtained is reliable."[145]

A fortiori is this true of judges. They must take pains to ensure that they (and their clerks) safeguard the accuracy and traceability of materials secured online. As they navigate the complexities of the digital age, they must similarly be mindful of the role of search engines in shepherding data and the potential for distortion as well as the above-stated common law uneasiness with independent judicial research.[146]

In sum, in the interim, the following simply stated principles may serve to guide judicial use of cyber searches:

- Refine judicial training, emphasizing proper citation practices for online sources, differentiating between proper and improper sources; foster awareness of the important role of search engines in data results and ordering.
- Avoid Wikipedia and other modifiable cyber sources. A certain static character is required for reliability.
- Select a cyber search only when a more traditional avenue is unavailable.
- Keep paper records of all cyber sources consulted and link to "primary sources whenever possible, unless the secondary source is central to your coverage."[147]

As a viable alternative, in the United States, the Ninth Circuit has its own collection of archives of every web page cited in a court opinion, in PDF format. If a link goes dead, one can head to the Ninth Circuit's own website archive of PDF copies.[148]

Recall that half the links cited by the US Supreme Court are alleged to be rotten.[149] Thus, there needs to be a protocol for identifying the potential time-stamped archive of an URL being referenced. As Harvard law professor Jonathan Zittrain argues, however, simply because something has been preserved digitally and centralized does not mean it cannot be

---

145 New York State Bar Association Committee on Professional Ethics, *Opinion 709* (16 September 1998) at 3.

146 However qualified, generally by the demands of competence, as noted above and expressly by the *Daubert* rule in the United States, as per Cheng, "Independent Legal Research," above note 29.

147 Leighton Walter Kille, "The Growing Problem of Internet 'Link Rot' and Best Practices for Media and Online Publishers" *Journalist's Resource* (16 February 2015), online: http://journalistsresource.org/studies/society/internet/website-linking-best-practices-media-online-publishers#sthash.uDETVdeE.dpuf [Kille].

148 Online: www.ca9.uscourts.gov/library/webcites/.

149 Liptak, above note 116.

altered.[150] The protean nature of such information often means that, indeed, it cannot be trusted to remain in the same form as when it was first written.[151]

Here is an outline of measures, some quite broad in scale, for ensuring that reliable digital information remains accessible in its original form.

Use perma links to archive references.

Perma links, as Zittrain explains, are authoritative archived versions of referenced URL material. They allow a court or academic to archive a page, which could then be accessed for future reference and viewed exactly as it was seen by the original citer. Their use thereby avoids the pervasive problems of link and reference rot, ensuring that the original source is permanent and verifiable, regardless of whether the content was later altered or removed.

Judges and legal scholars who are generating links through judgments or scholarship can choose to be custodians of their own links and host them on their in-house perma servers. These links are mirrored by more than sixty partners, mostly law school libraries and the Internet Archive, to allow for access to the pages being stored. The process entails a perma.cc link to the archived page that is then created and "vested" by a registrar with such privileges (libraries, and those deemed fit by libraries) in order to be stored forever as a citation. This system allows for regular access to the web page as long as it has not been altered since the citation was implemented. If the website author changes the content of the page or deletes it altogether, the perma.cc link directs to the older, archived version.[152]

Professor Zittrain also advocates the increased use of time capsule encryptions, which cannot be accessed until the requisite time has been reached. Such encryptions avoid legal challenges for access to the information because it is unattainable. The information can be permalinked and mirrored to libraries in order for it to be saved and eventually made public at the desired moment.

Develop a free centralized site that publishes all pertinent caselaw.

For the United States, another solution could be to create an authoritative, citable, and freely available site featuring US caselaw to be reached

---

150 Jonathan Zittrain, "Preserving Our Digital Trail: A Call to Arms" (Keynote speech delivered at the Georgetown University Law Library Symposium, *404/ File Not Found: Link Rot, Legal Citation and Projects to Preserve Precedent*, 24 October 2014), online: www.law.georgetown.edu/library/404/keynote.cfm.

151 *Ibid.*

152 Kille, above note 147.

through a single URL.[153] The site would be de-indexed from search engines.[154]

Establish guidelines for the use of reliable online journals.
Many poor-quality academic journals are flooding the Internet and often being promoted by search engine results.[155] To help identify reliable sources for legal information, libraries should create guidelines for the use of online journals and "establish a line" as to which journals are best to consult.[156] Courthouse libraries might consider adopting this practice, as well.

Use persistent URLs, or PURLs.
PURLs also offer greater longevity, but there is some debate over the wisdom of using them for archival purposes.[157]

---

153 Zittrain, above note 150; Canada already has something of this spirit in CanLII.org.
154 Please see Chapter 3 for a more detailed discussion.
155 *Ibid.*
156 *Ibid.*
157 Kille, above note 147.

CHAPTER 3

The Open Courts Principle, Litigant Privacy, and Electronic Court Records

A. INTRODUCTION

Courts, not unlike many others actors in society, have been eager to show that they are not lagging behind the times, and so they have tended to embrace technology, whose promises of simplicity and efficiency are difficult to ignore. However, in so doing — and in a sincere effort to promote and expand access — they have overlooked some of the perils inherent in the uninformed or impulsive use of complex innovative tools.

This assessment is particularly true with respect to electronic or online court documents. These tend to raise significant issues, only now attracting sober thought, amid the unbridled enthusiasm that originally greeted them. In particular, I refer to the inadvertent disclosure of personal information in ways *unanticipated by existing rules* and the resulting affront to the very access to justice that digital files were meant to promote. Canada's privacy commissioner pointed to this emerging predicament, offering this caution: "the open-court rule — which is extremely historically important — has become distorted by the effect of massive search engines."[1] Information of this nature has always been public — with excellent reason. The distinction between the past and present circumstance lies in the new conception of "accessibility," namely, that there is now an audience of incalculable numbers with indiscriminate access to bits and pieces of sensitive, personal information in an unprecedented fashion.[2]

1 Kirk Makin, "Online Tribunal Evidence Leaves Citizens' Data Open to Abuse" *The Globe and Mail* (20 August 2008) A5.

2 See Canadian Judicial Council, *Model Policy for Access to Court Records in Canada* (Ottawa: Judges Technology Advisory Committee, 2005), online: www.cjc-ccm.gc.ca/cmslib/general/news_pub_techissues_AccessPolicy_2005_en.pdf

Not surprisingly perhaps, new technology can and has produced some very unfortunate by-products, ranging from identity theft, to participants in the justice system receiving threatening messages from parties entirely removed from the case. Take, for example, the 9/11 *United States v Moussaoui* case[3] where, in order to promote transparency in such a high-profile matter, the United States District Court for the Eastern District of Virginia decided to "broadcast" the proceedings on the Internet. Testimony, evidence, and related material were made available to the general public in the interest of a public trial. It turned out that strangers to the case began to threaten witnesses and others outside the courtroom.

Whereas the above-recounted incidents in *Moussaoui* were isolated and presumably spontaneous, the United States Department of Justice warns of *an entire web-industry* organized and dedicated to collecting information from Internet court dossiers, with an eye towards intimidation and retaliation. Consider one of the many instances of witness bullying, enabled — or at the very least greatly facilitated — by electronic records,[4] as Snyder recounts:

> Arrested for interstate drug trafficking in New Mexico, "Stewart" agreed to cooperate with authorities and testify against his co-defendants. The government filed Stewart's plea agreement with the court, and an electronic version became available for download to the Public Access to Court Electronic Records ("PACER") service. Shortly thereafter, Stewart's PACER files were featured on *whosarat.com*, a website that claims to have exposed the identities of more than 4,300 cooperating witnesses and undercover agents. In an effort to intimidate Stewart from testifying, his co-defendants plastered the *whosarat.com* materials, which labeled Stewart a "rat and a snitch," on utility poles and windshields in

---

[*Model Policy for Access*]. See also Rebecca Fairley Rainey, "The Jury Is Out on Online Court Records" *Online Journalism Review* (25 January 2002), online: www.ojr.org/ojr/law/1015015443.php. Rainey refers to two policies issued by both the Judicial Conference of the United States and the California Judicial Council in which certain restrictions were placed on online posting of court records with a particular focus on limiting the personal information available in electronic versions of court records. According to Rainey, "[t]he reasoning, in both policies, is that releasing records to a broad audience on the Internet would expose plaintiffs, defendants and jurors to the risk of identity theft through the publication of the extensive personal information collected in civil proceedings."

3 483 F3d 220 (4th Cir 2007) [*Moussaoui*].

4 See, for example, David L Snyder, "Nonparty Remote Electronic Access to Plea Agreements in the Second Circuit" (2008) 35:5 *Fordham Urban Law Journal* 1263.

> Stewart's neighborhood, and sent them by direct mail to residents in the area.[5]

In addition to the embarrassment it can generate, unrestricted digital access may dissuade individuals in sensitive contexts, such as in the now infamous Ashley Madison privacy scandal, from availing themselves of legal remedies for fear of being further exposed or even re-victimized.[6] Moreover, free-for-all admission to court records online significantly facilitates witness–litigant bullying and may even nourish an intimidation industry. This observation is certainly not to suggest that litigants could not be embarrassed or that witnesses could not be "reached" before the Internet age; it is, however, pertinent to note that due to the nature of the networked environment, these pre-existing difficulties are exponentially worsened by the indiscriminate posting of court records online.[7]

Blanket filing, therefore, although aimed at enhancing access, can, in fact, have the opposite effect online — inadvertently *deterring* participation in the justice system — thereby frustrating the very rationale underlying access.[8] This unintended consequence arguably speaks to a phenomenon known as "translation," which was coined by Justin Hughes in a different context. *Translation* is the need to find "legal tools to reach roughly the same balance of interests in the Internet that we have developed for the rest of our world."[9] The Internet demands a sober rethinking of how we define access to court information and assess the current balance struck between the important values of access and privacy.

---

5 *Ibid* at 1264.

6 See, for example, "One of my first reactions was that Ashley Madison may be less of a class action risk than we would usually see because I'm not sure there are going to be a lot of potential representative plaintiffs who will want to come forward," says Catherine Beagan Flood, a partner at Blake, Cassels & Graydon LLP. Jennifer Brown, "Will Ashley Madison Customers Launch Class Action over Hacking Incident?" *legal feeds* (22 July 2015), online: www.canadianlawyermag.com/legalfeeds/2808/will-ashley-madison-customers-launch-class-action-over-hacking-incident.html. Not surprisingly, those who have come forward as the ink here dries are a widower and a bachelor rather than the expected married individual who presumably sustained more harm on a site such as this.

7 See discussion on paper versus the Net in Section B, below in this chapter.

8 As the Supreme Court of Canada subsequently recognized in *AB v Bragg Communications Inc*, 2012 SCC 46 [*AB*].

9 Justin Hughes, "The Internet and the Persistence of Law" (2003) 44 *Boston College Law Review* 359 at 360, online: http://lawdigitalcommons.bc.edu/bclr/vol44/iss2/4.

As Lyria Bennett Moses explains in her paper on the general merits of revisiting norms in light of technological change, generally: "Existing rules were not formulated with new technologies in mind. Thus, some rules in their current form inappropriately include or exclude new forms of conduct."[10] For the purposes of our discussion, an approach to posting court documents that discounts the impact of the networked environment on justice participants' rights (primarily privacy and dignity) constitutes a far elevated — and perhaps at times intolerable — "transaction cost" for access to the courts and must therefore be reconsidered. Plainly put, courts may want to reconsider the advantages and, indeed, the constitutionality of unbridled disclosure of records online when the rationale underlying the practice is, in light of technological change, "explicitly or implicitly based on a premise that no longer exists, and [is] thus no longer justified."[11] The old premise we recall is that blanket divulgation of data promotes access and that privacy and transparency counterbalance each other in the cyber context.

It stands to reason that, in this evolving context, unrestrained disclosure can disturbingly *chill* access to the courts. What is more, engaging in a decontextualized "balancing exercise" between privacy and access becomes no more than an artificial enterprise if these values are not clearly defined or worse, if they are anachronistically conceived as adversarial in a virtual world where privacy can no longer be spatially confined and where "wholesale access" to data produces little meaningful information. As a result, "access" may no longer serve the rationales of openness and accountability; instead, it undermines the very entry to justice it was intended to foster.

More directly, I would suggest that litigant privacy, in particular, is as much about the "collective" dimension of privacy — in this case, the value of protecting faith in and access to the justice system — as it is about individual privacy rights and safeguarding litigants' "personal information" — a charged and dynamic term. Moving a step beyond, and with an eye towards striking the optimal contextual balance between the value of privacy (both individual and collective) on the one hand, and transparency of process on the other, it is incumbent upon courts to closely scrutinize the underlying rationale that the principle of open courts is intended to serve. For, as Australian scholar Sharon Rodrick argues, these perceived

---

10 Discussing the scope of rules, see Lyria Bennett Moses, "Why Have a Theory of Law and Technological Change?" (2007) 8:2 *Minnesota Journal of Law, Science, and Technology* 589 at 595.

11 *Ibid.*

purposes have had a significant bearing on how courts have responded and continue to respond to invocations of the right to privacy.[12]

What then are the fundamental values controlling the above-cited openness that Rodrick and others speak of?[13]

Chiefly, the public monitoring of judicial competence and impartiality. Not surprisingly, transparency of process serves to deter arbitrariness, as in the timeless words of Jeremy Bentham, open justice keeps the judge, "while trying, under trial"[14] or more broadly as Resnik observes,[15] "to educate the public and discipline the state."[16]

How might this rationale apply to the digital age? Its primary objective is to visit scrutiny upon government (including but not limited to the judicial branch), not upon the parties themselves.[17] As Chantal Bernier notes, "What was meant to ensure impartiality and excellence of the court brings shame to the parties."[18]

Tellingly, even Bentham, notwithstanding his ferocious advocacy of openness, recognized the ills of disproportionate publicity of judicial proceedings and did so without ever being able to factor in the tribulations of the networked environment. Eerily prescient (and today reminiscent of cases such as *Costeja* and *Savir*, and their paradoxical negative repercussions on otherwise victorious plaintiffs), he observed that "justifications for privacy included protecting participants from 'annoyance,' avoiding unnecessary harm to individuals through 'disclosure of facts prejudicial to their honour' or about their 'pecuniary circumstances,' and preserving both 'public decency' and state secrets."[19]

Today, of course, examples abound of successful plaintiffs "losing" in the above-cited terms. That is not surprising because, as Rodrick points out, "Most documents on the court record are created by the parties and often

---

12 Sharon Rodrick, "Open Justice, the Media and Avenues of Access to Documents on the Court Record" (2006) 29:3 *University of New South Wales Law Journal* 90 at 93.

13 In a different context.

14 Jeremy Bentham, *The Works of Jeremy Bentham*, ed by John Bowring (Edinburgh: William Tait, 1843) vol 4 at 316.

15 Speaking of terrorism, in particular, and the importance of open process in that vein.

16 Judith Resnik, "The Democracy in Courts: Jeremy Bentham, 'Publicity', and the Privatization of Process in the Twenty-First Century" (2013) 10 *NoFo* 77 at 78, online: www.helsinki.fi/nofo/NoFo10RESNIK.pdf.

17 Rodrick, above note 12 at 100 and 105–6.

18 Expressed in a blogpost by Bernier, 19 May 2015 (on file with author).

19 Bentham, above note 14 at 360, cited in Resnik, above note 16 at 85–86.

contain bald assertions and exaggerated allegations or claims which are completely untested and which may even be ruled inadmissible."[20]

Suffice it to cite a few.

In what is at times referred to as the Globe24h case, a Canadian mother of two teenaged sons googled herself to see if her email address had been changed back to her maiden name only to find that the court details of a "tense" and protracted dispute with her ex-husband figured prominently in the search.[21] Especially shocking was the fact that the disturbing details were gleaned from CanLII (Canadian Legal Information Institute), the Canadian website that publishes most court decisions despite their policy not to index such matters to avoid having them emerge in search engine result lists. Notwithstanding that precaution, it appears that the CanLII material was obtained by and posted on a foreign (Romanian) website, called Globe24h, that — to compound harms — was demanding money, with payment by credit card or PayPal accepted (between 19 and 200 Euros) in exchange for the suppression of personal details.[22]

Not surprisingly perhaps, these dubious practices of collecting and posting sensitive personal information without consent — that some considered tantamount to extortion[23] — gave rise to multiple complaints, brought before the Office of the Privacy Commissioner of Canada (OPC). Concluding that Globe24h's practices were unreasonable,[24] the OPC re-

---

20 Rodrick, above note 12 at 133.

21 Christine Dobby, "Canadians Upset with Romanian Website That Exposes Court Case Details" *The Globe and Mail* (4 January 2015), online: http://fw.to/CxGJdIc [Dobby].

22 Removal guaranteed by Globe24h within twelve hours for $200. Dobby, *ibid.* Based in Romania, Globe24h posts the full text of Canadian judicial decisions in a way that allows search engines, such as Google, to index the text of the decisions. As a result, decisions that contain deeply personal information (such as that often found in family law cases, bankruptcy cases, human rights complaints, and refugee law cases) have been made public.

23 Dobby, *ibid.* See also Christine Dobby, "How Cyber Shame Scams Are Playing on Our Privacy Fears and Scaling Up" *Financial Post* (29 March 2014), online: Postmedia Group http://natpo.st/1PTxYkD.

24 According to the *Personal Information Protection and Electronic Documents Act*, SC 2000, c 5, s 5(3) [*PIPEDA*]: "[a]n organization may collect, use or disclose personal information only for purposes that a reasonable person would consider are appropriate in the circumstances." The OPC found that Globe24h's purpose is not to make judicial decisions accessible freely to all on the Internet, as the decisions were already available. See *PIPEDA Report of Findings #2015-002* (5 June 2015), online: https://www.priv.gc.ca/cf-dc/2015/2015_002_0605_e.asp [*PIPEDA #2015-002*].

jected the website's argument that a free removal process was available because the character of the process was terribly onerous in comparison to its costly (remove-for-a-fee) counterpart.

Intriguingly, Globe24h had argued that Canadians' privacy would be protected only if the country's judicial opinions were anonymized before being published online.[25] It pointed to the demonstrated futility of de-indexing in this instance. To that the Commissioner opined:

> It is evident from the Model Policy that the CJC [Canadian Judicial Council] accepts, in spite of the importance of individuals' electronic access to judgments, that a restriction against web indexing is necessary to address a serious risk to individual privacy, and that the benefits of such a restriction outweigh the negative impacts on the open courts principle. The Model Policy also establishes that the "unintentional" finding of court decisions in the course of a web search unrelated to those decisions would not be in furtherance of the open courts principle, and is thus to be avoided.
>
> Furthermore, given the fact that Canadian courts, as well as CanLII and SOQUIJ, broadly respect the CJC's restriction on web indexing, the reasonable expectation of Canadians is that while court decisions may be available online, personal information contained in those decisions should not be discoverable via popular search engines.[26]

The Canadian Judicial Council's *Model Policy for Access to Court Records in Canada* states as follows:

> [I]f . . . judgments are posted on the Internet, it is a good practice to prevent indexing and cache storage from web robots or "spiders". Such indexation and cache storage of court information makes this information available even when the purpose of the search is not to find court records, as any judgment could be found unintentionally using popular search engines like Google or Yahoo. Moreover, when the judgment is cache stored by the search engine, it is available to Internet users even if the court decides to withdraw the judgment from public access.[27]

Similar policies are recommended by the OPC's guidance documents for administrative tribunals.[28]

---

25 Please see Chapter 4 on point.

26 *PIPEDA #2015-002*, above note 24 at paras 85–86.

27 Above note 2 at 12.

28 Office of the Privacy Commissioner of Canada, *Electronic Disclosure of Personal Information in the Decisions of Administrative Tribunals* (Ottawa: Office of the Privacy Commissioner, 2010).

That said, and as the Globe24h incident demonstrates, de-indexing, while helpful, may not be sufficient for purposes of preventing the sort of reputational harms that cannot be undone, as others can easily manage to "re-index" deeply sensitive information naturally housed in such decisions.[29] Accordingly, the Commissioner found that Globe24h "has effectively undermined the balance between privacy and the open courts principle."[30]

Although eventually, and only following what might be considered significant pressure from the Privacy Commissioner, Globe24h agreed to delete some of the impugned personal data, there is no guarantee that these data have not been reproduced or will not otherwise resurface. That, in turn, provides little assurance to the victims whose profoundly personal details have already been exposed and cannot be unlearned.

Segueing from that cautionary tale, a second rationale offered in support of openness of proceedings is said to be that of "educating the public about the workings of the court."[31] Yet, a little knowledge is known to be a dangerous thing — particularly since the networked environment offers only decontextualized tidbits of otherwise sensitive information. In the words of Byrne J, the digital age "make[s] the curial and adjudicative process less and less comprehensible to the person in the public gallery," thereby prompting us to revisit the propriety of unbridled 'transparency.'"[32] To paraphrase privacy scholar Daniel Solove, it is of a Kafkaesque rather than Orwellian privacy nightmare that we must be wary due to the cyber world's fragmentary nature.[33]

B. PAPER VERSUS THE NET: THE MOVEMENT OF COURTS FROM BEING CUSTODIANS OF INFORMATION TO PUBLISHERS

In order to emphasize the extent to which the current "balancing" fails to achieve its purpose in light of technological change, it is useful to first consider how court documents on the Web differ from their paper counterparts. Although not the objective of this chapter to thoroughly set

---

29 A broader discussion of this conundrum is available in Chapter 4.

30 *PIPEDA #2015-002*, above note 24 at para 87.

31 Rodrick, above note 12 at 94.

32 *Ibid* at 92,

33 Daniel J Solove, *The Digital Person: Technology and Privacy in the Information Age* (New York: New York University Press, 2004) at 55 and 149.

out all distinctions between "paper and the Net," it is useful to highlight a few important differences.[34]

First, court documents are no longer protected by the "practical obscurity"[35] afforded by the paper records of years past. That translates into boundless, unprecedented, and unchecked distribution, with the ills commonly associated with most "good things" in unlimited and wholesale offering. "You were private by default and public by effort," says Electronic Frontier Foundation staff attorney Lee Tien. "Nowadays, you're public by default and private by effort."[36]

In addition, the courts have dramatically shifted from their traditional role of "custodians"[37] of information, or "passive repositories" of documents,[38] to active *publishers*, a distinct position clearly unanticipated by pre-existing disclosure rules and guidelines,[39] which feature a strong presumption in favour of wholesale publication and most stringently require "compelling" privacy interests to prevent disclosure.

---

34 For a discussion on the difference between paper records and electronic records, see Peter A Winn, "Online Court Records: Balancing Judicial Accountability and Privacy in an Age of Electronic Information" (2004) 79 *Washington Law Review* 307 at 315.

35 See, for example, *United States Department of Justice v Reporters Committee for Freedom of the Press*, 489 US 749 (1989).

36 Joel Stein, "Data Mining: How Companies Now Know Everything about You" *Time* (10 March 2011), online: www.time.com/time/business/article/0,8599,2058114,00.html#ixzz1GaK2nAg. Lee Tien is an attorney specializing in free speech and privacy issues at the Electronic Frontier Foundation, a non-profit civil liberties organization based in San Francisco, California.

37 Kenneth Withers (Speech delivered at the Privacy, Access, Technology, and the Future of Litigation in the United States conference, Princeton University, Center for Information Technology Policy, 13 May 2011) (webcast), online: http://citp.princeton.edu/event/privacy-access.

38 Grayson Barber (Speech delivered at the Privacy, Access, Technology, and the Future of Litigation in the United States conference, Princeton University, Center for Information Technology Policy, 13 May 2011) (webcast), online: http://citp.princeton.edu/event/privacy-access/.

39 Even the more recent. See, for example, The Sedona Conference, *The Sedona Guidelines: Best Practices Addressing Protective Orders, Confidentiality & Public Access in Civil Cases* (March 2007), online: http://citpsite.s3.amazonaws.com/events/privacy-access/WG2_Guidelines_March_2007.pdf.

C. DEROGATING SLIGHTLY FROM OPEN JUSTICE TO PROTECT ACCESS TO JUSTICE: *AB v BRAGG COMMUNICATIONS INC*[40]

In contrast to the above-painted discouraging picture, the Supreme Court of Canada has taken heed of the increasing and worrisome imbalance between privacy and transparency, and more important, its nefarious effect on access to justice. Like most courts, however, it had earlier adhered faithfully to unchecked transparency (with a few narrow exceptions) given the paramountcy of the open courts principle.[41]

In a landmark decision from 2012,[42] the Supreme Court significantly recognized the relationship between protecting litigant privacy (even anonymity) and access to justice, calling unmitigated transparency into question in the digital age. In a unanimous ruling in a matter preceding an action for defamation, Canada's highest court proved it was no longer insensitive to the burdens of unrestricted online posting considering the vicissitudes of the networked environment. It allowed a teenaged cyberbullying victim to proceed anonymously before the courts. This permission was given in order for the young person to unmask the identity of her online tormentor without exposing herself to additional ridicule and humiliation for no other reason than for seizing the courts.

Cognizant of the peculiar harms of the networked environment not only to the plaintiff (the value of individual privacy) but the deterrent effect on similarly situated individuals who might pursue justice (the value of access), the Court similarly issued a publication ban relating to the false sexualized Facebook profile forming the object of the action. In so doing, the Court took sober note of a significant change in circumstances (the advent of digital technologies), which must, in turn, give rise to a rethought-out approach to judicial publication.

Jennifer Stoddart, as privacy commissioner, praised the decision, noting:

> Victims willing to go to court face the extremely daunting prospect that, because information can now live on forever on the Internet, it can follow them around for the rest of their lives . . . . This decision shows that the courts understand the realities of today's technology and society, and that they will not allow those who seek justice to be re-victimized.[43]

---

40 Above note 8.

41 See, for example, *Nova Scotia (AG) v MacIntyre*, [1982] 1 SCR 175 at 189 [*MacIntyre*], *inter alia*.

42 *AB*, above note 8.

43 Office of the Privacy Commissioner of Canada, News Release, "Commissioner Welcomes Supreme Court Decision Recognizing the Importance of Protecting Young People's Privacy" (1 October 2012), online: www.priv.gc.ca/media/nr-c/2012/nr-c_121001_e.asp.

Although the opinion was handed down somewhat narrowly, accounting specifically for the "inherent vulnerability" of youth or children in its underlying rationale, it may nevertheless be extended to the publication of court records more generally, beyond the particular case of minors. All in all, *AB* may be deemed an important first step towards a new understanding of privacy protection in the justice setting.

D. LOSS OF CONTROL OVER COURT DOCUMENTS AND THE INABILITY TO "CORRECT" LATER

Although conceptions are changing in common law jurisdictions, it is significant that the general lack of a cohesive and institutionalized framework increasingly involves a loss of court control over the court's own materials. That is to say that once unleashed online — however inadvertently — most of these files cannot be edited, effectively redacted, or recalled, often despite the court's wishes and best efforts to do so. That, in turn, might do violence to the judge's duty to control court documents and, indeed, protect litigants before the court.

In this rapidly evolving area, no case better illustrates the erosion of judicial dominion or oversight over online documents than the following matter, which arose in Israel most recently.[44] Succinctly, a man (A) who purposefully kept his sexual orientation secret sued an Internet dating site (dedicated exclusively to same-sex couples). The company refused to delete postings by a former lover who, the plaintiff alleged, had assumed the man's online pseudonym in order to reveal his true identity and spread falsities regarding his HIV status. Following the standard practice, the pleadings were automatically and instantaneously posted online by the court system, including the very same impugned damaging details regarding the plaintiff's sexual orientation, sexual practices, and health that had prompted the suit. Although at the request of A's lawyer the judge did order the inflammatory details to be promptly redacted from the decision, immediately following publication, the first copy of the pleadings was left "floating" around cyberspace and could neither be tracked down nor effectively eliminated. Of course, counsel's tardy realization that the statement of claim would be posted online in accordance with the court's standard practice was presumably at least partially to blame for the lamentable result. However, this phenomenon is quite common, as attorneys, not unlike judges, gradually awaken to the darker side of technology —

44 *Doe v Doe* (*Ploni v Almoni*), (2006) Tel Aviv Magistrate Court 06/17485.

certainly at a far slower pace than that at which documents can be filed electronically and distributed worldwide.

What is clear from this unfortunate matter is the court's loss of mastery over its own materials, something that is contrary to one of the foundational principles of access. According to this principle, the court controls its documents, it "[h]as a supervisory and protecting power over its own records,"[45] and the "[a]uthoring judge, not publisher, is responsible for contents of judgment."[46] If the court loses control, it presumably undermines judicial authority, creating absurd situations in which official anonymized versions of court files coexist alongside unedited copies, floating around cyberspace.

Moreover, whereas judges take pains to draft judgments in restrained and respectful language, lawyers — not to mention self-represented litigants — are hardly as careful in phrasing their statements of claim and motions. With electronic records and e-filing, these often inflammatory declarations can be propagated on the World Wide Web for all to see. As noted, even if later "withdrawn," the damage caused is potentially irreparable.[47] As Winn cautions:

> The world of electronic information is a far less forgiving place . . . the simple abstract rules developed for a world of paper-based information may no longer suffice to resolve complex problems of judicial information management . . . . The failure of the legal system to maintain the ancient balance between access and privacy will lead to the greatest danger of all — inhibiting citizens from participating in the public judicial system.[48]

Accordingly, contingencies must be instituted promptly to mitigate these risks and their nefarious impact both on litigant privacy and access to justice itself.

---

45 *MacIntyre*, above note 41 at 189.

46 See Kate Welsh, "Court Records Access in Canada" (Presentation delivered at the 6th Conference on Privacy and Public Access to Court Records, Williamsburg, 6–7 November 2008) at slide 23, online: www.slidefinder.net/c/court_records_access_canada_prepared/courtrecordsaccessincanada/20803083.

47 As the case of *Benedikt v ChoicePoint*, No MRS-L-1084-07 (NJ Sup Ct 2009) [settled on the eve of trial] arguably illustrates.

48 Gary Dickson, "Administrative Tribunals, Privacy and the Net" (Paper delivered to a Canadian Bar Association audience, 30 January 2009) at 20, online: www.oipc.sk.ca/Resources/Administrative%20Tribunals.pdf.

E. A COMPARATIVE PERSPECTIVE

The European construction of litigant privacy in the digital age is illuminating and merits an overview,[49] however brief and superficial for our purposes.[50]

In France, not unlike most democracies, open proceedings remain the default rule, as explicitly set out in articles 6-1 and 8 of the *European Convention of Human Rights*[51] *inter alia*[52] and more specifically in *Directive 95*.[53] Thus, as the courts there have opined:

---

49 A more in-depth analysis of the complex national and supranational framework exceeds the scope of this book.

50 *Ibid.*

51 *European Convention for the Protection of Human Rights and Fundamental Freedoms, as amended*, Council of Europe 1950, ETS No 5, 213 UNTS 222 (entered into force 3 September 1953).

52 See Ramu de Bellescize, "Faut-il légiférer sur l'anonymisation des décisions de justice?" (2006) 188 *Petites affiches* 3 (Lextenso.fr) [footnotes omitted].

> Le Conseil d'État, dans un arrêt d'Assemblée du 4 octobre 1974, a jugé que « (. . .) la publicité des débats judiciaires est un principe général du droit; qu'il n'appartient dès lors qu'au législateur d'en déterminer, d'en étendre ou d'en restreindre les limites. » La publicité des débats judiciaires ayant ainsi été reconnue comme un principe général du droit, il en est de même, à plus forte raison de la publicité des jugements. En effet, quand les débats ne doivent pas avoir lieu en audience publique, le jugement doit, sauf exception expresse, être rendu en audience publique, cette audience étant le dernier rempart du principe de publicité.
>
> En droit international, les textes ratifiés par la France consacrant cette publicité sont nombreux. De l'article 6, § 1 de la Convention européenne de sauvegarde des droits de l'homme et des libertés fondamentales à la Déclaration universelle des droits de l'homme en passant par le pacte international de l'Onu relatif aux droits civils et politiques l'idée est toujours la même : le caractère public des décisions de justice ainsi que leur libre communication fait corps avec la justice elle-même. Or aucun de ces textes ne précise que les décisions rendues doivent être expurgées de certaines de leurs dispositions. Un courant doctrinal considère même que l'accès aux décisions de justice constitue une manifestation de la liberté d'expression que fondent les articles 11 de la DDH et 10 de la Convention EDH.

53 *Directive 95/46/EC of the European Parliament and of the Council of 24 October 1995 on the protection of individuals with regard to the processing of personal data and on the free movement of such data* [1995] OJ L 281. In French law the respect for privacy has its source in the general regime for civil liability (art 1382 of the *Civil Code*). In 1970, a more specific provision was added to art 9 of the *Civil Code* [translation]: "Everyone has the right to respect for their privacy. Judges may, without prejudice to compensation for the damage suffered,

putting a court decision containing personal information (be it regarding the judge, prosecuter, plaintiff, defendant or witnesses), at the public's disposal must be construed as constituting processing of personal information as defined in European Directive 94/46/CE, which protects such data. In fact, disseminating a court case containing such personal information is tantamount to processing personal data.[54]

. . . [Moreover,] the principle of finality (purposiveness) demands that we only use personal information for the purposes directly related to the data processing in question (in this case publication of court decisions). It is forbidden to stray from the initial purpose for which this personal data was obtained and utilise it in a manner incompatible with the said purpose. Accordingly, electronic publication of court decisions allows for widespread dissemination, thereby creating the temptation to access such personal information for reasons removed from the inital purpose of posting.[55]

---

prescribe any measures, such as sequestration, seizure, and others fit to prevent or stop an infringement of privacy; these measures may, if there is urgency, be ordered for interim relief." According to the Constitutional Council, the right to privacy is protected by art 2 of the *Declaration of the Rights of Man and of the Citizen* of 1789.

54 Cécile de Terwangne, "Diffusion de la jurisprudence via internet dans les pays de l'Union européenne et règles applicables aux données personnelles" (2005) 194 *Petites affiches* 4 at printed page 1, online: www.crid.be/pdf/public/5021.pdf [translated by author].

> La mise à disposition du public d'un jugement contenant des données sur des personnes physiques (qu'il s'agisse du juge, du Ministère public, des plaideurs, des parties, des témoins, etc.) correspond à un traitement de données à caractère personnel au sens de la directive 95/46/CE garantissant la protection des données personnelles. Par ailleurs, diffuser une décision de justice comportant de telles données [dites personnelles] implique une opération effectuée sur des données à caractère personnel et, partant, un traitement de données.

55 *Ibid* at printed page 4:

> le principe de finalité impose que l'on n'utilise les données personnelles qu'en vue de réaliser les finalités liées au traitement des données (le traitement étant, dans le cas qui nous occupe, la diffusion des décisions de jurisprudence). Il est interdit de détourner la finalité et de traiter les données dans un but incompatible avec le but initial . . . . Or, la publication des décisions de jurisprudence sur support électronique permet techniquement, et en conséquence offre la tentation, de consulter les bases de données dans un but différent de celui d'être éclairé sur un courant jurisprudentiel dans une matière particulière.

The rationale underlying this comparatively restrictive approach, as espoused by France's *Commission nationale de l'informatique et des libertés* (CNIL), is that the Internet allows for unintended searches divorced from the original purposes of disclosure, such as gathering information about a job or housing candidate, or viewing the credit rating of a neighbour or friend without that person's knowledge.[56]

The Belgian Commission for Privacy Protection (La Commission Belge sur la protection de la vie privée) for its part confirms the relevance of these concerns, cautioning that "free Internet searches using only the name or names of the parties or even a witness allow parties removed from the case to obtain and decontextualize personal information."[57]

In light of the above, European caselaw adapted more nimbly to digital realities — not surprisingly given the civil law's inherent principle-based approach and flexibility. As the Belgian Privacy Commission stated, "Notwithstanding certain exceptions provided by law, the purpose of publishing court decisions is to stimulate discussion on caselaw as a source of law — not to divulge participants' names to third parties."[58]

Take, for instance, the LEXEEK decision in France,[59] a matter which involved an association whose stated objective is to allow for free and

---

Furthermore, the *Guide des bonnes pratiques dans l'utilisation des technologies de l'information et de la communication adopté par la Conférence des présidents des cours d'appel de l'Union européenne* [*Guide of Good Practices in the Use of Information Technology and Communication Adopted by the Conference of Presidents of the Courts of Appeal of the European Union*], approved in Dijon on 15 October 2011, states in art 5 on respect for privacy [in translation] that "[t]he judge must ensure that privacy and personal data are strictly respected, taking all material precautions necessary for this purpose in the use of ICT, in order to safeguard individual liberties in general as well as the privacy principles derived from jurisprudence of the European Court of Human Rights."

56 "Ce qui est techniquement possible lorsqu'une recherche documentaire via internet est entreprise [. . .] l'est aussi lorsqu'il s'agit de se renseigner sur un candidat à l'emploi, à un logement ou à un crédit, sur un voisin ou un proche et ce, à l'insu des personnes concernées." France, Commission nationale de l'informatique et des libertés (CNIL), *Délibération portant recommandation sur la diffusion de données personnelles sur internet par les banques de données de jurisprudence*, No 01-057 (29 November 2001).

57 Belgium, Commission for the Protection of Privacy, *Avis 07/98* (1998) [translated].

58 *Ibid.*

59 *Lexeek* (12 July 2011), 2011-238, online: CNIL www.cnil.fr. See Aurélie Mivielle, "L'anonymisation des décisions de justice en ligne: une composante du droit a l'oubli numérique réaffirmée par la CNIL" (30 November 2011), online : IREDIC

public access to legal resources. LEXEEK was fined for what was considered a practice harmful to the respect of personal privacy and the right to be forgotten, by reason of its failure to anonymize the decisions it posted on its website.[60] According to the CNIL, "mindful of the true — at times even dramatic — effect of disseminating such decisions, the sanction meted out reflects a commitment to protecting privacy and the right to be forgotten as enshrined in law."[61]

In that case, some of the plaintiffs, according to the CNIL, endured significant professional difficulties, such as being refused employment or experiencing professional ostracism within their current place of employment, due to tidbits of information that their current or potential employer found online in a few clicks. At times, the CNIL notes — underscoring the importance of preventing such mishaps — the information was twelve years old. To paraphrase the European Court of Justice in *Costeja* (which had not yet been decided at the time), the information was outdated and irrelevant.[62]

---

http://junon.univ-cezanne.fr/u3iredic/?p=7425. See also Olivier Robitaille, "Droit à l'oubli: la Cnil condamne lexeek.com à 10 000 euros d'amende" (10 October 2011), online: Clubic.com http://pro.clubic.com/legislation-loi-internet/cnil/actualite-451796-droit-oubli-cnil-condamne-lexeek-10-000-amende.html.

60 Description available at www.Lexeek.com.

61 In translation. Another pertinent example can be found in the case of *Volker und Markus Schecke GbR v Land Hessen* (9 November 2010), joined cases C-92/09 and C-93/09 (ECJ). In this affair, among others, the European Court of Justice confirms that the protection of privacy in the context of the publication of judgments is a right that must be understood "in relation to its function in society." This does not necessarily extend to the right to be forgotten in the criminal context. See Cass civ 1re, 20 November 1990, *Mme Monanges v Kern et al.* Ruling that respect for privacy in this case should outweigh transparency, the court considered in regard to the publication of the personal data of individuals, that institutions are required to demonstrate that they have carried out a balanced weighting "between the Union's interest in guaranteeing the transparency of its actions on the one hand, and the right of the concerned beneficiaries to respect for their privacy in general and the protection of their personal information in particular, on the other hand." See also Denys Simon, "Transparence et vie privée," Europe No 1, January 2011, comm 2.

62 *Google Spain SL, Google Inc v Agencia Española de Protección de Datos, Mario Costeja González* (13 May 2014), C-131/12 (ECJ), online: Info Curia http://curia.europa.eu/juris/document/document.jsf?text=&docid=152065&pageIndex=0&doclang=EN&mode=req&dir=&occ=first&part=1&cid=129070 [*Costeja*].

F. RECONCILING OPEN JUSTICE, PRIVACY, AND ACCESS: FLORIDA'S EXAMPLE OF *MINDFUL* POSTING

With an eye towards eventually striking a measure of equipoise between transparency and privacy, the following offers a brief aperçu of the US experience, considered illuminating for the change it has undergone.[63] It would appear that the shift is towards encouraging courts, especially attorneys, to reflect before posting online. The idea, therefore, is to opt for *thoughtful* online posting rather than relatively mindless posting done automatically, as was the custom in the United States at the federal level,[64] broadly speaking. The prevailing "public-is-public" view, which failed to account for the peculiarities of the digital age in the hopes of being or at least appearing progressive, proved problematic to many.[65] In contradistinction, and presumably in light of successive PACER fiascos, the state of Florida, for its part, opted for an avant garde approach which favours "practical obscurity." In other words, it institutes safeguards that mimic those inherent to paper, transplanting them to cyberspace in order to prevent abuses.

Simply put, whereas the "public-is-public" approach views all postings alike regardless of medium (paper or digital), its "practical obscurity" counterpart focuses on the specific concerns peculiar to posting personal data online. The United States (chiefly Florida at this time), in keeping with transparency and related values respecting open courts, provides full uninhibited access at the courthouse (as was the case in the bricks-and-mortar world, prior to the advent of the Internet). An option to print is available,[66] and, in some cases, the courthouse provides electronic access via intranet kiosks, both of which otherwise limit widespread e-access.

---

63 For a more detailed discussion on the state of the law in the United States, see DR Jones, "Protecting the Treasure: An Assessment of State Court Rules and Policies for Access to Online Civil Court Records" (2013) 61 *Drake Law Review* 375.

64 "PACER was established in 1988 as a dial-up service. In the last decade, through the implementation of CM/ECF — that would be the electronic case filing system — PACER has evolved into an Internet-based service." The Honorable Ronald Leighton, Joe Cecil, Michael Ishakian, and Edward Felten, "Panel Three: Implementation—What Methods, If Any, Can Be Employed To Promote the Existing Rules' Attempts to Protect Private Identifier Information From Internet Access?" (2011) 79 *Fordham Law Review* 45 at 47.

65 Jones, above note 63.

66 However, in New Jersey a result similar to the above-mentioned typical problems arose, with a court noting in *Burnett v County of Bergen*, 198 NJ 408 at 430 (2009) that even if the social insurance numbers of litigants are public information in the sense that they are available at the court, "bulk disclosure of

Proponents of this approach are presumably sensitive to the perils inherent to widespread, knee-jerk posting where what are superfluous details for most readers could have a potentially devastating impact on litigants, witnesses, and others. Accordingly, they endeavour to limit the propagation of personal data (broadly defined), recognizing that dissemination would do little or nothing to improve transparency.[67]

It is for this reason *inter alia* perhaps that Florida courts considered it wise to revisit the framework and policies pertaining to court records in light of the advent of the digital age. As a result, they concluded that these must adapt accordingly. The reformation implicitly mimicked the above-stated European view based on purposive electronic publication, predicated on the adopting of means least restrictive to the privacy rights of litigants (and other participants). The strategy developed by Florida courts (via a special committee) aimed at curtailing or minimizing the inclusion of sensitive personal information in court documents, featuring only those necessary to managing the case. As noted above, the chief objective was what may be deemed *mindful* (rather than default) online posting to minimize the inclusion of deeply sensitive personal data superfluous for purposes of transparency, guided by the principle of proportionality. Judges are thus allowed to regain control over court documents instead of mindlessly unleashing them online and contending with the fallout at a later time.

This purposive construction, not unlike the approach of the *Canadian Charter of Rights and Freedoms* to balancing rights,[68] more generally sees fit to tweak posting in light of the imperatives of the digital age, rather than rewrite the rules in an attempt to keep up with technological developments. The latter construction has proven futile in numerous other areas of law. Thus, for instance, the Florida committee questions whether a particular online posting corresponds to the underlying objective of transparency, endeavouring to restrict or limit the unnecessary inclusion of personal data. Finally, in an effort to eliminate information superfluous to trans-

---

realty records to a company planning to include them in a searchable, electronic database would eliminate the practical obscurity that now envelops those records at the Bergen County Clerk's Office."

67 According to Jones, above note 63. See also Peter W Martin, "Online Access to Court Records — From Documents to Data, Particulars to Patterns" (2008) 53 *Villanova Law Review* 855 at 872.

68 Part I of the *Constitution Act, 1982*, being Schedule B to the *Canada Act 1982* (UK), 1982, c 11.

parency, Florida also approved a rule of civil procedure which restricts the inclusion of personal data at the discovery stage.[69]

G. SHIFTING CONCEPTIONS: ISRAEL AS AN EXAMPLE OF ONGOING CHANGES IN COMMON LAW JURISDICTIONS

The change in Florida's approach is indicative, it is submitted, of an increasingly broader departure from the orthodoxy of the bricks-and-mortar unbridled disclosure worldwide and, significantly, in common law jurisdictions outside Europe. A noteworthy example is Israel, where a committee on point was formed, headed by Itzhak Englard, a retired Supreme Court justice. The committee's mandate is to examine the propriety of blanket diffusion of court records online, particularly in more sensitive areas such as employment or criminal province.[70] Although it has not yet released its report, the committee appears to be "leaning towards a default position of not having names published at all on online versions in employment cases in particular & possibly criminal." According to the chair, Itzhak Englard: "[T]he question we are considering now is whether banning publication of names should remain the exception or become the rule."[71]

In fact, the three rulings released on point in one year alone (with the committee's findings pending) echo this persuasion, opining that, in certain sensitive contexts, "publishing a verdict without the name is generally sufficient for the public's right to know."[72]Attributing great weight to the changes wrought by the Internet,[73] Supreme Court Justice (and former attorney general) Elyakim Rubinstein cautioned: "Today when minimal effort of typing makes it possible to find an entire verdict, the potential harm to the person whose health details are revealed has grown (insurance); thus, it would appear it's possible and even appropriate to interpret

69 Fla R Civ P 1.280(f). For a more detailed explanation, see Jones, above note 63.

70 "To formulate recommendations on where the line between these conflicting principles should be drawn": Revital Hovel, "Courts Granting Defendants Right Never to Be Known" *Haaretz* (22 August 2014), online: www.haaretz.com/news/israel/.premium-1.611933.

71 *Ibid*: "a trend toward barring the publication of identifying details in court rulings had been taking shape in Israel."

72 *Ibid*. See also *Anonymous v The National Database for Automobile Insurance*, CA 438/14 (Israel CA 2014); *Eliahu Insurance v Anonymous*, 482/13 (Israel CA 2014) NA 13359/12/31 [in Hebrew].

73 Hovel, above note 70.

the term *serious harm* in a way that takes the aforementioned [Internet] into account and in a manner that leans towards respecting privacy."[74]

According to Labour Court Chief Justice Pilman (in the second of these cases):

> Even though nobody disputes the lofty status of the principle of public hearings, given the availability of large amounts of information in electronic media and the ability to store this information, there have been growing calls for changing the way it is exercised . . . to avoid serious violations of other rights, first and foremost the right to privacy and to a good name . . . . One emerging solution to the need to balance these conflicting rights is to allow court rulings to be published without the names of the litigants or other parties mentioned in the ruling.

Chief Justice Pilman noted that "the last word hasn't yet been said" on this issue, and that "it seems the law — the legislature and the courts — will have to adjust itself to this developing reality and the challenges it poses."[75] Surely, such widespread dissemination of deeply sensitive personal information gleaned from court files of individuals merely seeking to avail themselves of access to the courts, an unfortunate by-product of revendicating their rights, would have been inconceivable prior to the digital age.

Pending the committee's findings, MK Koll, a member of Israeli parliament, or Knesset, sponsored a bill, commonly known as "Koll's law," which "bars publication of the plaintiff's identity in any civil suit where medical information might be revealed, unless the court decides otherwise."[76]

H. THIRD-PARTY ISSUES

In the United States, in particular, data aggregators actively seek out electronic court documents in order to sell them to "credit rating agencies," a practice that is not without significant consequences. The practice creates burdens that raise the cost of participating in the justice system to the point where, in certain instances, availing oneself of one's rights before the courts may become prohibitive. Thus, for instance, ChoicePoint (a prominent US credit rating agency) reported that an individual named Karl Benedikt had been convicted of "kidnapping and coercion." The re-

---

74 *Ibid.*

75 *Ibid.*

76 *Ibid*; further information on bill available [in Hebrew], online: www.pmo.gov.il/Secretary/GovDecisions/2014/Pages/des1413.aspx.

port, based on an official court record from the Judicial Electronic Filing System (JEFIS), was, in fact, false, reflecting only ChoicePoint's *interpretation* of a numerical code from the JEFIS record.[77]

According to the brief of *amicus curiae*, or EPIC Brief:

> A judicial determination of expungement is important as a legal matter, as a policy issue, and as a matter of social justice. After someone has been rehabilitated, having paid the prescribed debt to society, he or she should not be penalized in perpetuity. Expungement reflects a judicial determination of fairness that should be respected, regardless of new business practices or technological change.
>
> However, data mining companies ignore judicial determinations and attempt to make conviction records live forever when they buy these records from state governments, repackage and sell them for employment background checks, credit ratings, and other commercial uses. Data aggregators such as ChoicePoint, Experian, and DataTrace advertise that their products are accurate because they get their data, including court records, from the government. Their claim is a legal falsity; the publication of the expungement record is itself proscribed. N.J.S.A. 2C:52-30.
>
> To omit the fact of an individual's expungement introduces error into these databases — both the databases sold by the states and the commercial databases sold by data mining companies. Absent the enforcement of the state interest in expungement, there is no avenue to correct these errors, either the data aggregators' or the government's.
>
> The impact of these errors in criminal justice records is not trivial. Individuals who are mistakenly listed as criminals or suspects can face consequences ranging from inconvenience to loss of liberty . . .[78]

---

77 *Benedikt v ChoicePoint*, above note 47. See *GD v Kenny*, Docket No 65,366, Appeal No A-16-09, "Brief of *Amicus Curiae*" (NJ Sup Ct) at 8, online: Electronic Privacy Information Center https://epic.org/amicus/KennyMeritsBrief.pdf [EPIC Brief], stating that Karl Benedikt was the citizen described in the Supreme Court of New Jersey, *Report of the Supreme Court Special Committee on Public Access to Court Records* (29 November 2007) at 52, online: www.judiciary.state.nj.us/publicaccess/publicaccess.pdf. Benedikt sued ChoicePoint and eventually settled.

78 EPIC Brief, above note 77. See also Ellen Nakashima, "A Good Name Dragged Down" *Washington Post* (19 March 2008). According to the EPIC Brief, above note 77 at 4: "Police work is affected as well, as errors are introduced into criminal databases. As Justice Ginsburg stated recently, 'Negligent recordkeeping errors by law enforcement threaten individual liberty, are susceptible to deterrence by the exclusionary rule, and cannot be remedied effectively through other means.' *Herring v. U.S.*, 129 S. Ct. 695 (2009), Ginsburg J, dissenting."

> But there is no incentive to update or maintain records that have been purchased from the courts. Once the government has published information about an individual, it cannot punish others who publish the same information when it is obtained by lawful means. *Cox Broad. Corp. v. Cohen*, 420 U.S. 469 (1974); *Florida Star v. B.J.F.*, 491 U.S. 524 (1989).
>
> The state has an interest in limiting access to public records, when used for commercial purposes, see *Los Angeles Police Dept. v. United Reporting Pub. Corp.*, 528 U.S. 32 (1999), and for governmental purposes as well . . . . This has repercussions for citizens' faith in the judiciary.[79]

This is particularly true as there do not seem to be robust remedies for such errors and omissions, with dire and plausibly permanent (but often inadvertent) consequences for participants in the court system.

As the EPIC Brief cautions: "It is impossible to know how frequently similar mistakes affect the lives of New Jersey citizens. As reported in the *New York Times*, it is entirely possible to be listed as a criminal because of a speeding ticket."[80]

In fact, some counsel have expressed concerns that their clients have been pressured into settling prematurely, unnecessarily, or against their advice, simply for fear of having personal information — or, indeed, what they consider disinformation or outright falsehoods — posted online, for all to see. The harm occasioned by such postings, particularly professionally injurious allegations, outweighs the desire to see justice done (or at least to have one's "day in court"). The effect presumably is to encourage frivolous suits with outlandish allegations aimed at extracting settlement by striking fear into potential defendants.[81] As noted above, it is not that court documents were not previously accessible; it is instead that today an effortless Google search — even one not intended to extract that sort of information — can inadvertently and permanently damage an individual or corporation in a variety of contexts, something that a targeted informa-

79 EPIC Brief, *ibid* at 8 citing, for example, Winn, above note 34.

80 *Ibid* at 9. The newspaper article referenced is Brad Stone, "If You Run a Red Light, Will Everyone Know?" *The New York Times* (3 August 2008) BU4.

81 Author's conversation with former labour and employment lawyer and employment law specialist Professor Finn Makela of the Faculty of Law, University of Sherbrooke, at Responsibility, Fraternity, and Sustainability in Law: A Legal Symposium in Honour of Justice Charles D Gonthier, McGill Faculty of Law, Montréal, Québec, 20–21 May 2011.

tion request could not cause, both in terms of magnitude, breadth, and permanence.[82]

Somewhat less dramatically, but presumably no less disruptively, Internet postings have precipitated important difficulties in the commercial (particularly the trade secret) context. Such was the case, for example, with memoranda filed electronically by the United States Federal Trade Commission (the FTC). The FTC failed to properly redact sensitive and potentially damaging business plans about Whole Foods Market Incorporated in a merger matter, prior to posting the documents online. Sensitive facts included plans to close a number of stores. By the time the oversight was detected, and despite the FTC's best efforts, it was too late.[83] Although technical or clerical errors have long occurred and cannot be entirely avoided, the magnified harms that they can cause in the Internet context must be weighted and factored into the balance and into our understanding of access and privacy.

More important, "access" is a misleading term in the Internet age. The electronic court document debate should not simply be framed in terms of the public's "right" to arbitrarily hoard information en masse, irrespective of its accuracy or relevance. Instead, precision and preservation of the integrity of data are tremendous issues here, as the Internet, in Cass Sunstein's words, "doesn't have quality control."[84] Plainly put, as data abound, transparency (not to mention accountability) no longer relates to the ability to gather information per se — erroneous, misleading, or simply meaningless data posted or collected indiscriminately can surely not be said to satisfy those values traditionally underlying access. Rather, transparency is about triage, and about the quality and accuracy of the data available to citizens.

Online disinformation can just as readily be fostered by too much access as by the absence of worthy data. In the words of Ejan Mackaay: "There is, if anything, an abundance of information; amongst the overload, the problem is how to select what information you need. This depends

82 Conversations with Professor Finn Makela regarding anecdotal evidence in the context of Québec's Commission des relations du travail (CRT). Therein, for example, Professor Makela quotes a conciliator who cautioned a complainant "that one of the factors he should consider was the fact that the CRT's decisions are published on-line and that if he lost, all of his future employers would be able to see the decision relating the misconduct he was accused of."

83 Lisa C Wood & Marco J Quina, "The Perils of Electronic Filing and Transmission of Documents" (2002) 22:2 *Antitrust* 91.

84 Noam Cohen, "Courts Turn to Wikipedia, But Selectively" *The New York Times* (29 January 2007), online: http://nyti.ms/1OHPaI7.

not merely on relevance but also on reliability or trustworthiness."[85] As the old adage cautions, a little information can be more dangerous than none, particularly in light of what Daniel Solove labels the problem of "aggregation of data,"[86] which stems from the Internet's "searchability." This problem stems from the fact that previously *disparate* pieces of information concerning an individual floating in cyberspace can be assembled (incorrectly or even maliciously) to form a "comprehensive" digital profile of that person. As noted above, unlike an access-to-information request or paper record, a search engine expedition can reap misleading, but nevertheless persuasive data, an aggregate of unreliable yet compelling morsels concerning a given litigant, witness, or even judge — as the *Cosgrove* case, discussed in Chapter 5, illustrates.

It therefore stands to reason that a misguided insistence on unbridled access to court information and intransigence in its regard, not only fails to promote transparency in respect of quality, but also can paradoxically undermine many of the very objectives publication is meant to serve. Surely, inhibiting participation cannot serve the rationale underlying systems that promote online posting, such as the US Public Access to Court Electronic Records system, or PACER, whose stated objective, as previously noted, was to bring "the citizen ever closer to the courthouse" via technology.[87]

What is more, distortions of court-generated information floating around cyberspace and masquerading as "official" records can eventually risk bringing justice into disrepute. If a high court judge's reputation can be called into question (as in Cosgrove J's case), what can be said of precarious litigants or witnesses? It would therefore appear that an understanding of access divorced from considerations relating to the protection of litigants' rights, privacy among them, is irreconcilable with transparency and accountability. Such access fails to achieve its purpose in light of technological change — and, therefore, must be reconsidered.

Only a quality-centred approach can serve the goals of transparency and accountability. Not only does unbridled admission to data frustrate access to justice by litigants or others fearing humiliation or intimidation,

---

85 Ejan Mackaay, "What's So Special about Cyberspace — Reflections on Elkin-Koren and Salzberger" (2006) 10:3 *Lex Electronica* at 5, online: www.lex-electronica.org/articles/v10-3/mackaay.htm.

86 Solove, above note 33.

87 See Administrative Office of the United States Courts, "Public Access to Court Documents: Better, Faster . . . and Cheaper Than Ever Before" *The Third Branch Newsletter* (April 2001).

as previously described, but it also risks creating the illusion of transparency or accuracy by inundating Internet surfers with a barrage of inaccurate, if not dangerously misinforming data. It thus frustrates the integrity of the justice system.[88]

So, what must we do?

As noted above, the Supreme Court of Canada did take what may be considered an important step towards recognizing the need to revisit the presumption of "openness" in light of the violence potentially done both to vulnerable litigants (a matter of individual rights) and access to the justice system (a collective value) in *AB* (see Section B, above in this chapter). That case presumes a renewed understanding of the relationship between privacy and access in light of technological change, anchored in comparative thinking. It serves as an important counterweight to what may be labelled a knee-jerk "balancing" of ill-defined values that arguably no longer serves the intended rationale and comports with the global trend on point.

As already observed and in sharp contrast to the common law tradition, the civilian vision of privacy, encapsulated by the French experience, favours a more flexible construction. Privacy is considered to be a "personality right" — an idea central to the civilian tradition, but alien to the common law. What that means, in a nutshell, is that privacy attaches to persons rather than property, irrespective of special constraints. Focus is on the *être* — the being — in contrast with the *avoir* — the having; it is divorced from special constraints, that is, the notion of seclusion.

Conceiving the right to privacy as a personality right predicated on dignity and free of territorial constraints allows the civilian legal method to grasp privacy as a zone of intimacy delineated not by space or ownership but by the basic needs of personhood. This conception is of great interest on point as a flexible interpretation lends itself to the protection of privacy in an era of constant technological and social change.

In this vein, privacy may be construed as an *ally* of access rather than as an adversary, for it can be more easily reconciled with both the court's commitment to openness and its responsibility to protect litigants and control its own records. In other words, courts might construe safeguarding privacy as a means of encouraging participation in the justice system (crucial to dignity) in an age when so doing exposes individuals to

88 In Joel Reidenberg's words, "overtransparency is challenging the Rule of Law": Berkman Center for Internet & Society, Harvard University, "Joel R Reidenberg on Transparent Citizens and the Rule of Law" (10 February 2010), online: http://cyber.law.harvard.edu/interactive/events/lawlab/2010/02/reidenberg.

countless risks. Additionally, safeguarding privacy may be seen as a way of enabling courts to maintain essential control over their own materials.[89]

Consequently, it is not merely that the balance between transparency and privacy has shifted tremendously online; it may be that safeguarding privacy can become a way towards ensuring access to justice and willingness to participate in light of the challenges of the Internet age. The duty to protect privacy can and must be construed as part of courts' responsibility to maintain access to justice and prevent disinformation. As noted, the Internet's fragmentary nature, coupled with a significant loss of judicial control over online information, eventually risks fostering a disinclination to participate in the justice process. Paradoxically, the very access to justice that paperless records were meant to enhance is undermined. If privacy is more broadly understood as a flexible concept not contingent on physical space or expectations but on personhood, then it can be viewed as a facilitator of access, not as something that impinges on it.

I. IMPLEMENTING REASONABLE DELAYS

There is, however, an important practical dimension to help assuage the concerns before and until the conceptual challenge can be properly addressed.

As previously noted and evidenced by the above-cited Israeli case, judges, but particularly attorneys and, most of all, self-represented litigants, are not yet aware of the imperatives of digitizing court documents and of their broad privacy implications. They might fail to request redaction by reason of sheer ignorance or make their requests tardily, with significant ramifications to themselves, their clients, and, indeed, the justice system as a whole.

Needless to say, fostering awareness among the judiciary, litigants, and the self-represented is key, but that clearly takes time. In the meantime, there are simple steps that courts can take to lessen the above-described harms to both the integrity of the justice system and litigants themselves. One such proposed step is to implement reasonable delays prior to publishing court documents online. Doing so would presumably allow litigants to ponder the need to request redaction or at the very least prevent

89 For a more detailed account, see Karen Eltis, "The Judicial System in the Digital Age: Revisiting the Relationship between Privacy and Accessibility in the Cyber Context" (2011) 56:2 *McGill Law Journal* 289.

or minimize incidents where the court, upon realizing the ramifications, is powerless to retract information already "unleashed" online.[90]

In other words, imposing reasonable delays (rather than publishing decisions online when rendered) will afford litigants, their representation, and, of course, the courts themselves the time that they need to adjust to technological change and to soberly evaluate, challenge, and, if necessary, correct the information that goes online, in order to at the least manage the risk of permanent deformation. Deformation in an Internet of infinite memory not only brings what is potentially permanent harm to participants in the justice system, but it can also bring the very courts into disrepute.

90 As in *Doe v Doe* (*Ploni v Almoni*), above note 44.

CHAPTER 4

"De-anonymization" and "Re-anonymization"

Why Traditional Assumptions No Longer Apply

Notwithstanding what was said previously, and in a sincere but at times misguided effort to enhance access, courts and quasi-judicial bodies are increasingly eager to digitize. Not only are individual judges (for the most part) electing to go digital, judicial associations such as the Canadian Judicial Council (CJC) actively encourage online publication,[1] and some jurisdictions legally require it.[2] Thus, for instance, "Quebec has perhaps the most distinct legislative framework of all for publication of decisions made by tribunals. Quebec access to information law captures administrative bodies, but, unlike other jurisdictions, the legislation specifically requires public disclosure of tribunal decisions . . . ."[3] Thus, the regulation applicable to Québec's access and privacy legislation reads as follows:

> A public body that makes reasoned decisions in the exercise of adjudicative functions must send the decisions to the Société québécoise d'information juridique, which must distribute them, in accordance with the by-law made under section 21 of the Act respecting the Société

---

1 David Loukidelis, *Privacy and Openness in Tribunal Decisions* (Victoria, BC: Office of the Information & Privacy Commissioner for British Columbia, 2008), online: www.cba.org/cba/cle/pdf/loukidelis_david.pdf. At 13, Loukidelis indicated that the Canadian Judicial Council "concluded in a 2005 publication that all judgments should be published on the internet to enhance access to justice and facilitate legal research."

2 For example, the United States. See Loukidelis, *ibid* at 6, citing Canadian Judicial Council, Judges Technology Advisory Committee, *Model Policy for Access to Court Records in Canada* (2005) at para 19, online: CJC www.cjc-ccm.gc.ca/cmslib/general/news_pub_techissues_AccessPolicy_2005_en.pdf.

3 Loukidelis, above note 1 at 10.

québécoise d'information juridique (R.S.Q., c. S-20), through its website on which the decisions of the courts, administrative tribunals and other bodies are published.[4]

Similarly, movements like "free access to justice"[5] aim to incentivize digital court records worldwide. This course of action is particularly attractive to courts in developing countries, due to the low cost of electronic records, as compared to their paper counterparts (which require court reporters, as well).[6]

But how is it that courts progressively shift towards online records, given the dangers outlined above?

One answer is the ostensible promise of anonymization or simply "omitting personal data identifiers which by their very nature are fundamental to an individual's right to privacy."[7] Yet seemingly innocuous morsels of information (such as zip codes[8]) can almost effortlessly be compiled or contextualized to make out individuals,[9] as Latanya Sweeney's groundbreaking research[10] and more recent incidents such as the Netflix

---

4 *Regulation respecting the distribution of information and the protection of personal information*, CQLR c A-2.1, r 2, s 6.

5 Legal Information Institute, 4th Law via the Internet Conference, Montréal, 3 October 2002; Legal Information Institute, 5th Law via the Internet Conference, Sydney, Australia, 26–28 November 2003.

6 The World Legal Information Institute is a free, independent, and non-profit global research facility developed collaboratively by some national legal information institutes and other organizations. See the "About" page of the WorldLII, online: www.worldlii.org.

7 Loukidelis, above note 1 at 13. See also *ibid*: "It identifies certain information, such as name and date of birth, social insurance number and financial account numbers, as being worthy of protection in written decisions because of the risks associated with disclosing them."

8 "California Retailers Sued following Zipcode Privacy Ruling" *CBS San Francisco* (15 February 2011), online: http://sanfrancisco.cbslocal.com/2011/02/15/california-retailers-sued-following-zip-code-privacy-ruling.

9 Latanya Sweeney, *Computational Disclosure Control: A Primer on Data Privacy Protection* (PhD Dissertation, Massachusetts Institute of Technology, 2001) at 110, online: http://groups.csail.mit.edu/mac/classes/6.805/articles/privacy/sweeney-thesis-draft.pdf.

10 Latanya Sweeney, "Uniqueness of Simple Demographics in the U.S. Population," Working Paper LIDAP-WP4 (Pittsburgh: Carnegie Mellon University, Laboratory for International Data Privacy, 2000); Paul Ohm, "Broken Promises of Privacy: Responding to the Surprising Failure of Anonymization" (2010) 57 *UCLA Law Review* 1701 at 1719:

case,[11] where some financial information of Netflix's customers was inadvertently disclosed, and the AOL[12] fiasco respectively, clearly illustrate.[13]

Simply put, these measures are of questionable use at best. What is most worrisome, however, is that they provide a dangerous false sense of security, particularly in the judicial context. In his insightful piece on point, Paul Ohm warns that computer scientists are now able to "'reidentify' or 'deanonymize' individuals hidden in anonymized data with astonishing ease."[14] In his words:

> For decades, technologists have believed that they could robustly protect the privacy of people by making small changes to their data, using techniques surveyed below. I call this the *robust anonymization assumption* . . . .
>
> But in the past fifteen years, computer scientists have established what I call the *easy reidentification result*, which proves that the robust anonymization assumption is deeply flawed . . . .[15]

And to summarize:

> Anonymization has become "privacy theater"; it should no longer be considered to provide meaningful guarantees of privacy.[16]

Needless to say, there are inherent problems with "anonymized" data: problems that may not only render current anonymization techniques

---

Recall from the Introduction the study by Latanya Sweeney, professor of computer science, who crunched 1990 census data and discovered that 87.1 percent of people in the United States were uniquely identified by their combined five-digit ZIP code, birth date (including year), and sex. According to her study, even less specific information can often reveal identity, as 53 percent of American citizens are uniquely identified by their city, birth date, and sex, and 18 percent by their county, birth date, and sex.

11 George Gombossy, "Netflix under Legal Attack over Privacy Concerns" *ctwatchdog* (5 April 2011), online: http://ctwatchdog.com/2011/03/28/netflix-under-legal-attack-over-privacy-concerns. See also Steve Lohr, "Netflix Cancels Contest after Concerns Are Raised about Privacy" *The New York Times* (12 March 2010), online: http://nyti.ms/1i49s2s, or, generally, "On 'Personally Identifiable Information,'" online: http://randomwalker.info/social-networks/On_Personally_Identifiable_.html.

12 See Michael Geist, "Why the AOL Search Fiasco Matters" (8 August 2006), *Michael Geist* (blog), online: www.michaelgeist.ca/content/view/1346/.

13 Ohm, above note 10 at 1717 and 1720.

14 *Ibid* at 1701.

15 *Ibid* at 1706–7 [emphasis in original].

16 *Ibid* at 1743.

obsolete but also cause them to give participants in the justice system a false sense of security regarding the safety and privacy of their personal information. Thus, for instance, in the now infamous Netflix context, University of Texas at Austin researchers Arvind Narayanan and Vitaly Shmatikov demonstrated how simple the de-anonymization of purportedly "anonymized" data really was.[17] By so doing, they pointed to some fundamental problems inherent to such popular techniques. Compounding the issue, prohibiting the use of the sorts of methods employed by Narayana and Shmatikov is unlikely to succeed due to acute enforcement problems.[18]

Whereas identity thieves and the like seem the most likely suspects, liable to "re-identify" purportedly "de-anonymized" information housed within court documents, seemingly disinterested members of the public are surprisingly also able — and prepared — to do the same. Thus, for example, in Oshawa, Ontario, members of the public "de-anonymized" (or "re-identified") information in a criminal murder trial, notwithstanding the court-ordered publication ban on the names of both the victim and accused.[19] The case involved a toddler, allegedly killed by his mother's boyfriend.[20] Despite a court-imposed publication ban, aimed at protecting the respective identities of the mother and toddler, random members of the public, outraged by the heinous events and eager to express sympathy, "de-identified" information in order to "openly mourn Keagan Davis" on a Facebook tribute site set up by the young victim's father.[21] The Crown

17 Bruce Schneier, "Why 'Anonymous' Data Sometimes Isn't" *Wired* (13 December 2007), online: https://www.schneier.com/essays/archives/2007/12/why_anonymous_data_s.html.

18 "A reidentification ban is sure to fail, however, because it is impossible to enforce": Ohm, above note 10 at 1758.

19 "Writing in The Toronto Star in January, reporter Jesse McLean described a case where a tribute website for a murdered two-year-old Oshawa boy was breaking a court-ordered publication ban that was supposed to protect the identity of the boy and his mother and — since he was the mother's 26-year-old boyfriend — the accused. People posting to the site apparently theorized about the manner of the toddler's death and posted photos of the victim, thereby breaking the ban": Pam Frampton, "Judge, Jury and Facebook" *The Weekend Telegram* (11 September 2010), online: www.thetelegram.com/Opinion/Columns/2010-09-11/article-1741631/Judge,-jury-and-Facebook/1.

20 Emily Mathieu, "Publication Ban Lifted in Oshawa Toddler's Death" *Toronto Star* (12 January 2010), online: www.thestar.com/news/ontario/article/749754--publication-ban-lifted-in-oshawa-toddler-s-death.

21 Jesse McLean, "Does Facebook Page Break the Law?" *Toronto Star* (11 January 2010); "Publication Ban on Toddler in Oshawa, Ont., Lifted" *CBC News*

(and, of course, the court) eventually lifted the ban, presumably realizing its ineffectiveness but also cognizant of the fact that the boy's father, seeking to memorialize him, would in so doing be inadvertently violating the ban.

It is significant that this incident speaks not only to the ease of re-identification, but to the above-mentioned *loss of court control* over the court's own documents. There is the risk of tainting the justice system when "personal identifier"–focused publication bans have unintended effects online, such as preventing a father from memorializing his son. That is also the case when courts are unable to enforce their own publication bans. When the ban was broken in this case, the court ostensibly had little choice but to lift it, as it officially did for the respective names of the accused and victims.[22] Of course, in this case, the use made of the information was relatively innocuous.

Sometimes, though, information is put to more disconcerting uses, as illustrated by the following examples raised by David Loukidelis when he was BC privacy commissioner.

The first case Loukidelis points to, *Alberta (Attorney General) v Krushell*,[23] involved an individual who "had requested a copy of a list of the names of accused individuals found in each Alberta criminal court docket between 1990 and 2005. He apparently hoped to sell the information on the Internet. In holding that the requested records were not covered by Alberta's freedom of information law, Bielby J said the following about posting such information online:"

> The mischief which could be created by allowing ready public access to the names of unconvicted accused is not difficult to imagine. Statutorily prescribed punishments for the convicted would pale in many cases in comparison to the *de facto* punishment created by posting information on the criminally charged for the benefit of the gossip and the busybody. Similarity of names might create defamatory impressions. Same-day internet postings would create concern about courthouse security and judge-shopping which could affect the administration of justice and

---

(12 January 2010), online: www.cbc.ca/news/canada/toronto/story/2010/01/12/oshawa-publication-ban643.html.

22 Jesse McLean, "Facebook Page for Slain Oshawa Boy Raises Questions about Possible Violation of Publication Ban on Case" *Guelph Mercury* (11 January 2010), online: www.guelphmercury.com/news/article/470193--facebook-page-for-slain-oshawa-boy-raises-questions-about-possible-violation-of-publication-ban-on-case.

23 2003 ABQB 252 [*Krushell*], cited in Loukidelis, above note 1.

> thus judicial independence in ways the Legislature clearly attempted to avoid by so carefully exempting all matters relating to the judiciary in other subsections of s. 4 [of the Alberta *Freedom of Information and Protection of Privacy Act*] . . . . While there is currently limited public access to this information via the physical daily posting of the criminal dockets on site, that does not justify posting world-wide for all time to all of those with access to the internet.[24]

Indeed, as Reza has written: "Criminal accusation stigmatizes. Merely having been accused of a crime lasts in the public eye, damaging one's reputation and threatening current and future employment, relationships, social status, and more."[25]

So, too, does Loukidelis cite a 2005 Saskatchewan incident in which that province's information and privacy commissioner investigated an individual's complaint against the Automobile Injury Appeal Commission [AIAC].[26] "The AIAC had begun posting decisions on its website that contained applicants' first and last names, as well as personal medical information and detailed financial information. The AIAC tried to justify its practice relying, in part, on the open court principle. [Saskatchewan] Commissioner Dickson concluded that publication of applicants' personal information online violated Saskatchewan's privacy law, asking, "[w]hat value is added to the goal of accountability and transparency by refusing to mask the particular identity of a claimant?'"[27] Again, it is not only about masking, but doing so effectively.

At this juncture, it is worth emphasizing that the overly broad — yet paradoxically overly narrow — notion of "personal information" — or in this context, "personal identifiers" — lies at the core of the conundrum. Consider that the first generation of privacy laws focused on distinguishing between personal and non-personal data; however, this focus is increasingly inoperable and has left us anonymous in name only. The better view of privacy harm is one able to distinguish between otherwise trivial (oftentimes publicly available) information once labelled "personal" and the information that is central to identity in context. It is this view that

---

24 Loukidelis, *ibid* at 6–7, citing *Krushell*, above note 23 at paras 49 & 50.

25 Sadiq Reza, "Privacy and the Criminal Arrestee or Suspect: In Search of a Right, in Need of a Rule" (2005) 64 *Maryland Law Review* 755.

26 Loukidelis, above note 1 at 7, citing Saskatchewan, Office of the Information and Privacy Commissioner, *Investigation Report 2005-001* (27 January 2005), online: www.oipc.sk.ca/Reports/IR2005-001.pdf.

27 Loukidelis, *ibid* at 7, citing Commissioner Dickson's comments in *Investigation Report 2005-001*, above note 26 at para 113.

empowers courts to differentiate between the two for purposes of protecting litigants before them.

As a report of the Minnesota Supreme Court Advisory Committee on Rules of Public Access to the Judicial Branch rightly cautioned:

> Internet publication of nonmeritorious allegations can harm a person's reputation even if a final court order finds that the allegations are without merit. Those who really need access for a legitimate purpose (such as the media reporting on the development of a case) can obtain the information from the courthouse. Internet publication of allegations made in these types of actions can harm a person's reputation even if a final court order finds that the allegations are without merit . . . . Internet publication of allegations prior to a decision on the merits by a court compounds the injury that a false allegation can cause. As discussed over the next several sections of the report, advisory committee members have conflicting views on whether such publication serves valid public policy.[28]

Finally, as discussed in Chapter 3, a practice of de-indexing, while immensely helpful, may alone be insufficient for preventing the sorts of injustices perpetrated by the likes of the Globe24h incident *inter alia*. Very often it appears that pseudonyms can be reversed and auxiliary information can serve to identify an individual even when "personal information," strictly speaking, is omitted.[29] In the end, the uncertainty associated with de-identification prompts us all the more to avoid putting an unhealthy reliance upon it. It also further militates against blanket online disclosure, as was censured in Chapter 3, because of its highly negative impact both on individual privacy and access to justice.

---

28 *Recommendations of the Minnesota Supreme Court Advisory Committee on Rules of Public Access to Records of the Judicial Branch*, State of Minnesota in Supreme Court, Final Report, No C4-85-1848 (28 June 2004) at 11 and n 14, online: www.lawlibrary.state.mn.us/access/accessreport.htm, quoting from the National Criminal Justice Association. See also *Justice Information Privacy Guideline: Developing, Drafting and Assessing Privacy Policy for Justice Information Systems* (September 2002) at 54, online: www.ncja.org/sites/default/files/documents/Justice-Information-Privacy-Guideline.pdf.

29 See Simson L Garfinkel, "Understanding Identifiers" (July 2015), online: www.dropbox.com/sh/idfmlmfebf3m90o/AABQnhcfINzQi7OBVfu1A60ha/Understanding%20Identifiers%20(Simson%20L.%20Garfinkel).pdf?dl=0.

CHAPTER 5

"Googling" the Judge and the Perception of Impartiality

Out-of-Court Speech, the Internet, and Judicial Ethics

A. INTRODUCTION

The Internet's effect on the boundaries of acceptable out-of-court judicial speech and association,[1] particularly in an era of ubiquitous social networking, is a matter of increasing substance to courts and litigants.[2]

For evident reasons pertaining to the public's confidence in the judicial system and the perception of its integrity, it behooves judges to take pains to avert the slightest appearance of bias. In Canada, the *Charter of Rights and Freedoms* is, of course, only properly satisfied when fairness and impartiality are both "subjectively present and objectively demonstrated to the informed and reasonable observer,"[3] as justice must be done

---

1 See Ed Ratushny, "Speaking as Judges: How Far Can They Go?" (2000) 11 *National Journal of Constitutional Law* 293 at 296: "[T]he judge is not speaking as a judge but as a member of society . . . . The issue here is whether such speech may reflect adversely on the impartiality of the office of the judge as constituting 'unjudicial' conduct even though not performed in the capacity of a judge. In the second situation, the judge is engaging in judicial conduct, but in doing so, may be fulfilling the judicial role improperly."

2 For said purposes, I borrow a broad working definition of "judicial ethics," namely: "Judicial ethics are the morals that guide the comportment of judges." Justice Georgina R Jackson, "The Mystery of Judicial Ethics: Deciphering the Code" (2005) 68 *Saskatchewan Law Review* 1 at 2.

3 As discussed by Bryden's enlightening piece in great detail. See Phillip Bryden, "Legal Principles Governing the Disqualification of Judges" (2003) 83 *Canadian Bar Review* 555. See the *Canadian Charter of Rights and Freedoms*, s 11(d), Part 1 of the *Constitution Act, 1982*, being Schedule B to the *Canada Act 1982* (UK), 1982, c 11 [*Charter*], which states: "Any person charged with an offence has the

and be seen to be done. This duty unquestionably extends to judges' extra-judicial or out-of-court speech, conduct, and associations.[4]

Sparing an outline of the normative framework, well exposed elsewhere,[5] the obligation in question and the related requirement of general "*retenue*," or acting in a "reserved manner,"[6] are enshrined at various levels of the

---

right . . . (d) to be presumed innocent until proven guilty according to law in a fair and public hearing by an independent and impartial tribunal." See *R v RDS*, [1997] 3 SCR 484 at para 31 [*RDS*]. See also *Rex v Sussex*, [1924] 1 KB 256 at 259, Lord Hewitt CJ. See also Stanley De Smith, *Judicial Review of Administrative Action*, 4th ed (London, Sweet & Maxwell, 1980) at 250, and Robert Reid & Hillel David, *Administrative Law and Practice*, 2d ed (Toronto: Butterworths, 1978) at 231, and the Québec *Charter of Human Rights and Freedoms*, CQLR c C-12, s 23, which states: "Every person has a right to a full and equal, public and fair hearing by an independent and impartial tribunal, for the determination of his rights and obligations or the merits of any charge brought against him." See *2747-3174 Quebec Inc v Quebec (Régie des permis d'alcool)*, [1996] 3 SCR 919, as cited by Bryden.

4 The appearance of bias, then, may originate from both the words and conduct of the judge, indicating prejudice. Justice Mahoney considered *in dicta* in *Weerasinge v Canada (Minister of Employment and Immigration)*, [1994] 1 FC 330 at para 13 (CA), the question of whether or not "consultation by a decision maker before publishing a decision, including consultation by the judge with a law clerk" could be abused so as to entail reasonable apprehension of bias. The answer lies in "whether an informed person, viewing the matter realistically and practically, and having thought it through, would think it more likely than not" that the decision was influenced by the clerk.

5 For the Canadian framework, see, for example, Bryden, above note 3, and Ratushny, above note 1. See also Adam Dodek, "Second Opinion: Help Wanted: A Judicial Code of Conduct" *Law Times* (25 February 2008), online: http://lawtimesnews.com/200802252322/commentary/second-opinion-help-wanted-a-judicial-code-of-conduct.

6 See Gonthier J in *Ruffo v Conseil de la magistrature*, [1995] 4 SCR 267 at para 108 [*Ruffo*], citing the *Universal Declaration on the Independence of Justice*, adopted unanimously at the final plenary session of the First World Conference on the Independence of Justice, Montréal, 10 June 1983 [internal footnotes omitted, emphasis in original]: "2.10. Judges shall always conduct themselves *in such a manner as to preserve the dignity of their office* and the impartiality and independence of the judiciary. *Subject to this principle*, judges shall be entitled to freedom of belief, expression, association and assembly."

Justice Gonthier, *ibid*, also approved the following from United Nations, High Commissioner for Human Rights, *Basic Principles on the Independence of the Judiciary*, adopted by the Seventh United Nations Congress on the Prevention of Crime and the Treatment of Offenders, Milan, 26 August–6 September 1985 [emphasis added]: "8. In accordance with the Universal Declaration of

normative hierarchy, including constitutional, codal/statutory rules, rules on disqualification,[7] and ethical principles, both formal[8] and unwritten.[9]

Human Rights, members of the judiciary are like citizens entitled to freedom of expression, belief, association and assembly; *provided, however, that in exercising such rights, judges shall always conduct themselves in such a manner as to preserve the dignity of their office and the impartiality and independence of the judiciary.*"

7 For a thorough and excellent discussion of judicial disqualification, see Bryden, above note 3. In Québec, the *Code of Civil Procedure*, CQLR c C-25, Book II, Title IV, c V, sets out rules governing the recusation of judges in civil proceedings in the province (arts 234–35) as well as a procedural framework for making decisions concerning the recusation of judges in such proceedings (arts 236–42).

8 See Canadian Judicial Council, "Ethical Principles for Judges" (1999) 10 *National Journal of Constitutional Law* 261; Canadian Judicial Council, *Ethical Principles for Judges* (Ottawa: CJC, 1998) [CJC, *Ethical Principles*]. See Justice Georgina Jackson, "'Teaching' Judicial Ethics: The Canadian Methodology" (Paper delivered at the 2d International Conference on the Training of the Judiciary: Judicial Education in a World of Challenge and Change, Ottawa, 2 November 2004) at 2: "the *Ethical Principles* set out the main principles and provide commentary and examples intended to sustain what is already an ethical judiciary."

9 This analysis, however, concerns itself only with *extra-judicial* or out-of-court conduct, including speech and association. For a broader discussion, see Professor Martin L Friedland, *A Place Apart: Judicial Independence and Accountability in Canada* (Ottawa: Canadian Judicial Council, 1995) at 84–87. See also *Report to the Canadian Judicial Council of the Inquiry Committee Established Pursuant to Subsection 63(1) of the* Judges Act *at the Request of the Attorney General of Nova Scotia* (Ottawa: Canadian Judicial Council, 1990), which is better known as the Marshall Inquiry Committee Report [Marshall Report]. For a broader discussion, see Jacob S Ziegel, "Judicial Free Speech and Judicial Accountability: Striking the Right Balance" (1996) 45 *University of New Brunswick Law Journal* 175; Peter H Russell, "Judicial Free Speech: Justifiable Limits" (1996) 45 *University of New Brunswick Law Journal* 155 at 158; and William Mackay, "Judicial Free Speech and Accountability: Should Judges Be Seen and Not Heard?" (1993) 3 *National Journal of Constitutional Law* 159. American Bar Association, *Model Code of Judicial Conduct* (Chicago: Center for Professional Responsibility, American Bar Association, 2011) comment [3] to Rule 3.1:

> Discriminatory actions and expressions of bias or prejudice by a judge, even outside the judge's official or judicial actions, are likely to appear to a reasonable person to call into question the judge's integrity and impartiality. Examples include jokes or other remarks that demean individuals based upon their race, sex, gender, religion, national origin, ethnicity, disability, age, sexual orientation, or socioeconomic status. For the same reason, a

These find echo in democracies the world over.[10] As Yigal Mersel observes: "ethical norms aspire to regulate the judge's comportment not only when s/he hears a specific case, but far more generally; they are overarching norms, permeating all facets of judicial conduct, embracing that which transpires outside the courtroom, extending to judicial expression and social activities."[11]

In that vein, the guiding principle in Canada (as in various sister democracies) appears to be that "judicial freedom of expression stops where serious undermining of public confidence in the judiciary begins."[12]

But how does technology — specifically the Internet and even social networking in particular (discussed in Chapters 6 and 7) — affect the scope and substance of acceptable out-of-court activities, including, but not limited to, those (verbal and non-verbal) associational engagements previously sheltered from the public view? How indeed might online search engines, in particular, prompt courts to redefine the time-honoured judicial duty to "act in a reserved manner"[13] and the perception-based standards for appropriate speech and conduct for judges outside the courtroom? To raise these questions is to begin grappling with them, as we now must.

Before the digital age, a judge's external affiliations, most notably those of cultural, familial, religious, or merely leisurely ilk (as distinguished from partisan or political activity) were generally considered innocuous

---

judge's extrajudicial activities must not be conducted in connection or affiliation with an organization that practices invidious discrimination.

10 See, for example, Institute for Democracy in South Africa (Political Information and Monitoring Service), *Judicial Accountability Mechanisms: A Resource Document* (March 2007), online: www.deontologie-judiciaire.umontreal.ca/fr/textes%20int/documents/Judicial_Accountability_SOUTH_AFRICA.pdf.

11 See Yigal Mersel, *Judicial Discretion* [in Hebrew] (Jerusalem: Israel Bar Editions, 2006) at 33ff [translated by author].

12 See Leo Barry, "Judicial Free Speech and Judicial Discipline: A Trial Judge's Perspective on Judicial Independence" (1996) 45 *University of New Brunswick Law Journal* 79 at 80 & 81, summarizing the reasons of Gonthier J in *Ruffo*, above note 6; and Gonthier J's comments in *Ruffo*, *ibid*. See also Bryden's instructive article on point, above note 3. Using Bryden's classification, such cases might fall under his "fifth situation" category, *ibid* at 586: "The final situation where disqualification arguments may succeed is where the judge has made some form of statement or engaged in behaviour that would lead a reasonable observer to conclude that the judge was either incapable of acting impartially or had failed in his or her duty to act impartially."

13 *Ruffo*, above note 6 at para 1, referring to *Judicial Code of Ethics* [now RRQ, c T-16, r 1], s 8.

so long as they were appropriate in substance.[14] Deemed acceptable in essence, these doings were, quite significantly, by and large beyond public access and, therefore, scrutiny; consequently, they were unlikely to taint the *perception* of impartiality.[15]

Whereas the *substantive* nature of said activities and the rationale governing their tolerability have remained unchanged, the *perception* thereof, for its part, has likely changed. Why? *Discrete* Internet postings (verified or false) may *cumulatively* serve to generate a generally unreliable, ad hoc "digital portrait" of the judge. Such data — accurate or not — have become universally available with unprecedented ease. Plainly put, the Internet generally and search engines specifically make "googling" the judge a far less onerous — however no more dependable — activity. When resulting tidbits are amateurishly or even maliciously compiled, an increased number of presumably frivolous allegations of partiality is likely to arise.

The latter occurred when revered Australian High Court judge Michael Kirby was defamed by identity thieves using the Internet site Myspace: "A profile page, claiming to have been written by the Australian judge, also contains sordid and sexually charged material."[16]

Although the outlandish allegations contained therein would probably be disregarded by anyone with good sense, other, more subtle forms of judicial besmirching — liable to be widely believed — offer cause for concern. The ready availability of often false or unrelated morsels of data purportedly respecting a judge's out-of-court (presumably otherwise proper) expression — rather than the questionable nature or substance of the data — now potentially renders the data problematic. They are problematic because aside from possibly misleading parties, the awareness of such data might, in turn, serve to further unnecessarily restrict the (painfully

14 Examples of such "benign" forms of expression or associations include church membership, family reunions, involvement in cultural activities relating to one's ethnic or religious background (such as participation in a St. Patrick's Day parade), or even academic writing.

15 Perception oftentimes being divorced from substance or reality, it stands to reason.

16 Reid Sexton, "Judge a Victim of MySpace Fraud" *The Age* (7 January 2007), online: www.theage.com.au/news/security/judge-a-victim-of-myspace-fraud/2007/01/06/1168104896791.html. See also Reid Sexton, "High Court Judge Kirby Targeted by Malicious Internet Fraud" *The Age* (7 January 2007), online: www.theage.com.au/news/national/high-court-judge-kirby-targeted-by-malicious-internet-fraud/2007/01/06/1167777325037.html?page=2.

narrow)[17] scope of a judge's private expressional and associational activities.[18] This restriction could conceivably even invite *Charter* scrutiny.[19]

The medium alone therefore, it stands to reason, might suffice to alter the notion of acceptable judicial expression and perceived prejudice, and is visibly liable to affect the culture of judicial comportment emerging therefrom.[20] It can go as far as impugning the judge's very core identity, as discussed below. More specifically, the problem can perhaps best be expressed as one of "aggregation" of otherwise presumably inoffensive data,[21] inadvertently producing an artificially constructed "digital biography"[22]

---

17 As Russell queries in his important piece on point, above note 9 at 156, "to what extent should judges in their private lives as citizens be constrained from enjoying the freedoms available to all other citizens? Clearly, the constraints on judges *qua* citizens should be minimal and based solely on what is required to maintain their capability in the first realm — to discharge properly the distinctive civic and professional responsibilities of a judge."

18 See Yves-Marie Morissette, "Figure actuelle du juge dans la cité" (1999) 30 *Revue de Droit de l'Université de Sherbrooke* 1. According to Professor Morissette (as he then was) at para 14, the trend is towards greater openness to judicial expression: "L'idée, cependant, que le juge puisse invoquer un droit de parole, ou un droit à la liberté d'expression, progresse au Canada . . . ." And at para 17: "La tendance est vers l'ouverture . . . ." See also Justice John Sopinka, "Must a Judge Be a Monk — Revisited" (1996) 45 *University of New Brunswick Law Journal* 167, and Ratushny, above note 1.

19 Former Chief Justice Brian Dickson observed that "today's reality of an independent, bilingual, multicultural Canada in which civil liberties are protected by an entrenched *Charter of Rights and Freedoms* poses new and different challenges of a jurisprudential nature." Brian Dickson CJC, "The Path to Improve the Accessibility of the Law in Canada" (Address delivered to the AGM of the Canadian Bar Association, Winnipeg, 28 August 1984), cited in H Mellon, "Meeting the Public: The *Charter*, Public Debate, and the Judiciary" (2002) 21 *Windsor Yearbook of Access to Justice* 33. See also Morissette, above note 18 at 7–9, regarding judges' *Charter* right to free expression, where he suggests that judges, of course, do enjoy freedom of expression, however limited. See also CJC, *Ethical Principles*, above note 8, ch 6 (Impartiality), commentary D.5.

20 As well as the application of principles pertaining to recusal or disqualification.

21 This term was coined by Daniel J Solove, "Access and Aggregation: Privacy, Public Records, and the Constitution" (2002) 86:6 *Minnesota Law Review* 1137 [Solove], in a different context.

22 *Ibid*. Solove coined the term "digital biographies" to describe the same phenomenon that Rosen refers to as the "dossier society." See Solove, *ibid* at 1184–94. In *The Unwanted Gaze: The Destruction of Privacy in America* (New York: Random House, 2000), Jeffrey Rosen highlighted the danger of assem-

of the judge, one that litigants and others can inexpertly assemble, misread, or even manipulate.[23] As Daniel Solove observes in a different context:

> Computer databases contribute significantly to what I call the "aggregation problem." The aggregation problem stems from the fact that the digital revolution has enabled information to be easily amassed together. We often sprinkle small details about ourselves in a variety of settings as we go about our daily lives . . . . But imagine if every person or entity we ever came into contact with during our lives pooled everything that they knew about us. A fact here and a detail there add up. (p. 14)[24]

In this aggregative manner, the accessibility of data (often irrespective of reliability or accuracy) can increasingly cause judges' impartiality to be frivolously censured.

Not only are data purportedly pertaining to the judge's own expression and association "fair game" but that relating to the judge's family, colleagues, and former associates might also inadvertently attach or be involuntarily or erroneously attributed to the judge. For as Gary Marx explains, in the technology age "information that refers to an individual can be personal or impersonal. Any information that can be tagged to an individual is, in one sense, personal, but not all personal information involves expectations of privacy, nor, when it does, is this to the same degree."[25]

In the Internet era, therefore, decontextualized and deceptive aggregations of online data ostensibly respecting a particular judge can effectively spark the apprehension of bias.[26] Tautologically, they even render it reasonable.

---

bling data from disparate sources. Decontextualized, these tidbits can be used to draw inaccurate and potentially damaging conclusions about individuals.

23 Can include views expressed publicly by judges in their private capacity, prior to their appointment.

24 See Solove, above note 21 at 1185, online: www.privacyrights.org/cc/ar/onlinepubrecs.htm.

25 Discussing privacy generally, from a sociological perspective. See Gary T Marx, "What's in a Concept? Some Reflections on the Complications and Complexities of Personal Information and Anonymity" (2006) 3:1 *University of Ottawa Law & Technology Journal* 1.

26 See also *Wewaykum Indian Band v Canada*, 2003 SCC 45 at para 66 [*Wewaykum Indian Band*] [emphasis in original]: "[T]he relevant inquiry is not whether there was *in fact* either conscious or unconscious bias on the part of the judge, but whether a reasonable person properly informed would apprehend that there was."

Consider the case of Alex Kozinski, a Ninth Circuit (US Federal) judge, who some commentators believe was a potential candidate for the US Supreme Court. The judge was conducting an obscenity trial when the *Los Angeles Times* broke a story alleging that he collected pornography, bordering on bestiality, on his personal computer server.[27] The server in the judge's home was connected to the Internet, and the images on his personal website had become publicly available, via that same connection.

Mired in scandal (the *Times* piece having spread throughout cyberspace in a matter of minutes), Kozinski J disqualified himself from hearing the prominent case and proceeded to declare a mistrial. As for the newspaper, it later averred that a disgruntled former litigant may have found a way to access these files in order to impugn the (already outspoken and controversial) judge's character. Justice Kozinski's wife subsequently explained that the so-called pornography videos were their twenty-one-year-old son Yale's jokes (albeit in poor taste) and not the judge's,[28] but the mere story (and its prominent voyage "across" the Internet) served to raise suspicion of the court's bias in favour of the defendants in what was an obscenity case. Needless to say, it similarly harmed the judge's reputation and the perception of his impartiality in a far broader sense.

Indeed, in addition to being censured and held to account for the contents of their — or their family members' — personal computers/servers, judges can have their impartiality brought into question for arguably improper motives. Motives might relate to the judge's very identity, such as gender, ethnicity, religious observance (or lack thereof), and sexual orientation.[29] These are deemed "prohibited grounds" per section 15(1) of the *Charter*,[30] and anti-discrimination provisions much like it exist in similar-minded jurisdictions.

At worse, ill-intentioned individuals, from judge shoppers to prejudiced parties, can easily manipulate Internet data to fashion the appearance of bias, using the judge's "core identity" against her. Thus, in addition to further constricting judicial expression (whose narrowness is already

---

27 Scott Glover, "9th Circuit's Chief Judge Posted Sexually Explicit Matter on His Website" *Los Angeles Times* (11 June 2008), online: http://fw.to/GXuyhnU.

28 "Alex Kozinski's Wife Speaks Out" *Patterico's Pontifications* (16 June 2008), online: http://patterico.com/2008/06/16/alex-kozinskis-wife-speaks-out/.

29 That is to say parties requesting attorneys of the same gender or cultural/religious, socio-economic background as themselves.

30 Thus arguably leading to claims discriminating against judges of certain backgrounds, the effect of which might be to exclude them from sitting in a manner contrary to s 15(1) of the *Charter*, above note 3.

decried),[31] technology might serve to reprimand a judge's very identity (gender, cultural, religious, or other) — in terms of either appointment or recusal[32] — as cultural affiliations enter disputes in an increasingly multicultural society.[33]

Perhaps the most prominent illustration of the above-described (non-scholarly) "judicial profiling" is that of Hazel Cosgrove J, the first female Supreme Court judge in Scotland, who stood accused of bias in a recent immigration case. Justice Cosgrove faced charges that her Jewish background and membership in the International Association of Jewish Lawyers and Jurists[34] should have disqualified her from hearing a case involving the denial of asylum to a Palestinian refugee, Fatima Helow.[35]

---

31 See Sopinka, above note 18 at 171:

> Some support a rule of total silence on the basis that almost any issue may in future come before the court. My response to this is that it is accepted that judges have views with respect to issues of the day. The fact that these views are not expressed in the context of a specific case should not be a basis for recusal. The scope of the constraint on judicial free speech should be no greater than necessary. This means it should be confined to politically contentious issues and legal questions that may become the subject of adjudication.

32 *Ibid.*

33 For example, Lamer CJC was a Catholic and appears on Wikipedia as a Canadian Roman Catholic and member of the Roman Catholic Church. See Wikipedia entry on "Canadian Roman Catholics" online: http://en.wikipedia.org/wiki/Category:Canadian_Roman_Catholics. What is more, "Lamer drew condemnation not only for supporting the striking down of Canada's abortion law in the pivotal 1988 *Morgentaler* case, but also for admitting afterward he did so on the basis of public opinion. 'Had you asked me at a hearing if I was for or against (abortion), I would have said against,' he said at the University of Toronto in 1998." Could his belonging to a church or his being Catholic for that matter, today constitute reason for disqualification? See "Antonio Lamer 'Liberated' Canada for Abortion" (15 March 2008), online: www.thefreelibrary.com/Antonio+Lamer+%22liberated%22+Canada+for+abortion.-a0173373293. An Internet search can also reveal whether a judge served in the military (as did Lamer CJC, a former member of the Royal Canadian Artillery and Intelligence Corps, and Dickson CJC, with its own ramifications for the above-discussed).

34 For a broader description, see www.intjewishlawyers.org/main.

35 "Lady Cosgrove's impartiality when ruling on an immigration case of a Palestinian woman was compromised by being part of the International Association of Jewish Lawyers and Jurists." See Damien Henderson, "Judge Cleared of 'Jewish Bias'" *The Herald* (17 January 2007), online: www.heraldscotland.com/news/12753594.Judge_cleared_of__apos_Jewish_bias_apos_/. See also

This happened after the party's attorneys googled the judge and found that she was a member in this Jewish professional association[36] and notwithstanding the crucial fact that their client did not in any way claim that the judge's decision *itself* disclosed or reflected any bias. Although the House of Lords (as it then was) cleared the judge in this case of "lacking impartiality,"[37] as did the Lords of Appeal,[38] the mere incident stands as a warning to judges regarding the ready dissemination of personal and unrelated information over the Internet and its availability to litigants and potential frivolous claims or manipulation.[39]

In this manner, technology can be said to reawaken and, indeed, transform the recurring issue of the relevance of a judge's personal traits.[40] It

---

"Accusation of Judge's Bias Rejected" *The Journal of the Law Society of Scotland* (17 January 2007), online: www.journalonline.co.uk/news/1003819.aspx:

> The Association's aims include the advancement of human rights, the prevention of war crimes, the punishment of war criminals and international co-operation based on the rule of law and the fair implementation of international covenants and conventions. It "is especially committed to issues that are on the agenda of the Jewish people, and works to combat racism, xenophobia, anti-Semitism, Holocaust denial and negation of the State of Israel."

36 The court's opinion can be read, online: www.refworld.org/pdfid/47f9d62e4f2.pdf. See para 16 of the decision:

> Upon receiving intimation of the judge's decision, those representing the petitioner chose, for whatever reason, to make further inquiry about the judge. By means of the Internet search engine Google they discovered information about her which was (and is) publicly available on various websites. One such website was that of The International Association of Jewish Lawyers and Jurists ("the Association"), www.intjewishlawyers.org.

37 *Ibid.*

38 Appeal judgment available, online: www.publications.parliament.uk/pa/ld200708/ldjudgmt/jd081022/helow-1.htm.

39 The judge's ethnicity is well known, as she is the first Jewish appointment to that court level in Scotland.

40 See, for example, Bertha Wilson, "Will Women Judges Really Make a Difference?"(1990) 28 *Osgoode Hall Law Journal* 507; Peter McCormick & Twyla Job, "Do Women Judges Make a Difference? An Analysis by Appeal Court Data" (1993) 8:1 *Canadian Journal of Law and Society* 135; and Constance Backhouse, "The Chilly Climate for Women Judges" (Paper delivered at the Adding Feminism to Law: The Contributions of Madame Justice L'Heureux-Dubé workshop, Ottawa, September 2002). See also Justice Maryka Omatsu, "On Judicial Appointments: Does Gender Make a Difference?" (also citing the work of Carol Gilligan regarding social context) in Peter Fletcher, ed, *Ideas in Action: Essays on Politics and Law in Honour of Peter Russell* (Toronto: University of Toronto

prompts the notion of legitimately entertaining, if not approving a party's explicit request for a "custom-made judge," that is, a judge whose gender and ethnicity conform to the litigant's specifications or correspond to his or her own portrait.[41] In other words, as the debate regarding "individualized justice" attracts consideration and the notion of incorporating cultural sensitivity and "cultural pluralism into the law"[42] — with its benefits and foibles — gains momentum,[43] the enhanced capability to look up and "re-create" a judge's (or judicial nominee's) identity online is bound to enliven the issue of a party's entitlement to a judge conforming to their ethnic, gender, or religious specifications.[44]

Press, 1999) at 176. For a US perspective, see Carol Gilligan, *In a Different Voice* (Cambridge: Harvard University Press, 1982); and John Gruhl, Cassia Spohn, & Susan Welch, "Women as Policymakers: The Case of Trial Judges" (1981) 25:2 *American Journal of Political Science* 311.

41 See James Stribopoulos & Moin A Yahya, "Does a Judge's Party of Appointment or Gender Matter to Case Outcomes? An Empirical Study of the Court of Appeal for Ontario" (2007) 45:2 *Osgoode Hall Law Journal* 315; and Cass R Sunstein, David Schkade, & Lisa Michelle Ellman, "Ideological Voting on Federal Courts of Appeals: A Preliminary Investigation" (2004) 90 *Virginia Law Review* 301.

42 See Pascale Fournier, "The Ghettoisation of Difference in Canada: 'Rape by Culture' and the Danger of a 'Cultural Defence' in Criminal Law Trials" (2002) 29:1 *Manitoba Law Journal* 1, and Jennifer Choi, "The Viability of a 'Cultural Defence' in Canada" (2003) 8:1 *Canadian Criminal Law Review* 93. According to Choi at 96: "a good starting point for defining 'cultural defence' is put forth by Lyman, as a defence to . . . negate or mitigate criminal responsibility where acts are committed under a reasonable, good-faith belief in their propriety, based upon the actor's cultural heritage or tradition." Professor Etherington (see Choi, *ibid* at 96) gives a similar definition in a working document on reform of multiculturalism and justice issues: ". . . an independent substantive defence or, as an alternative, the manner in which evidence of cultural differences could be allowed to buttress the assertion of one of our traditionally accepted defences, excuses or justifications."

43 Up to now particularly with regard to cultural defences. See Choi, *ibid*.

44 Composition of juries remains a contentious matter in the United States. See, for example, *Batson v Kentucky*, 476 US 79 (1986); *Powers v Ohio*, 499 US 400 (1991); *Edmonson v Leesville Concrete Co Inc*, 500 US 614 (1991); *Georgia v McCollum*, 505 US 42 (1992); *JEB v Alabama*, 511 US 127 (1994); *Norris v Alabama*, 294 US 587 (1935); *Carter v Texas*, 177 US 442 (1900); Sheri Lynn Johnson, "Litigating for Racial Fairness after *McCleskey v. Kemp*" (2007) 39 *Columbia Human Rights Law Review* 178; *McCleskey v Kemp*, 478 US 1019 (1986); Kenneth J Melilli, "*Batson* in Practice: What We Have Learned about *Batson* and Peremptory Challenges" (1996) 71 *Notre Dame Law Review* 447; Regina Graycar, "The

Whereas the impact of a judge's personal characteristics might form the object of proper study as per the "personal attributes" model,[45] other legitimate studies[46] — however, contentious — are distinguished by their scholarly objectives and by use of recognized scholarly methodology.[47] It bears repeating that beyond the legitimate discussion on point and emphasizing the contribution of social context edification,[48] digital judicial biographies, as compiled by litigants or parties external to the case, can easily serve as pretext for judge shopping and even racist, sexist, or homophobic accusations directed at members of the judiciary whereby integral

---

Gender of Judgment: Some Reflections on 'Bias'" (1998) 32 *University of British Columbia Law Review* 1; Tanya E Coke, Note, "Lady Justice May Be Blind but Is She a Soul Sister? Race Neutrality and the Idea of Representative Juries" (1994) 69 *New York University Law Review* 327 at 331: "that the public believes that all-white juries put minority defendants and victims at a disadvantage — is reason to worry about prevalence of non-representative trial juries."

45 C Neal Tate & Panu Sittiwong, "Decision Making in the Canadian Supreme Court: Extending the Personal Attributes Model across Nations" (1989) 51:4 *Journal of Politics* 900.

46 See, for example, Fiona M Kay, Cristi Masuch, & Paula Curry, "Growing Diversity and Emergent Change: Gender and Ethnicity in the Legal Profession" in Elizabeth Sheehy & Sheila McIntyre, eds, *Calling for Change: Women, Law and the Legal Profession* (Ottawa: University of Ottawa Press, 2006) at 203; Anne Boigeol, "Male Strategies in the Face of the Feminisation of a Profession: The Case of the French Judiciary" in Ulrike Schultz & Gisela Shaw, eds, *Women in the World's Legal Professions* (Portland: Hart, 2003) at 401 [Schultz & Shaw]; Eliane Botelho Junqueira, "Women in the Judiciary: A Perspective from Brazil" in Schultz & Shaw, *ibid* at 437; Patricia Yancey Martin, John R Reynolds, & Shelley Keith, "Gender Bias and Feminist Consciousness among Judges and Attorneys: A Standpoint Theory Analysis" (2002) *Signs: Journal of Women in Culture and Society* 665.

47 Initiated and performed by scholars using scientific methods as opposed to disgruntled or merely inexperienced parties to a case on an ad hoc basis.

48 See Margo L Nightingale, "Judicial Attitudes and Differential Treatment: Native Women in Sexual Assault Cases" (1991) 23 *Ottawa Law Review* 71 at 96, discussing social context education:

> When undertaking any analysis of cultural difference, a judge must be particularly aware of his or her own bias(es), whether in the form of race, class or gender bias. The judge must also try to be aware of bias in the information collected and presented. Is the information regarding the "community values or traditions" truly representative? . . .

Judges must be made aware of their own socio-cultural leanings and the means to overcome them, so as to achieve the proper balancing of rights in exercising their discretion and duties.

components of the judge's very identity can be invoked as in themselves indicative of prejudice[49] or unsuitability for judicial office.[50] Salient to this last point, newly appointed Canadian Supreme Court Justice Russell Brown was criticized by some for his blogging as a law professor (see Chapter 2).

B. WHAT THEN CAN AND MUST WE DO?

A helpful starting point for a pragmatic, flexible approach is one premised upon the rationale underlying the principles governing judicial expression. Far too often, jurists and lawmakers are prone to "extreme" reactions when it comes to new technologies. In other words, many of us tend to either ignore cyber problems as too complex to address or even impossible to regulate, while others try to over-regulate by "reinventing the wheel" and fashioning normative mechanisms far too specific or narrowly tailored to keep up with evolving technology. As Solove observes: "When they try to track existing technology too closely, they become too rule-like and lose the flexibility of a standard. Basic principles get lost or forgotten in the shuffle of technicalities."[51]

Taking such a tight approach can be especially problematic in the judicial context in countries such as Canada where, for reasons relating to flexibility and judicial independence, *inter alia*, ethical principles are aspirational rather than prescriptive.[52] Justice Georgina Jackson explains:

> First and foremost, it is not necessary to interpret the *Ethical Principles* as creating standards of conduct. The *Ethical Principles* booklet is written for an independent judiciary. Canadian judges have earned their

---

49 As the hypothetical Lamer CJC example, above note 33, seeks to demonstrate.

50 See Karen Eltis & Fabien Gélinas, "Constitutional Guarantees of the Independence of the Judiciary" (Paper delivered at the International Academy of Comparative Law, XVII International Conference of Comparative Law, Utrecht, July 2006).

51 Daniel J Solove, "Fourth Amendment Codification and Professor Kerr's Misguided Call for Judicial Deference" (2005) 74 *Fordham Law Review* 747 at 773.

52 CJC, *Ethical Principles*, above note 8, states as principle 2 in ch 1 (Purpose):

> The Statements, Principles and Commentaries are advisory in nature. Their goals are to assist judges with the difficult ethical and professional issues which confront them and to assist members of the public to better understand the judicial role. They are not and shall not be used as a code or a list of prohibited behaviours. They do not set out standards defining judicial misconduct.

> status first through rigorous training, and then by the respect and approval of their peers prior to appointment. A disciplinary code may be more important in a judicial system where judges are elected or enjoy less status than Canadian judges, but it is not needed for a judiciary that is free from political and financial pressures.
>
> Second, it is commonly believed that the test for sanctionable conduct is now established at a level that maximizes the exercise of impartial judicial thought. If the *Ethical Principles* are interpreted as creating a standard of conduct for disciplinary purposes, the ambit of what is considered sanctionable conduct may be broadened. This may result in an increase in complaints. As Professor Morissette indicates, "a series of complaints is likely to affect the judge where he or she is most vulnerable, namely in the ability to make impartial decisions with the appropriate degree of detachment on questions of general interest that are both very difficult and controversial."
>
> Third, one can, in my opinion, accomplish more with ethical principles than with a code of prohibited behaviours. Ethical principles are, by their nature, more stringent than any standard of conduct can ever be. They represent the ceiling to which judges strive . . . . Ethical principles leave more to the individual good conscience of the judge than a code that can lead simply to legalistic ritual.
>
> Fourth, any attempt to use the *Ethical Principles* as a standard of behaviour for discipline overlooks the fact that the booklet omits matters that we take for granted as sanctionable conduct and addresses matters which could be considered innocuous, For example, there is no mention of gifts, but there is extensive treatment of the circumstances in which a judge can give a letter of reference.[53]

Instead, a purposive, however progressive and contextual, interpretation of the flexible principles already in place, informed by the perspective of comparative inquiry, would appear to serve judges best.

Consequently, in order to carefully assess whether any impugned statements, conduct, or online data have given rise to a reasonable appre-

---

53 Justice Georgina R Jackson, "The Mystery of Judicial Ethics: Deciphering the Code" (2005) 68 *Saskatchewan Law Review* 1 at 16–17. This viewpoint was echoed in the review of the conduct of Matlow J by the Canadian Judicial Council (CJC) in 2008. The CJC explicitly stated "that the *Ethical Principles* are not written as a proscriptive conduct code and it is not possible to apply them as such": "Majority Reasons of the Canadian Judicial Council in the Matter of an Inquiry into the Conduct of the Honourable P Theodore Matlow" (3 December 2008) at para 103, online: www.cjc-ccm.gc.ca/cmslib/general/Matlow_Docs/Final%20Report%20En.pdf [Matlow Report].

hension of bias, we must — as we have always done — inquire the following: "[W]hat would an informed person, viewing the matter realistically and practically — and having thought the matter through — conclude[?] Would he think that it is more likely than not that [the decision maker], whether consciously or unconsciously, would not decide fairly?"[54]

In other words, the test is whether "a reasonably informed bystander could reasonably perceive bias on the part of an adjudicator"[55] or as expressed in the Matlow case before the Canadian Judicial Council, whether the expression "would severely undermine public confidence in the administration of justice."[56] The wording, though not identical, is again, similar in most like-minded jurisdictions.[57]

It is important to reinforce that the Canadian judiciary benefits from a strong "presumption of judicial integrity" and that judges are "assumed to be [persons] of conscience and intellectual discipline, capable of judging a particular controversy fairly on the basis of its own circumstances."[58]

---

54 See *Committee for Justice and Liberty v Canada (National Energy Board)*, [1978] 1 SCR 369 [*Justice and Liberty*].

55 *Newfoundland Telephone Co v Newfoundland (Board of Commissioners of Public Utilities)*, [1992] 1 SCR 623 at para 22. It is clearly beyond the scope of this endeavour to provide a comprehensive discussion of judicial recusal. Such discussions are widely available, however. See, for example, Bryden, above note 3. The test encompasses a twofold requirement, namely, the person considering the bias must be reasonable and so must the apprehension of bias in the context. See also *Wewaykum Indian Band*, above note 26.

56 Matlow Report, above note 53 at para 9.

57 CJC, *Ethical Principles*, above note 8 at 25, 41. See also United Nations, Economic and Social Council, "Bangalore Universal Principles of Judicial Conduct" Annex of ECOSOC 2006/23, Value 4.6, online: www.unodc.org/pdf/corruption/corruption_judicial_res_e.pdf: "A judge, like any other citizen, is entitled to freedom of expression, belief, association and assembly, but, in exercising such rights, a judge shall always conduct himself or herself in such a manner as to preserve the dignity of the judicial office and the impartiality and independence of the judiciary."

58 *RDS*, above note 3 at paras 28 and 32, in the latter instance citing *US v Morgan*, 313 US 409 at 421 (1941). This crucial presumption emanates from two distinct sources: the Judicial Oath of Office and the provisions of the *Judicial Code of Conduct* respecting impartiality; see the discussion in *R v Smith & Whiteway Fisheries Ltd*, [1994] NSJ No 362 at paras 60–61 (CA); *R v Lin*, [1995] BCJ No 982 at para 34 (SC). As Richard Devlin observes: "The law will not suppose a possibility of bias in a judge, who is already sworn to administer impartial justice, and whose authority greatly depends upon that presumption and idea": see Richard F Devlin, "We Can't Go On Together with Suspicious Minds: Judicial Bias and Radicalized Perspective in *R v. R.D.S.*" (1995) 18 *Dalhousie Law*

It remains that a judge must avoid engagements in activities whereby his impartiality or the appearance of impartiality "may reasonably be questioned."[59] Nevertheless, and while a thorough exposition of the normative framework evades present purposes and scope, "the threshold for a finding of real or perceived bias is high[60] and evaluated contextually."[61] Again and plainly put: "In light of the strong presumption of judicial impartiality, the standard refers to an apprehension based on serious

---

Journal 408 at 417, quoting from William Blackstone, *Commentaries on the Laws of England III* (Oxford: Clarendon, 1788) at 361. As judges are presumed to be both fair and impartial, disqualification, in practice, is quite rare. Thus, in the words of L'Heureux-Dubé J, quoted in *RDS*, above note 3 at para 49: "Before concluding that there exists a reasonable apprehension of bias in the conduct of the judge, the reasonable person would require some clear evidence that the judge in question had improperly used his or her perspective in the decision-making process; this flows from the presumption of impartiality of the judiciary."

59 The test for judicial disqualification is one of reasonable apprehension of bias: see de Grandpré J in *Justice and Liberty*, above note 54 at 394, and *R v Valente*, [1985] SCJ No 77 at paras 11–12. This is to say that if the judge's words or conduct give rise to such an apprehension, he is deemed to have exceeded his jurisdiction, thereby warranting disqualification. The test being an objective one, actual bias need not be shown, nor must it exist for that matter. A similar test exists in England, as per Lord Denning in *Metropolitan Properties Ltd v Lannon*, [1968] 3 All ER 304 at 310 (CA): "in considering whether there was a real likelihood of bias, the court does not look at the mind of the justice himself . . . it does not look to see if there was a real likelihood that he would, or did, in fact favour one side at the expense of the other. The court looks at the impression which would be given to other people. Even if he was as impartial nevertheless, if rightminded persons would think that, in the circumstances there was a real likelihood of bias on his part, then he should not sit. And if he does sit, his decision cannot stand." See also *R v Higgins*, [1895] All ER Rep 914, [1895] 1 QB 563; and *R v Sunderland Justices*, [1901] 2 KB 357.

60 "[A]llegations of perceived judicial bias will generally not succeed unless the impugned conduct, taken in context, truly demonstrates a sound basis for perceiving [bias] . . . . One overriding principle from these cases is that the impugned comments or other conduct must not be looked at in isolation. Rather it must be considered in the context of the circumstances, and in light of the whole proceeding": in *RDS*, above note 3 at para 141.

61 This is to say that "if the words or conduct of the judge, viewed in context, do not give rise to a reasonable apprehension of bias, the findings of the judge will not be tainted, no matter how troubling the impugned words or actions may be": *RDS*, *ibid* at para 100.

grounds. Each case must be examined contextually and the inquiry is fact-specific."[62]

For purposes of Internet "judicial profiling," the direction offered by the above-stated principles, it would appear, is threefold.

First, the logic underlying the expressed desire for a multicultural judiciary of varied experience[63] dictates that attention best be focused more concretely on a judge's expression and activities rather than on the judge's (immutable) core identity and personal characteristics.[64] Adopting this focus better serves us in circumscribing the apprehension of bias and further aids in averting frivolous — if not discriminatory — allegations.[65] In "Judgment, Diversity, and Relational Autonomy," Jennifer Nedelsky puts "individualized" justice into some context. She writes that "although no given litigant at either the trial or appellate level could expect a judge who shares their background and experience, every litigant could expect a judge with wide experience in talking with, listening to, trying to persuade people from diverse backgrounds."[66]

A second (and related) direction is to take a purposive interpretation of the principles of apprehension of bias, in other words, to consider what the principles are intended to address. In the Internet age, doing so is most relevant to ensuring that we stay the course and maintain a principled stand (rather than be swayed by knee-jerk responses). An interpretation of the principles is well expressed by Buergenthal J of the International Court of Justice:[67]

---

62 *Wewaykum Indian Band*, above note 26, Summary.

63 See Eltis & Gélinas, above note 50.

64 *Ibid*. With regard to appointments as well. In that regard generally, see Justice Michael J Bryant, "Judging the Judges: Judicial Independence and Reforms to the Supreme Court of Canada Appointment Process" (2004) 24 *Supreme Court Law Review* (2d) 29 at 38–39. See also Sébastien Grammond, "Transparence et imputabilité dans le processus de nomination des juges de la Cour suprême du Canada" (2006) 36:4 *Revue générale de droit* 739.

65 This is not to say that the notion of "individualized" justice cannot and should not be properly entertained. Instead, it is merely to suggest that Internet search engines do not constitute a proper and reliable mechanism for advancing such claims in a serious fashion.

66 Jennifer Nedelsky, "Judgment, Diversity, and Relational Autonomy" in Ronald Beiner & Jennifer Nedelsky, eds, *Judgment, Imagination and Politics: Themes from Kant and Arendt* (Lanham, MD: Rowman & Littlefield, 2001).

67 In his dissenting opinion regarding the legal framework governing disqualification in the Israeli Fence case re petition to disqualify Elaraby J: *Legal Consequences of the Construction of a Wall in the Occupied Palestinian Territory*,

> A court of law must be free and, in my opinion, is required to consider whether one of its judges has expressed views or taken positions that create the impression that he will not be able to consider the issues raised in a case or advisory opinion in a fair and impartial manner, that is, that he may be deemed to have prejudged one or more of the issues bearing on the subject-matter of the dispute before the court.[68]

Third, the principles of justice and fairness (encapsulated in the traditional standard) need to be shored up in light of the concerns relating to constructing or misperceiving a spurious digital portrait of the judge.[69] Doing so can be achieved by placing careful emphasis on the "reasonable" criteria by which the apprehension of bias is assessed. In other words, would the impugned judicial expression or association lead a *reasonable* person to apprehend bias?[70] That criterion is nothing new. The standard mandating recusal if and whenever "impartiality might reasonably be questioned" or in the presence of the "reasonable apprehension of bias" remains unaltered. But the renewed emphasis of reasonableness as an *aide-mémoire* is of the essence, for while the reasonable person may well be tech savvy and avail herself of the use of Internet search engines, the sensibleness of assembling a "digital judicial biography" based on an ad hoc compilation of data from unverified sources that may or may not be accurate at best, or could be misleading or based on improper considerations pertaining to the judge's identity at worse, is, by most accounts, of questionable prudence.

Although technological evolution invites renewed reflection, it does not necessarily follow that the normative framework must be reinvented. Rather, the concerns that new technologies raise can be properly addressed at the level of *interpretation* of what are often malleable standards, fashioned to survive these advances and others. For reasons that are easily understood, "true impartiality does not require that the judge have

---

Advisory Opinion, [2003] ICJ Rep 136 at 240ff, online: www.icj-cij.org/docket/files/131/1534.pdf.

68 *Ibid* at para 11, cited in Yuval Shany & Sigall Horovitz, "Judicial Independence in The Hague and Freetown: A Tale of Two Cities" (2008) 21:1 *Leiden Journal of International Law* 113 at 117, n 20 (discussing judicial impartiality and disqualification in the international context). See also Theodor Meron, "Judicial Independence and Impartiality in International Criminal Tribunals" (2005) 99:2 *American Journal of International Law* 359.

69 Or even misrepresenting and distorting judicial activities.

70 See "Disqualification of Federal Judges for Personal Bias" (1949) 16:2 *University of Chicago Law Review* 349, online: http://links.jstor.org/sici?sici=0041-9494(194924)16%3A2%3C349%3ADOFJFP%3E2.0.CO%3B2-C.

no sympathies or opinions; it requires that the judge nevertheless be free to entertain and act upon different points of view."[71] This requirement is particularly critical given that the desirability of maintaining a multicultural, diverse judiciary[72] mandates the acceptance, if not encouragement of cultural affiliations. Anything less, if it is tendered, would surely have an undesired chilling effect on judges, causing them, to paraphrase Sopinka J, to completely withdraw from society[73] or, indeed, voiding judges of the very humanity that we expect them to exhibit.

C. JUDICIAL APPOINTMENTS: COMPROMISING CYBER DATA AND THE DUTY TO SEARCH AND DISCLOSE

Having broached the question of "innocent" judge-related data being manipulated or distorted, as well as the issue of the potential exclusion of cultural or other "alternative life-experience" minority individuals from the bench, let us now turn briefly to less innocuous cyber data: data that may either be compromising to, or at the very least influence, the nomination process and the integrity of the justice system.

More concretely, the Lori Douglas incident in Manitoba stands as a prominent illustration of this preoccupying phenomenon. This senior judge and associate chief justice was asked to be "relieved in the interests of the judiciary and of the court," after nude photos of her surfaced online.[74] Before her appointment, she had allegedly posed for her husband (allegedly engaging in bondage and oral sex), and years later he gave the pictures to a client who, in turn, proceeded to post them online.[75] Although the Canadian Judicial Council investigation into the judge and the propriety

---

71 Canadian Judicial Council, *Commentaries on Judicial Conduct* (Ottawa: CJC, 1991) at 12 [emphasis added].

72 As part of society and enshrined in the *Charter*, above note 3. On the merits of a diverse judiciary, see Richard Devlin, A Wayne MacKay, & Natasha Kim, "Reducing the Democratic Deficit: Representation, Diversity and the Canadian Judiciary, or towards a 'Triple P' Judiciary" (2000) 38 *Alberta Law Review* 734.

73 As some presumably had when the Marshall Report emerged, above note 9. Justice Sopinka explains: "Some had withdrawn completely from society": Sopinka, above note 18. See also Mellon, above note 19.

74 "Man. Judge in Nude Photo Scandal Steps Aside" *CBC News* (2 September 2010), online: CBC www.cbc.ca/1.901778.

75 And filed a complaint against the judge with the Manitoba law society. See Judith Timson, "The Net Killed Sexual Privacy" *The Globe and Mail* (2 September 2010), online: http://fw.to/0cbpY8T.

of her conduct ended with the judge agreeing to retire,[76] the very word of the compromising photos served to unleash a public and media storm.[77] The focus was chiefly on the judge's duty to disclose the existence of the images prior to her appointment and, indeed, the appointing authority's obligation to inquire into such matters, in an effort to prevent subsequent shame being visited upon the judiciary and its good name.

As Irwin Cotler, a former minister of justice, has repeatedly stated, admirable personal characteristics,[78] in general, and forthrightness, in particular, are determinant in making a judicial appointment.[79] Indeed, "impeccable personal and professional ethics: honesty, integrity and forthrightness" are deemed especially pertinent in fact and as emerged from the minister's speeches *sine qua non* to judicial appointments.[80] These characteristics are valued all the more at a time when the appointment process is increasingly impugned for lack of transparency on the one hand and a plethora of data, some of it unreliable, is discoverable online on the other. Accordingly, any qualms about disclosure and one's Internet presence can give worrisome pause to any judicial candidate.

In light of the Lori Douglas incident and as "private" space increasingly contracts, it stands to reason that a candidate for judicial (or quasi-judicial) office has a specific duty to divulge — to explicitly reveal — any behaviour that might reasonably risk disparaging the integrity of the judiciary.[81] Certainly, candidates (like anyone who values their reputation) must search themselves online regularly and thereafter without delay reveal any finding (such as images) that might imperil respect for judicial office, even by virtue of mere perception. As perception is of the essence, candidates need to divulge whether the information is true or false. (The

76 See "Judge Lori Douglas's Offer to Retire Early Accepted by Judicial Panel" *CBC News* (24 November 2014), online: CBC www.cbc.ca/1.2846980; a transcript of the hearing is available online at www.cjc-ccm.gc.ca/cmslib/general/Douglas_Docs/CJC-Douglas-transcript-2014-10-28.pdf.

77 "Manitoba Judge in Alleged Sex Scandal Halts Administrative Duties Pending Review" *Hamilton Spectator* (10 February 2011), online: www.thespec.com/news-story/2193762-manitoba-judge-in-alleged-sex-scandal-halts-administrative-duties-pending-review/. See also Kirk Makin, "Watchdog Partially Clears Manitoba Judge Caught Up in Sex Scandal" *The Globe and Mail* (5 January 2011), online: http://fw.to/08zzdcQ.

78 Along with professional capacity and diversity.

79 See again appointing minister's comments, for example, here: www.huffingtonpost.ca/irwin-cotler/judges_b_4032593.html?utm_hp_ref=tw.

80 *Ibid.*

81 By the reasonable person, as per the existing normative framework.

latter sort can — and must — be dealt with swiftly.) Such a duty has, needless to say, always existed. New technologies only reinforce it, given the Internet's infinite memory and potential for distorting information and cloaking falsehoods in the guise of truths.

As Frank Work, Alberta's information and privacy commissioner, observed: "I am all the more concerned as communications technology evolves and presents a world where nothing — no indiscretion, no stupid, regrettable word, no fit of pique, no foot in mouth — will be forgotten. Your permanent record is now . . . permanent."[82] In other words, and for our purposes, a candidate for judicial (or equivalent) office must alert the appointing authorities or committee to the existence of potentially compromising details whether they are true or false, decontextualized, reproduced without consent, or even fabricated. Further, in order to do so and avoid embarrassing the office later on, the candidate must conduct diligent searches online, recognizing the networked environment's unique potential for rapidly spreading and magnifying information (regardless of its accuracy).

As observed earlier, technology serves only to enhance and fortify the pre-existing requirements that both candidates and their appointing authorities must respect. The Internet (or networked environment, more broadly speaking) is a public place or to quote *The Wall Street Journal*, the Internet "[l]ets it all hang out."[83] It renders the notion of private space most elastic, and it must be navigated with great care in order to avoid committing "the digital-age sin of assuming privacy exists in a medium intended for disclosure."[84]

We are all, therefore, to the extent reasonably feasible, responsible for protecting our personal information online, and this responsibility is all the more serious for judges and aspiring judges. Although the focus in the post-Second World War era has correctly been on rights, corresponding responsibilities, as per the civil law tradition, are not to be neglected, and individuals, especially judges and members of the legal profession, have a duty to avoid inappropriate exposure or even overexposure that might be misconstrued online.

---

82 Quoted in Christie Blatchford, "Winnipeg Judge's Story a Cautionary Tale with a Modern Twist" *The Globe and Mail* (7 September 2010), online: http://fw.to/Y0GlpJP.

83 L Gordon Crovitz, "The Internet Lets It All Hang Out" *The Wall Street Journal* (13 June 2011), online: http://on.wsj.com/mTsP7r.

84 *Ibid.*

Appointing authorities, too, must conduct reasonable inquiries, online and off, with candidates' consent; indeed, chief judges and judicial administrators might periodically consider doing the same. However, the chief burden of disclosure rests reasonably on candidates themselves. As in the Douglas example, compromising information may surface online only years later, therefore arguably making it difficult to detect (or even undetectable, in some cases) prior to its posting.

Yet it is significant to note that a decontextualized image of a candidate or manipulated comments erroneously or maliciously attributed to a judge or a judicial candidate does not mean automatic disqualification, particularly bearing in mind the unjust effect of these on women, who are often the object of cyber intimidation. On the contrary and since, as Frank Work correctly notes, no indiscretion, even those of one's tender youth, is now forgotten, such data, if assessed properly in context, must not *prima facie* render a candidate ineligible for judicial office — unless a human or diverse judiciary is not the goal.

Sossin and Bacal point out that as judges are increasingly appointed with "digital baggage," older posts might progressively appear less "scandalous" or improper as social values evolve and social media connections become even more commonplace for a new generation of judges:

> What might have shocked the public a generation ago (an openly gay or lesbian judge, judges with children out of wedlock, etc.) today barely attracts notice. Similarly, the scenario of groups or individuals who are parties to litigation and who come before the court with Facebook connections to the judge may cause anxiety today but may well appear quaint a generation from now. In other words, if the ability to adjudicate free from bias is the standard, social media has the potential to reshape the relevance of a judge's background to the perception of his or her impartiality.[85]

In this vein, Sossin and Bacal highlight the onerous task of assessing when a judge is speaking *qua* judge online, which might give rise to a reasonable apprehension of bias. They consider the nebulous distinction between "private" and "public" online.[86] Indeed, with online profiles outfitted with complex and difficult-to-navigate privacy settings, it can be hard to determine when a judge is speaking in an official capacity or

---

85 Lorne Sossin & Meredith Bacal, "Judicial Ethics in a Digital Age" (2013) 46:3 *University of British Columbia Law Review* 629 at 637.

86 *Ibid* at 641–42.

speaking as a private citizen.[87] That said, and mindful that judges lead private lives and have the right to free speech, the difficulty of this distinction provides a strong argument in favour of additional reserve and caution online. In summary, online data are particularly susceptible to manipulation and must not be taken at face value — certainly not to evaluate a candidate's moral calibre or integrity; the data must, however, be considered in the full context of circumstances by the relevant appointing bodies (or chief justice for sitting magistrates).

87 *Ibid* at 641.

CHAPTER 6

Facebook, Social Networking, and the Appearance of Impropriety

For Judges Less Is More

A. INTRODUCTION

It was said in 2010 that 40 percent of all US judges engage in social networking practices.[1] Needless to say, the statistics are far higher for attorneys generally, if only due to the median age.

Although the benefits are clear to most users, the perils remain unknown to many judges and lawyers, who could easily avoid unnecessary humiliation or worse by taking simple precautions. As David Mangan correctly asserted, "The belief that social media is 'only' another medium for oral discussion remains ubiquitous, thereby oftentimes engendering a 'disconnect' between users' perceptions of the medium and legal distinctions"[2] between oral discussion and social media. Indeed, this general lack of awareness is evidenced by one such attorney getting caught in an embarrassing lie by the judge in front of whom she was pleading: the latter had simply checked the lawyer's Facebook page:[3] "The lawyer had asked for a continuance because of the death of her father. The lawyer

1 Conference of Court Public Information Officers, *New Media and the Courts: The Current Status and a Look at the Future* (26 August 2010), online: CCPIO http://ccpio.org/wp-content/uploads/2012/02/2010-ccpio-report-summary.pdf.

2 David Mangan, "A Platform for Discipline: Social Media Speech in the Workplace" 2015 *Osgoode Legal Studies Research Paper Series*, Paper No 85, online: http://digitalcommons.osgoode.yorku.ca/cgi/viewcontent.cgi?article=1084&context=olsrps.

3 Molly McDonough, "Facebooking Judge Catches Lawyer in Lie, Sees Ethical Breaches #ABAChicago" *ABA Journal* (31 July 2009), online: www.abajournal.com/news/article/facebooking_judge_catches_lawyers_in_lies_crossing_ethical_lines_abachicago/.

had earlier posted a string of status updates on Facebook, detailing her week of drinking, going out and partying. But in court, in front of [Judge] Criss, she told a completely different story."[4]

Interestingly, the magistrate in question, Susan Criss, an (elected) state judge in Texas, was herself the source of controversy with respect to social networking as she used Facebook to "friend" lawyers for possible future campaign purposes. It appears that "[Judge] Criss gets around the ethical rules prohibiting *ex parte* communications between judges and lawyers by asking lawyers to 'de-friend' her when they're trying cases before her."[5]

Attempting to respond to the prevalence of this phenomenon, some states (Florida, in particular) have gone so far as to ban judicial social networking between judges and attorneys.[6] Thus, for instance, a Florida judge needed to recuse herself from a case after sending a Facebook friend request to a litigant who was appearing before her in a divorce case.[7] The litigant had refused the request, and her lawyer then claimed that the judge retaliated against his client by awarding her "most of the marital debt."[8] What's more, another Florida judge had to recuse himself because he was "friends" with a prosecutor on Facebook.[9] As Gross J (concurring) colourfully warns in this vein:

> Judges do not have the unfettered social freedom of teenagers. Central to the public's confidence in the courts is the belief that fair decisions are rendered by an impartial tribunal. Maintenance of the appearance of impartiality requires the avoidance of entanglements and relationships that compromise that appearance. Unlike face to face social interaction, an electronic blip on a social media site can become eternal in

---

4 *Ibid*. See also Dahlia Lithwick & Graham Vyse, "Tweet Justice: Should Judges Be Using Social Media?" *Slate* (30 April 2010), online: www.slate.com/id/2252544.

5 *Ibid*.

6 Florida Supreme Court, Judicial Ethics Advisory Committee, "Opinion 2009-20" (17 November 2009), online: www.jud6.org/LegalCommunity/LegalPractice/opinions/jeacopinions/2009/2009-20.html ["Opinion 2009-20"]. See also John Schwartz, "For Judges on Facebook, Friendship Has Limits" *The New York Times* (10 December 2009), online: http://nyti.ms/1TD3xR0.

7 Jacob Gershman, "Judge Disqualified over Facebook 'Friend' Request" (27 January 2014) *The Wall Street Journal* (blog), online: Law Blog http://blogs.wsj.com/law/2014/01/27/judge-disqualified-over-facebook-friend-request/?mod=WSJBlog.

8 *Ibid*.

9 *Domville v Florida*, No 4D12-556 (Fla Dist Ct App 16 Jan 2013), online: www.4dca.org/opinions/Jan%202013/01-16-13/4D12-556.rehg.pdf [*Domville*].

> the electronic ether of the internet. Posts on a Facebook page might be of a type that a judge should not consider in a given case. The existence of a judge's Facebook page might exert pressure on lawyers or litigants to take direct or indirect action to curry favor with the judge. As we recognized in the panel opinion, a person who accepts the responsibility of being a judge must also accept limitations on personal freedom.[10]

Other US jurisdictions, such as Ohio, have been far more permissive, ruling that judges can "friend" lawyers appearing as counsel before them provided that the "judge's participation on a social networking site . . . be done carefully" in order to comply with ethical rules.[11] Delaware, for its part, has stressed "[c]omplete separation of a judge from extra-judicial activities is neither possible nor wise [as] a judge should not become isolated from the society in which a judge lives."[12]

That middle-of-the-road approach was echoed in the state of New York,[13] where judges are to "exercise discretion" in order to "avoid impropriety"[14] such as that apparently fostered by a Staten Island judge transferred to Manhattan by reason of his offending Facebook posts regarding pending cases.[15] Since then, however, New York issued *Advisory Opinion 13-39* which states "that the mere status of being a 'Facebook friend,' without more, is an insufficient basis to require recusal. Nor does the committee believe that a judge's impartiality may reasonably be questioned or that there is an appearance of impropriety based solely on having previously

---

10 *Ibid.*

11 Supreme Court of Ohio, Board of Commissioners on Grievances and Discipline, "Opinion 2010-7" (3 December 2010) at 1, online: www.supremecourt.ohio.gov/Boards/BOC/Advisory_Opinions/2010/default.asp.

12 Judge Thomas E Hornsby (ret), "The American Bar Association (ABA) 2007 *Model Code of Judicial Conduct*: What Does It Mean to Juvenile and Family Court Judges?" (2011) 62:1 *Juvenile and Family Court Journal* 67 at 80, online: http://onlinelibrary.wiley.com/doi/10.1111/j.1755-6988.2010.01057.x/pdf. See also Comparison of the Judicial Canons of Florida, New York, South Carolina, Texas and the ABA, online: http://bruceacampbell.com/category/judges.

13 New York State Unified Court System, "Opinion 08-176" (29 January 2009), online: www.nycourts.gov/ip/judicialethics/opinions/08-176.htm.

14 *Ibid.*

15 John M Annese, "Staten Island Criminal Court Judge to Be Transferred to Manhattan after Facebook Postings, Sources Say" *silive.com* (15 October 2009), online: www.silive.com/news/index.ssf/2009/10/criminal_court_judge_to_be_tra.html.

'friended' certain individuals who are now involved in some manner in a pending action."[16]

In comparison, North Carolina reprimanded a judge who "friended" counsel in a pending divorce case, labelling this an "ex parte" contact and conversation,[17] which failed to "promote confidence in the integrity and impartiality of the judiciary," in accordance with the relevant rules of ethics.[18]

Certainly, the appearance of impropriety generated by the judge's online friendship with an attorney or *a fortiori* a defendant[19] suffices to give us pause, particularly when the nature of such relationships (especially indirect) has yet to be clearly defined.

That said, the Arizona Supreme Court's Judicial Ethics Committee,[20] for its part, seems to follow a specific, circumstance-based approach. Although it does not entirely proscribe judicial social media use, it does appear to scrutinize the purpose and effects of such online connections. Thus, for instance, according to the committee, the standard for whether a judge should be disqualified for being friends with a lawyer on Facebook "is whether the judge's impartiality in a proceeding might reasonably be questioned." "Friending" lawyers per se does not disqualify the judge, but points to the idea that judges should disclose any personal relationship and let the parties decide if they want to seek recusal. In comparison, the professional networking platform LinkedIn specifies that judges should not recommend lawyers known to argue before them; judges are, however, permitted to use this medium to recommend a

16 George D Marlow, "Opinion 13-39" (28 May 2013), online: www.nycourts.gov/ip/judicialethics/opinions/13-39.htm.

17 State of North Carolina, Judicial Standards Commission, "Inquiry No 08-234" (1 April 2009).

18 See also *In the Matter of J Patrick McArdle, County Court Judge for the First Judicial District*, 2010 Neb LEXIS 108 (Supreme Court of Nebraska), and *Onnen v Sioux Fall Independent School District*, 2011 SD 45; 801 NW2d 752; 2011 SD LEXIS 102 (Supreme Court of South Dakota).

19 For information about a Philadelphia matter where the judge's Facebook friendship with the defendant was impugned, raising serious issues, see Ian Bush, "Facebook 'Friendship' between Judge and Defendant Raises Questions" *CBS Philly* (8 November 2011), online: http://cbsloc.al/1oWsRq7.

20 Arizona Supreme Court, Judicial Ethics Committee, "Use of Social and Electronic Media by Judges and Judicial Employees" Advisory Opinion 14-01 (5 August 2014), online: www.azcourts.gov/azcjc/Judicial-Ethics-Advisory-Opinions/2014.

former law clerk.[21] In terms of blogs, the committee warns that certain uses could raise ethical considerations, but seems to leave it to the judges' discretion to ensure that their blogging conforms to the rules of ethical behaviour.

Perhaps somewhat similarly, the Judicial Ethics Committee of the California Judges Association issued a more detailed and balanced start. It said that judges "are not required to isolate themselves from their communities" and that social networking should be analyzed under "the same rules that govern a judge's ability to socialize and communicate in person, on paper and over the telephone."[22] It proceeded to observe: "As a general rule, a judge's extrajudicial activities are governed by Canon 4A which states: 'A judge shall conduct all of the judge's extrajudicial activities so that they do not (1) cast reasonable doubt on the judge's capacity to act impartially; (2) demean the judicial office; or (3) interfere with the proper performance of judicial duties.'"[23] Social media thus provide another medium through which judges run the risk of clear ethical violations. Judges should not use social networking to comment on pending cases. Additionally, they should avoid posting anything on their profiles that may give the suggestion of bias or prejudice. Similarly, their profiles should not demean the judiciary. "While it may be acceptable for a college student to post photographs of himself or herself engaged in a drunken revelry, it is not appropriate for a judge to do so."[24] Further, endorsing or opposing political candidates is just as impermissible online as it is in person.

Can judges include lawyers in their social networks? Usually, judges are allowed to befriend attorneys, even ones that practise in their jurisdiction.[25] Under Canon 4A of the California opinion, judges are allowed and even encouraged to join bar associations and other legal organizations to promote civility and professionalism. Associating with lawyers over social media is thus permissible to promote the same ends.[26]

Florida is a notable exception to this trend of allowing judges and lawyers to associate over social media. While acknowledging that the term

---

21 *Ibid* at 1–2.

22 California Judges Association, Judicial Ethics Committee, "Online Social Networking" Opinion 66 (23 November 2010) at 4 & 3 respectively, online: www.caljudges.org/docs/Ethics%20Opinions/Op%2066%20Final.pdf ["Opinion 66"].

23 *Ibid* at 3–4.

24 *Ibid* at 5.

25 Andrew Sternlight, "Judges on Facebook" (5 April 2010), *En Banc* (blog), online: http://lacbablog.typepad.com/enbanc/2010/04/judges-on-facebook.html.

26 "Opinion 66," above note 22 at 6.

"friend" carries a different meaning with social media, the Florida Judicial Ethics Advisory Committee found that social networking may violate the judiciary's obligation to avoid even the appearance of impropriety.[27] Notably, however, this position received some criticism for not realizing that social networking is now a part of modern life. "Judges do not 'drop out of society when they become judges.' . . . The people who were their friends before they went on the bench remained their friends, and many of them were lawyers."[28] Some judges may also distinguish between Facebook friends and an intimate circle of close friends. Although judges generally can befriend other attorneys, at least one judges association found that they cannot remain friends with lawyers who have cases pending before them. In order to avoid the appearance of impropriety, the attorneys must be "defriended."[29]

Interestingly, there appears to be an ongoing exchange between the various districts of the Florida Court of Appeals on the point of digitally related recusal. Thus, although the court in the "Chase case"[30] ordered recusal, it explicitly stated its disagreement with the decision in the *Domville* case (in which a judge recused himself by reason of his Facebook friendship with a prosecutor).[31] Opined the court:

> We have serious reservations about the court's rationale in *Domville*. The word "friend" on Facebook is a term of art. A number of words or phrases could more aptly describe the concept, including acquaintance and, sometimes, virtual stranger. A Facebook friendship does not necessarily signify the existence of a close relationship. Other than the public nature of the internet, there is no difference between a Facebook "friend" and any other friendship a judge might have. *Domville*'s logic would require disqualification in cases involving an acquaintance of a judge. Particularly in smaller counties, where everyone in the legal community knows each other, this requirement is unworkable and unnecessary. Requiring disqualification in such cases does not reflect the true nature of a Facebook friendship and casts a large net in an effort to catch a minnow.[32]

---

27 "Opinion 2009-20," above note 6.

28 Schwartz, above note 6.

29 "Opinion 66," above note 22 at 10–11.

30 See Gershman, above note 7, for an outline of how lawyer Damon Chase came to challenge a judge's impartiality.

31 Above note 9.

32 *Chace v Loisel*, No 5D13–4449 (Fla Dist Ct App 24 Jan 2014), online: http://caselaw.findlaw.com/fl-district-court-of-appeal/1655565.html.

B. THE AMERICAN BAR ASSOCIATION: PROCEED, BUT WITH CAUTION

An encouraging development towards uniformity (or harmonization of principles) in the United States, going beyond the ad hoc state approach, is the following. In February 2013, the American Bar Association (ABA) released an opinion on judges' social media use.[33] Although the ABA does not expect judges to refrain entirely from using social media, it encourages them to proceed with caution, warning:

> Judges must assume that comments posted to [social media] will not remain within the circle of the judge's connections . . . . Comments, images or profile information — some of which might prove embarrassing if publicly revealed — may be electronically transmitted without the judge's knowledge or permission to persons unknown to the judge or to other unintended recipients. Such dissemination has the potential to compromise or appear to compromise the independence, integrity and impartiality of the judge, as well as to undermine public confidence in the judiciary.[34]

Thus, unlike many (although not all) of its state counterparts, the ABA appears to take a moderate stance, commensurate with the above-suggested "balance" or least restrictive means, as dictated by the imperatives of judicial office. In effect, the bar association recognizes that, "when used with proper care, judges' use of [social media] does not necessarily compromise their duties under the Model Code any more than use of traditional and less public forms of social connection such as U.S. mail, telephone, email or texting."[35] Not insignificantly, the ABA similarly highlights the community immersion rationale, opining "[s]ocial interactions of all kinds, including [social media], can be beneficial to judges to prevent them from being thought of as isolated or out of touch."[36]

The ABA, it is important to note, flags issues related to third-party use and loss of control over information posted, urging caution and sobriety. Plainly put, and somewhat more explicitly, judges should be wary not only of their own posts but of those of their family, friends, and (former) associates who may (often unbeknownst to them) use their name or image

---

33 American Bar Association, "Formal Opinion 462, Judge's Use of Electronic Social Networking Media" (21 February 2013), online: ABA www.americanbar.org/content/dam/aba/administrative/professional_responsibility/formal_opinion_462.authcheckdam.pdf.

34 *Ibid* at 1–2 [footnote omitted].

35 *Ibid* at 4.

36 *Ibid* at 1.

in their own social networking pursuits. In fact, although an unreported case dismissed an appeal where the trial court judge's daughter was a "Facebook friend" of the victim's sister (because the defendant apparently did not explicitly invoke recusal),[37] the case foreshadows issues to come.

Finally, the ABA opinion remains nebulous on matters of disqualification and has been criticized in some circles for failing to provide clear guidelines on what constitutes "reasonable" electronic social media (ESM) conduct more generally. Notwithstanding, it is submitted that in an emerging and dynamic context such as this, open-ended, flexible positions may be preferable to their more dogmatic or detailed counterparts, which risk being outpaced by technology even before the ink dries.

C. INTERNATIONAL AND NATIONAL PERSPECTIVES ON PRINCIPLES AND PRACTICES

Preceding this view, in 2012, the International Bar Association (IBA) released a report titled "The Impact of Online Social Networking on the Legal Profession and Practice."[38] The report, which examined social media activity by lawyers, judges, and jurors, surveyed members of various international bar associations. Important report findings include the following:

- Almost 70 percent of respondents believed it was acceptable for lawyers and judges to be in contact with one another on social networks.
- More than 90 percent of respondents deemed it unacceptable for lawyers and judges to post online comments or opinions about lawyers, judges, parties, or cases in progress.
- Only 15 percent of respondents believed that the presence of lawyers on social networks negatively affected the public's confidence in the integrity of the legal profession.[39]
- In contrast, almost 40 percent of respondents thought that judges' use of social networks negatively affected the public's confidence in the

---

37 *Illinois v Schiller*, 2012 IL App (2d) 110677-U, No 2-11-0677 (19 Dec 2012) at para 43, online: http://illinoiscourts.gov/R23_Orders/AppellateCourt/2012/2nd District/2110677_R23.pdf, cited in Brian Wassom, "Social Media and Judicial Ethics" (18 July 2013), *Wassom.com* (blog), online: www.wassom.com/social-media-and-judicial-ethics-guest-post.html.

38 International Bar Association, Legal Projects Team, "The Impact of Online Social Networking on the Legal Profession and Practice" (London: IBA, 2012), online: www.ibanet.org/Committees/Divisions/Legal_Practice/Impact_of_OSN_on_LegalPractice/Impact_of_OSN_Home.aspx.

39 *Ibid* at 12.

integrity and impartiality of the judiciary, undermining judicial independence.[40]

As a response to the survey, the IBA released "International Principles on Social Media Conduct for the Legal Profession" in 2014. The purpose of these principles is to "assist bar associations and attorney regulatory bodies around the world to promote social media conduct within the legal profession that conforms to relevant rules of professional responsibility as well as considerations of civility."[41] The six principles outlined by the IBA are as follows: (1) professional independence — legal professionals should consider how online relationships might affect their independence, or the appearance of independence; (2) integrity — legal professionals should consider how information posted online (even "privately") might affect their integrity; (3) responsibility — legal professionals should have a responsibility to properly understand the media they are using, to clarify how they are using it (e.g., giving legal information or advice), to use media appropriately, and to adhere to the professional codes of conduct; (4) confidentiality — lawyers must consider how posting information online might breach client confidentiality; (5) maintaining public confidence — legal professionals should monitor their online activities; and (6) policy — firms and professionals should develop clear and coherent policies for their professional social media accounts.[42]

As for the Canadian Judicial Council, it has expressed disapproval of social networking practices, but that expression is neither binding nor clear. The Council did, however, release articles in January 2014 with an eye towards better explaining the myriad of arguably un-navigable social media privacy settings to judges, without making any direct recommendations.[43] It similarly updated its explanatory pieces on the judicial use of Skype that same year, highlighting best practices for the use of Skype, its privacy settings, and the workings of VoIP (Voice over Internet Protocol).[44]

---

40 *Ibid* at 16.

41 International Bar Association, "IBA International Principles on Social Media Conduct for the Legal Profession" (London: IBA, 2014), online: www.ibanet.org/Article/Detail.aspx?ArticleUid=4f410090-8de0-438d-b81e-f4a21d31501f.

42 *Ibid.*

43 Martin Felsky, "Facebook and Social Networking Security" (Paper prepared for the Canadian Judicial Council, Judges Technology Advisory Committee, 17 January 2014), online: www.cjc-ccm.gc.ca/cmslib/general/Facebook%20security%202014-01-17%20E%20v1.pdf.

44 Martin Felsky, "Is Skype Safe for Judges?" (Paper prepared for the Canadian Judicial Council, Judges Technology Advisory Committee, 17 January 2014),

In the same vein, it released the fifth edition of "Ten Things Judges Can Do Now to Improve the Security of Judicial Data," including advice on how to create a secure password and use encryption.[45]

D. THE CANADIAN CENTRE FOR COURT TECHNOLOGY REPORT

In May 2015, the Canadian Centre for Court Technology (CCCT) issued a discussion paper on social media use by *individual* judicial officers after appointment. "The Use of Social Media by Canadian Judicial Officers," which endeavoured to glean better insight into such practices and offer recommendations on point,[46] began with a survey of 678 judicial officers.[47] The survey indicated that 48 percent of Canadian judges visit or use social media sites.[48]

The report proceeded to find that "73 per cent believe a [social media] policy would be useful." Counterintuitively in light of the above said perhaps, it also noted, "Judicial officers responding to the survey tend[ed] to believe that using social media websites in a personal capacity is more acceptable than engaging in similar activities from a professional standpoint."[49] This belief, coupled with how "unsure" judicial officers are about the ethical aspects of social media use, led the authors to conclude that there is a "lack of clear understanding" or knowledge of the social media concepts at play and the risks or the ethical issues they may or may not raise in a professional context.[50] That recognized lack, in turn, points

---

online: www.cjc-ccm.gc.ca/cmslib/general/Is%20Skype%20Safe%20for%20Judges%202014-01-17%20E%20v2.pdf.

45 Online: Canadian Judicial Council www.cjc-ccm.gc.ca/cmslib/general/Ten%20Things%20Judges%20Can%20Do%20Now%20to%20Improve%20the%20Security%20of%20Ju%20E%20v2.pdf.

46 The discussion paper includes the following as stated objectives: to "assess and determine the needs of courts and develop best practices; and consider best practices amongst the judiciary in their use of social media": Canadian Centre for Court Technology, "The Use of Social Media by Canadian Judicial Officers," Discussion Paper (May 2015) at 1, online: wiki.modern-courts.ca http://wiki.modern-courts.ca/pub/Social-Media-Report.pdf [CCCT Report].

47 Defined as judges and tribunal members.

48 CCCT Report, above note 46 at 8–9.

49 *Ibid* at 12.

50 *Ibid* at 14: "a general lack of social media policies for judicial officers in Canadian courts and tribunals and a lack of awareness by chief judges/justices of use of social media by members of their courts/tribunals."

to a need for both more specific policies and education for judicial officers.[51]

In the interim, the discussion paper noted the following:

1. All judicial officers have a duty to ensure that they understand the advantages, disadvantages and risks of the use of social media in personal and professional contexts and conduct themselves accordingly.
2. Existing policies, principles, codes of conduct or guidelines are inadequate to respond to that duty.
3. Until such time as more guidance is provided, judicial officers should use social media with caution, keeping in mind the above principles.[52]

The report also recommended the creation of "mandatory education programs to address the advantages, disadvantages and risks of the use of social media in personal and professional contexts for all judicial officers" *inter alia*.[53]

E. THE NEED TO ACHIEVE A DELICATE BALANCE

Although very helpful, the various above-cited opinions — the CCCT Report, which goes much further in terms of helpful guidance, aside — do not appear to fully flesh-out the risks specific to the Internet age, which "lets it all hang out,"[54] and of social networking more particularly. Furthermore, the implications of online activities such as Facebook and Twitter conducted by judges' spouses, former associates, and family members — which, as we have seen, can be significant — must be addressed, again within flexible principles.[55]

---

51 *Ibid.*

52 *Ibid* at 36.

53 *Ibid* at 37.

54 L Gordon Crovitz, "The Internet Lets It All Hang Out" *The Wall Street Journal* (13 June 2011), online: http://online.wsj.com/article/SB10001424052702304259304576377522779707418.html.

55 In Canada, the Canadian Judicial Council has created a Judicial Ethics Advisory Committee, whose role is to offer confidential advice to members of the judiciary facing an ethical dilemma, but ultimately leaving the decision in such matters to individual judges. Although the committee may have already (presumably) issued opinions on social networking, these are available only to judges. See also Richard F Devlin, "(Re) Constructing Judicial Ethics in Canada" (2010) 42 *McGeorge Law Review* 19 at 24.

Providing clearer guidance on point will, of course, require achieving a delicate balance between judges', and certainly their family members', freedom of expression and association and the general imperatives of the justice system and judicial ethics. But family members and business partners (past or present) are not immune from ethical rules, as the rules respecting judicial disqualification for pecuniary interest teach us by analogy. A judge's spouse or children, for example, may choose to "like" a particular (even controversial) political figure on Facebook, post pictures of themselves with that politician, or openly affiliate with a particular party or candidate. What control, in such a case, can or should the judge be reasonably expected to have over that family member's online activities and "likes"?

F. "LIKING" AS A FREE SPEECH RIGHT

To further complicate matters and compound this already nuanced conundrum, "liking" or even social media expression more broadly in some cases — and in more than one jurisdiction — has been deemed fundamental expression or constitutionally protected speech. Thus, a US court recently ruled that Facebook "likes" are considered speech protected by the First Amendment. "Liking," the Fourth US Circuit Court of Appeals held in *Bland v Roberts*, is the "Internet equivalent of displaying a political sign in one's front yard, which the Supreme Court has held is substantive speech."[56] As summarized by Alicia Sklan:

> In *Bland*, a suit was brought against the recently re-elected, Sheriff B.J. Roberts, alleg[ing] that the Sheriff violated the plaintiff's First Amendment rights to freedom of speech and freedom of association when he fired them for supporting the candidacy of his election opponent through their "speech" on Facebook.[57]

The ruling against the Sheriff's department, reversing the trial court's decision, is regarded as groundbreaking in the Internet age as the First Amendment now applies to digital phenomena,[58] confirming that cyber speech merits robust constitutional protection.

---

56 No 12-1671 (4th Cir 2013) at 40.

57 See Alicia D Sklan, "@SocialMedia: Speech with the Click of a Button? #SocialSharingButtons" (2013) 32 *Cardozo Arts & Entertainment Law Journal* 377 at 389–90.

58 Joe Palazzolo, "Court: Facebook 'Like' Is Protected by the First Amendment" (18 September 2013), *The Wall Street Journal* (blog), online: Law Blog http://

Finally, it may be worth noting that, in an otherwise negligible unreported case, *Re Andre B*,[59] the California District Court of Appeal struck down the prohibition on inmate (convicted felon) use of social media as infringing upon the First Amendment. That is not surprising as the US Supreme Court has made clear that First Amendment protections for speech extend to Internet communications, as well as to anonymous speech.[60]

Mindful of the above, precluding judges from engaging in social media culture altogether now appears an extreme response to a very nuanced and complex challenge. "As noted by the European Court of Human Rights, social media (as a form of communication via the internet) 'has now become one of the principal means by which individuals exercise their right to freedom of expression and information, providing as it does essential tools for participation in activities and discussions concerning political issues and issues of general interest.'"[61]

G. PERTINENCE OF CHANGING VIEWS ON SOCIAL MEDIA TO THE JUDICIARY

Although importing notably distinct considerations, the above-cited cases' relevance to the judiciary is that social networking (and Internet access more broadly) is increasingly being construed as a *basic right*. Accordingly, it stands to reason that absolutist policies seeking to entirely proscribe, rather than moderately or reasonably regulate judicial use (and certainly family use) in the digital age will be met with resistance (as unnecessarily infringing on freedom of expression as well fostering judicial isolation).[62]

---

blogs.wsj.com/law/2013/09/18/court-facebook-like-is-protected-by-the-first-amendment.

59 No J227937, 2012 WL 5353806 (Cal App 4 Dist 31 31 Oct 2012).

60 See *Reno v American Civil Liberties Union*, 521 US 844 (1997).

61 Mangan, above note 2, citing *Yildirim v Turkey*, [2012] ECHR 2074.

62 See Karen Eltis, *Courts, Litigants and the Digital Age* (Toronto: Irwin Law, 2012), the first edition of this book. There, I suggested that judges would do best to abstain from social media entirely, whenever possible: it is far preferable "that judges temporarily abstain from such practices altogether unless and until clearer guidelines emerge. In the alternative, a social network reserved for judges and their families exclusively, although for obvious reasons not a panacea, can perhaps fill some of the vacuum" (at 96). While that is still ideal, in light of recent caselaw, particularly in the United States (where social media have been explicitly brought under the First Amendment's ambit), isolating judges entirely from this ever prevalent form of communication would overly infringe on their freedom of expression (see, for example, *Bland v Roberts*,

Instead, it appears more likely that policies imposing narrowly tailored restrictions, logically related and *adapted* to the judicial office (and values such as restraint and impartiality) will prevail. Restricted judicial use of social media (guided by the adoption of proportional or minimally intrusive limitations) appears to be the burgeoning direction of most jurisdictions, as views on the point crystallize. In this vein, as noted above, mandatory social media training can assist in further fleshing-out the content of such proportional or least restrictive restrictions, with particular emphasis on the indelible nature of social media, the illusory perception of anonymity that tends to embolden unnecessarily, and the risk of third-party use of replicated posts.[63]

Surely, and as most of the guidelines have yet to tackle, social networking presents specific challenges, unique or particular to it, of which judges and, indeed, attorneys must be mindful. In the interim, the time-tested principle of avoiding the appearance of impropriety, whatever the medium, is helpful.[64] When in doubt, participants in the justice system (above all, judges) must take pains to avoid any appearance of impropriety. As the American Bar Association *Model Code of Judicial Conduct* states: "A judge shall uphold and promote the independence, integrity, and impartiality of the judiciary, and shall avoid impropriety and the appearance of impropriety."[65]

---

above note 56 and accompanying text). Accordingly, restrictions that are contextual to the digital age and represent the least restrictive means, commensurate with judicial obligations, better lend themselves to a sober balance between judicial duties and rights and would more likely withstand constitutional muster in Canada, the United States, and similarly situated constitutional democracies.

Moreover, although abstinence is best, it might be unreasonable to expect or demand it from all judicial players in light of constitutional constraints and given the strong temptation to engage in these now near ubiquitous social practices. Therefore, the current edition of *Courts, Litigants, and the Digital Age* proposes more concrete guidelines for judicial social media use.

63 Heila Garrido Hull, "Why We Can't Be Friends: Preserving Public Confidence in the Judiciary" (2012) 63 *Syracuse Law Review* 175. See also Judicial Conference of the United States, Committee on Codes of Conduct, "Resource Packet for Developing Guidelines on Use of Social Media by Judicial Employees" (2010), online: www.uscourts.gov/uscourts/RulesAndPolicies/conduct/SocialMediaLayout.pdf.

64 As the California guidelines suggest.

65 American Bar Association, ABA *Model Code of Judicial Conduct* (Chicago, IL: ABA, 2011) Canon 1 [ABA *Model Code*].

In consequence, judges — and attorneys as officers of the court — would do well to review the privacy settings on all websites visited and electronic devices used (particularly those with locational tracking features) and ensure that they are properly updated and set to the highest privacy setting. That having been said, they must also bear in mind that privacy settings are *by no means* a guarantee of discretion or panacea and that breaches and transfers of information to unscrupulous third parties are commonplace. Thus, for instance, it is now well known (from recent controversy) that purposefully turning off the GPS tracking function on Apple devices (iPhones, in particular) is of no avail.[66] Therefore, judges, especially those operating under threat or concerned about malicious, dangerous, or simply disgruntled stalkers, should be aware that many "smartphones" and equivalent devices not only feature tracking capabilities, which may be harnessed by ill-doers, but that turning "off" these tracking functions may not always disable them.[67]

Thus, for instance, in Canadian employment law cases, greater emphasis is increasingly placed on an awareness of privacy settings "and how employing stricter settings demonstrates an intention to control to whom the remarks are made. Conversely, failure to amend settings imputes an intention that the remark was made to an unlimited audience . . . ."[68]

Certainly, and as noted above, a judge should not be isolated from the community. As former Israeli Supreme Court president Aharon Barak cautions, the judge "cannot dissociate himself or herself from [the] legal community [as she or] he is always acting within the framework of shared values and principles."[69] Practically speaking, this approach might also allow judges to happen upon and uncover those who would try to mislead them, as the Judge Criss example that opened this chapter somewhat humorously illustrates.

But in terms of social networking in particular, and in light of the above said, it is far preferable (although not without controversy, as noted) that judges temporarily abstain from such practices unless and until clearer

66 Brian X Chen, "iPhone's Location-Data Collection Can't Be Turned Off" *Wired* (25 April 2011), online: www.wired.com/gadgetlab/2011/04/iphone-location-opt-out.

67 Apple has now developed software aimed at turning off tracking functions. The software, however, must be expressly downloaded and installed.

68 Mangan, above note 2.

69 Aharon Barak, "Comparative Law, Originalism and the Role of a Judge in a Democracy: A Reply to Justice Scalia" (Paper delivered at the Fulbright Conference Law Symposium: International Influences on National Legal Systems, Haifa, 29 January 2006) at 20.

guidelines emerge.[70] In the alternative, a social network reserved for judges and their families exclusively, although for obvious reasons not a panacea, can perhaps fill some of the vacuum.

In assessing the wisdom of social networking practices in regard to isolation, it stands to reason that the test, broadly speaking, should be much like that associated with judicial pecuniary interest (by mere analogy). Namely, is it necessary[71] to immerse oneself in these activities in order to prevent unreasonable isolation from community life under the totality of the circumstances? The balance to be achieved, in consequence, is between the need to maintain judicial connection to the legal and larger community and the need to preserve the bench's integrity. Indeed, "the honour, dignity and independence of the Bench demand that the remotest suspicion of bias on the part of a Judge should be most scrupulously guarded against and most tenaciously avoided."[72]

H. PRACTICAL GUIDELINES

That having been said, judges who do choose to use such public sites are wise to adopt the following practical guidelines:

- Exercise tremendous care and restraint in accepting "friend" requests on Facebook and the like.
- Limit "friends" to closest and most trusted friends in the traditional sense. (The term has, of course, expanded considerably and taken on a looser meaning with the advent of social networking.)
- Minimize the amount of personal information volunteered online generally and on social networking sites specifically. For example, avoid posting photos; do not disclose date of birth, especially the day and month; the year is generally known, as the judge's age is customarily a matter of public record.

---

70 Concordant with the Canadian Judicial Council's expression of "concern" regarding social networking by judges. The recommendation here was earlier made in the first edition of this book: see above note 62. See, for example, Martin Felsky, "Facebook and Social Networking Security" (November 2009), online: www.cjc-ccm.gc.ca/cmslib/general/JTAC-Ssc-Report-to-JTAC-2010-01-29-Appendix-C-Facebook-ArticleE.pdf.

71 ABA *Model Code*, above note 65, of guidance to Canadian judges. See also T David Marshall, *Judicial Conduct and Accountability* (Toronto: Carswell, 1995).

72 *Cotton v Stack* (1876), 16 NBR 424 at 431 (CA).

Further to the point above, consider the effect of new and increasingly popular and controversial facial recognition technologies.[73] These can intersect with other technologies and publicly available data, most prominently one's date of birth, to effectively "re-identify" an individual (to borrow Ohm's term, used in Chapter 4). Thus, an ill-doer (most obviously a disgruntled litigant) can collect pictures of the judge or family members available online and presumably arrive at their personal information (social security and more) for an array of illicit objectives. In light of facial recognition technologies, court administrators should revisit how they post pictures of judges online. Although the latter issue will necessarily involve a long process of reflection (and balancing between crucial values such as transparency and judicial privacy and safety), judges can reduce overall risks by reducing the number of pictures that they and their families volunteer on social networking sites.

- Be wary of "dropping" decontextualized morsels of information, which can be maliciously assembled or misinterpreted. Indeed, as Nate Anderson observes: "It's useful to remember just how far your data trail extends behind you on the Internet . . . and just how well determined researchers can follow the digital bread crumbs."[74]
- Disable geo-tagging functions on portable devices whenever feasible (noting above iPhone caveat).
- Google yourself once a day or at least once a week, and report suspicious content to administrators.[75] In this manner it may be possible to discover online judicial officer social media impersonation, as in the case of the judge in the high-profile Luka Magnotta case.[76] Someone

73 Professors Alessandro Acquisti, Ralph Gross, and Fred Stutzman at Carnegie Mellon conducted a study showing "how three converging technologies are undermining privacy. By mining public sources, including Facebook profiles and government databases, the researchers could identify at least one personal interest of each student and, in a few cases, the first five digits of a social security number." The study is available, online: http://repository.cmu.edu/jpc/vol4/iss2/2/. See also Julia Angwin, "Face ID Tools Pose New Risk" *The Wall Street Journal* (1 August 2011), online: http://online.wsj.com/article/SB10001424053111903341404576480371062384798.html?mod=WSJ_business_whatsNews; and "Anonymous No More" *The Economist* (30 July 2011), online: www.economist.com/node/21524829.

74 Nate Anderson, "Pulling Back the Curtain on 'Anonymous' Twitterers" *Ars Technica* (31 March 2009), online: http://arstechnica.com/tech-policy/news/2009/03/pulling-back-the-curtain-on-anonymous-twitterers.ars.

75 Go to www.google.com/webmasters/tools/removals.

76 A Canadian accused of murdering and dismembering a Chinese student.

had apparently opened a fake Twitter account in the trial judge's name (with no tweets in it). Happily, it came to the attention of that judge who then convened the jury to deny any association with the fake account, thereby nipping any future consequences in the bud.[77]

- Beware of SafeSearch parameters on search engines such as Google; improper, including X-rated, results, images among them, may not surface unless these parameters are removed. On the other hand and somewhat paradoxically, removing the SafeSearch mode may yield results that, in turn, create the appearance of improper searches. In consequence, it might be wise for individual judges to stay in SafeSearch mode, whereas court administrators or chief justices might elect to turn them on under controlled circumstances, in order to ensure that judges' names and images are not being misappropriated in such contexts. (See Chapter 3 for examples of misappropriation of publicly available information on the Internet.)
- Use various and diverse passwords.
- Never post passwords on a sticky note in front of your computer screen or in your office (a surprisingly prevalent practice, even at reputable institutions).
- Refrain from using "free" wifi, particularly in hotels and coffee shops.
- Refrain from using USB keys or allowing for their use in the court computer system. Most viruses are transmitted in this way, and leaks can occur in this manner.
- Reset the browser or erase computer search history every day.

Bear in mind that information online does not disappear. Time machine–type websites (like the "wayback machine"[78]) allow surfers to retrieve seemingly "disappeared" sites and Facebook accounts that have not actually been shut down.[79] Remember that the web means "the end of forgetting"[80] and that information cannot easily (or sometimes ever) be deleted. The following is some general advice on how to minimize your "digital imprint."

- Counsel family members on Internet safety tips and advise discretion, bearing in mind your position and duties.

---

77 CCCT Report, above note 46 at 28.

78 Online: www.archive.org/web/web.php.

79 Kristi Oloffson, "Why Is It So Hard to Delete Your Facebook Account?" *Time* (14 May 2010), online: http://newsfeed.time.com/2010/05/14/why-is-it-so-hard-to-delete-your-facebook-account.

80 Jeffrey Rosen, "The Web Means the End of Forgetting" *New York Times Magazine* (21 July 2010), online: http://nyti.ms/w2wBvf.

- Avoid free online services. Seemingly "free" communication sites such as Skype may exact a non-pecuniary price, as in reduced privacy.[81] Thus, for instance, Martin Felsky, writing for Canadian Judicial Council's Judges Technology Advisory Committee (JTAC), counsels judges to take a number of precautions if they choose to use Skype or similar services.[82]
- Avoid tweeting or blogging altogether (as the purpose, of course, is to share intimate thoughts and views and "track" daily activities). If you do tweet, take care to avoid the sort of mistake made infamous by Anthony Weiner who, by pressing the wrong key, made private posts public inadvertently à la "Reply all."[83]

It would appear at this stage that, in addition to implementing the above-mentioned mandatory social media training more broadly, courts may wish to systematically put into practice coherent guidelines for judicial social media use. These "next-generation norms" would feature minimally intrusive restrictions on the use of social media, which are directly linked to the values of independence and impartiality. Further, impropriety, for purposes of developing the aforesaid guidelines, must be interpreted contextually, and such norms should be far clearer than the rules currently available, which, for the most part, cryptically counsel judges to use their "discretion" as they would in the bricks-and-mortar world. Conversely and further complicating matters, it is in the same breath important that next-generation guidelines, while clear, be brought to a relatively high level of abstraction in light of rapid, dynamic technological change and the fact that "what we don't know, we don't know"[84] might in the end

81 See, for example, Donald Melanson, "Skype Acknowledges Android, Privacy Vulnerability, Says It's 'Working Quickly' on a Fix" *Engadget* (15 April 2011), online: www.engadget.com/2011/04/15/skype-acknowledges-android-privacy-vulnerability-says-its-wor.

82 See Martin Felsky, "Is Skype Safe for Judges?" (Paper prepared for the Canadian Judicial Council, Judges Technology Advisory Committee, 6 July 2010), online: www.cjc-ccm.gc.ca/cmslib/general/JTAC-Ssc-Skype-security-article-FinalE.pdf; an updated report, version 3, was released in January 2014, above note 44.

83 Chris Cuomo, Chris Vlasto, & Devin Dwyer, "Rep. Anthony Weiner: 'The Picture Was of Me and I Sent It'" *ABC News* (6 June 2011), online: http://abcnews.go.com/Politics/rep-anthony-weiner-picture/story?id=13774605.

84 In Donald Rumsfeld's words, see US Department of Defense, News Transcript, "DoD News Briefing: Secretary Rumsfeld and Gen. Myers" (12 February 2002), online: http://archive.defense.gov/Transcripts/Transcript.aspx?TranscriptID=2636.

present the greatest challenge to those wishing to avail themselves of social media.

Somewhat more concretely, both training and guidelines would do well to focus on imparting a better understanding of the peculiarities of social media (which are not all "created equal") and, above all, emphasize that innocent comments can be misconstrued, compounded by the false sense of security individuals tend to have online. Although it is beyond the scope of this present endeavour to outline steps to be taken in any great detail, suffice it to note that mastering privacy settings and hiding one's social networking profile from search engines is helpful,[85] as is opting out of instant personalization programs (where one's name and image may be used for ads).[86] Preventing tagging, sharing little, and avoiding third-party apps are, needless to say, desirable.

I. A FINAL THOUGHT INFORMED BY COMPARATIVE INQUIRY

Lastly, while entertaining more substantive recommendations in any great depth far exceeds the scope of this present reflection, it should suffice to remark on the worth of comparative inquiry in examining the standards governing proper out-of-court judicial expression in the Internet age. While the usefulness of traditional standards has by no means passed — subject, as noted, to a purposive, contextual interpretation and to added emphasis on reasonableness — it is worth noting that conceptions of the boundaries of judicial expression are subject to diverging understandings.[87] Most notably, in contradistinction to the traditional English or common law conception of said limitations, whereby judges must err on the side of refraining from any activity that might be perceived as having a political flavour,[88] the European and particularly German view is one

85 Account/Privacy Settings/Search and unchecking the Public Search Results box. This is by no means to say that the profile could still not be found.

86 Account/Privacy Settings/Applications and Websites/Instant Personalization Pilot Program, click on the Edit Setting button, and uncheck the box.

87 See Justice Barbara Krix, "The 'Political Judge' and the Principle of Impartiality in Germany" (Presentation at the 3d International Organization for Judicial Training (IOJT) Conference, Barcelona, Spain, 21–25 October 2007) [unpublished, on file with author] [Krix].

88 As summarized by Shimon Shetreet: "Judges do not make public comments on particular cases tried in their courts nor, generally, are they available for press interviews on general questions or on matters relating to law, courts and the administration of justice. Moreover, they do not reply to criticisms passed upon them by the Press. As Lord Denning said in one case 'from the nature of

that tolerates — if not welcomes — the "political judge,"[89] cognizant of the counterproductive effect of complete judicial isolation from society (the so-called "chilling effect"). Although curious and perhaps even radical in Canada, which at one time barred judges from even voting, the civil and specifically German perspective is of interest in that it conceives a measure of judicial social and political involvement — even active involvement — as appropriate if not desirable.

Having deemed that such participation allows judges to immerse themselves in their community, such immersion, which for historical reasons can easily, however painfully be understood,[90] is considered necessary for

---

our office we cannot reply to criticism. We cannot enter into public controversy. We must rely on our conduct itself to be its own vindication.'" See Shimon Shetreet, *Judges on Trial: A Study of the Appointment and Accountability of the English Judiciary* (Amsterdam: North-Holland, 1976) at 319. Bryden discusses the "modern" approach to disqualification generally (rather than expression specifically) in greater detail: "the modern English approach employs a bifurcated analysis, in which a distinction is drawn between situations where disqualification is automatic and situations in which disqualification flows from a reasoned perception that the judge may lack impartiality. The second approach, which I will describe as the Canadian approach — though it seems to have found favour in Australian, New Zealand and South African decisions as well — employs a unified 'reasonable apprehension of bias' test": See Phillip Bryden, "Legal Principles Governing the Disqualification of Judges" (2003) 82:3 *Canadian Bar Review* 555 at 559. Significantly, that is changing in Canada, as indicated by Justice John Sopinka, "Must a Judge Be a Monk — Revisited" (1996) 45 *University of New Brunswick Law Journal* 167, and by Professor Yves-Marie Morissette (as he then was), "Figure actuelle du juge dans la cité" (1999) 30 *Revue de droit de l'Université de Sherbrooke* 1. See also Karim Benyekhlef, "L'indépendance institutionnelle du pouvoir judiciaire: légitimité et participation au débat public" (1996) 45 *University of New Brunswick Law Journal* 37; and William Mackay, "Judicial Free Speech and Accountability: Should Judges Be Seen and Not Heard?" (1993) 3 *National Journal of Constitutional Law* 159.

89 See H Patrick Glenn, "Limitations on Judicial Freedom of Speech in West Germany and Switzerland" (1985) 34:1 *International and Comparative Law Quarterly* 159.

90 See Krix, above note 87 at 25, n 90: "The image of the judge that we have in Germany today has been affected to a large extent by the experiences that the Germans have made with their judges during the Nazi era." See also Irwin Cotler, "Human Rights and the New Anti-Jewishness" (2004) 38 *Justice Magazine: The International Association of Jewish Lawyers and Jurists* 24, online: www.infolink.co.il/intjewishlawyers/docenter/viewDocument.asp?id=9285. See also Shannon Smithey, "The Study of the Past as Exercise in Political Theory and the History of Ideas" (2006) 7:2 *German Legal Journal* 233; Vivian

preventing that which is far worse than improper speech: silent acquiescence in the face of abuses or taken to the extreme, atrocities; silence by the guardians of democracy which legitimizes the unspeakable.[91] Lying at the heart of the approach is the idea that the duty to rise vocally against injustice is not stifled but is, indeed, bolstered when donning the judicial robe.

Accordingly, section 39 of the *German Judicial Act*[92] confirms and reflects this vision, one that is scornful of judicial neutrality and, instead, encourages socio-political involvement.[93] Thus, on the heels of the unfathomable intellectual and judicial silence compounding the atrocities of the Holocaust,

> the [German] Parliamentary Council (Parlamentarischer Rat), the legislative body assigned with the task to draft the constitution, discussed the image of the judge already in 1948/9. It was intended to create a new judge character that would typify the role of the judge as a representative of the judicature . . . . The judiciary should cease regarding political matters as something inferior that one should keep out of. According to the council it was a misinterpretation of the notion of impartiality to think that a judge could be politically neutral. In fact, they called for the political judge, but not for a judge active in or for a political party. The political judge should speak in the spirit of democracy, of social equal-

---

Grosswald Curran, "Formalism and Anti-formalism in French and German Judicial Methodology" in Christian Joerges & Navraj Singh Ghaleigh, eds, *Darker Legacies of Law in Europe: The Shadow of National Socialism and Fascism over Europe and Its Legal Traditions* (Oxford: Hart, 2003) 205 at 255.

91 As per Elie Wiesel, in his acceptance speech, on the occasion of the award of the Nobel Peace Prize, Oslo, 10 December 1986: "I swore never to be silent whenever and wherever human beings endure suffering and humiliation. We must always take sides. Neutrality helps the oppressor, never the victim. Silence encourages the tormentor, never the tormented."

92 *The German Judiciary Act*, in the version published on 19 April 1972 (Bundesgesetzblatt, Part I p 713) as last amended by art 1 of the Law of 11 July 2002 (Bundesdesetzblatt, Part I p 2592), ss 38–43 DRiG: Section 39 (Maintenance of Independence) reads: "In and outside office a judge shall conduct himself, in relation also to political activity, in such a manner that confidence in his independence will not be endangered," online: www.iuscomp.org/gla/statutes/DRiG.pdf. See also Krix, above note 87 at 3: "References to how judges are to conduct themselves ethically are to be found in the Basic Law (Articles 92, 97 GG), in *The German Judiciary Act* (sections 38–43 DRiG) and in the respective judiciary acts of the German *Länder*."

93 Justice Barbara Krix, "Ethic for Judges, a Worldwide Discussion" (2003) 81 DRiZ 149; and Krix, above note 87.

> ity, of social understanding and of human rights . . . . These were the guidelines of the Parliamentary Council for the *German Judiciary Act*.[94]

As Patrick Glenn taught:

> Continental judges have [traditionally enjoyed] greater individual political freedom than their common law counterparts. This phenomenon is related to that of judicial authority in general . . . . Standards of judicial performance and conduct are necessarily those which can be met and tolerated by large numbers of people whose adult and professional lives are still before them. It is therefore frequently accepted that a judge may engage in political activity, and membership in a political party or politically active union is often tolerated.[95]

It follows from the above said that ethical principles and, indeed, the boundaries respecting judicial political involvement in Germany specifically and the European continent (to some extent) generally are to a certain degree comparatively fluid.[96] This necessarily gives rise to the tension between the need to provide firm guidance and the nebulosity of certain activities in this context.[97]

---

94 Krix, *ibid* at 3.

95 See Glenn, above note 89 at 159.

96 *Ibid.* Interestingly, however, an illustration of the above-mentioned "cultural defence" is an incident of a German judge who apparently crossed even those "fluid" boundaries by asserting that religious imperatives excuse a Muslim man from bowing to the prohibition of spousal abuse. See "Paving the Way for a Muslim Parallel Society" *Der Spiegel* (29 March 2007), online: www.spiegel.de/international/germany/0,1518,474629,00.html:

> . . . the judge argued, the woman should have "expected" that her husband, who had grown up in a country influenced by Islamic tradition, would exercise the "right to use corporal punishment" his religion grants him. The judge even went so far as to quote the Koran in the grounds for her decision. In Sura 4, verse 34, she wrote, the Koran contains "both the husband's right to use corporal punishment against a disobedient wife and the establishment of the husband's superiority over the wife."

97 For an American perspective, see Merle W Loper, "Free Expression and Judicial Speech: A General Framework from One American Perspective" (1996) 45 *University of New Brunswick Law Journal* 105. See also Mackay, above note 88 at 171:

> There is beginning to emerge a more modern conception of the role of the judge which is more tolerant of elements of subjectivity. Those who support this version of the judge argue that to completely factor out all subjective perceptions would make judging mechanical and inhuman. It would also be virtually impossible to do. This more subjective and human judge is not to be substituted for the objective judge. The challenge is to put the two roles

Although Canadian thinking has traditionally allied itself with the *mère patrie*'s more reserved view of "when in doubt out,"[98] the German perspective appears to be gaining adherents.[99] The underlying rationale, beyond the previously noted, is that these are, of course, career judges who,

---

> together. The argument for representation in the judiciary follows from this paradigm: more perspectives leads to more open-mindedness, more ways of seeing things. This in turn destroys stereotypes that may otherwise not be confronted if the dominant image of objectivity is not challenged.

For a somewhat different perspective, see Benyekhlef, above note 88, who disagrees with Mackay's position but not his general criticism of excessive constraints on judicial expression.

98 See Bryden, above note 88 at 558 and generally at 555: "the Canadian law governing the disqualification of judges is steeped in English historical tradition . . . ." Bryden does however note an evolution: "over the past decade divergent strands have been emerging in the decisions of Commonwealth courts when addressing the issue of judicial impartiality." See also Ed Ratushny, "Speaking as Judges: How Far Can They Go?" (2000) 11 *National Journal of Constitutional Law* 293 at 296: "a judge must not engage in partisan public debate on controversial issues. To do so would detract from the perceived neutrality of such a judge."

99 See Mackay, above note 88 at 174. Particularly, Mackay seems to echo this view, arguing that

> knowing where individual judges stand on broad social and political issues is crucial to the administration of justice. Once one accepts that judges have views on broad social and political issues, the litigants are better served by knowing the judge's perspective in advance. The guarantee of freedom of expression contained within the *Charter* should thus expand and protect judicial expression outside the court. The judge must, of course, not prejudge the issue at hand. On the other side of the coin, the equality values entrenched in the *Charter* provide some limitations to judicial expression in and out of court. Prejudicial comments or views issued from the Bench regarding vulnerable groups, specifically those protected in section 15 of the *Charter*, ought to be censured. Needless to say, the values expressed by the *Charter* provide guidelines to judicial speech uttered outside the courtroom as well.

And at 175: "Any expansion of judicial free speech must be accompanied by effective mechanisms of accountability for abuse of this freedom. Judicial speech and accountability should go hand in hand."

See also Benyekhlef, above note 88, arguing:

> En raison de l'importance du nouveau rôle confié aux tribunaux par l'avènement de la *Charte canadienne* en 1982, ces derniers sont de plus en plus souvent l'objet d'une attention scrupuleuse de la part des médias et du public. Afin d'assurer l'indépendance de l'institution judiciaire, il convient alors de reconnaître aux juges et à l'institution elle-même une plus grande liberté d'expression. Cette liberté d'expression apparaît nécessaire afin de

unlike latecomers to the professions (broadly speaking) in the common law world, would be subject to a quasi-lifelong, therefore intolerable, muzzle. Pragmatically speaking — and for good reason — the above-exposed rationale pertaining to civil judges (in light of their training and career path) does not historically lend itself to direct application to Canadian circumstances; we might, nevertheless, glean a measure of perspective from the German (and broader continental) experience for interpretation of proper judicial conduct in the Internet age: we do not need to adopt it in its entirety. In other words, the German counterpoint can presumably smooth the progress of our understanding of how the time-honoured reasonable apprehension of bias standard might function in the Internet age, when ad hoc aggregations of cyber data risk eliciting knee-jerk reactions.

Although common law judges are not career judges, the rationale respecting the impossibility (or mere undesirability) of muzzling magistrates for an extended time (from their youth, when continental judges begin their career) now arguably applies to their Anglo-American counterparts. Given the Internet's infinite memory, thoughts expressed by common law judges years prior to their often late-life appointment are (as noted) now readily available, thus, it would seem, unnecessarily and detrimentally creating a "chilling effect" on attorneys who envision a judicial career.[100] In other words, even though these judges are appointed only late in life, the cyber world would impose a far earlier (career-long) code of silence for fear of later censure in a way similar to that faced by continental counterparts, were it not for the more relaxed approach to "political" expression, outlined above. Not surprisingly then, the conventionally stringent English view may have relaxed, edging closer to its continental counterpart.[101]

---

permettre aux tribunaux d'expliquer et, parfois, de justifier la portée et les conséquences socio-politiques de leurs décisions.

100 This is all the more true with changes to Facebook's features (called Timeline), which allow a user's entire history to be viewed. As per *The New York Times*: "This may be the first moment that many of Facebook's 800 million members realize just how many digital bread crumbs they have been leaving on the site — and on the Web in general. . . ." See Jenna Wortham, "Your Life on Facebook in Total Recall" *The New York Times* (15 December 2011), online: http://nyti.ms/1IntXjS.

For better or worse, the new format is likely to bring back a lot of old memories; however, it could also make it harder to shed past identities.

101 As evidenced by the (oft-criticized) *Pinochet* case in which "Lord Browne-Wilkinson went out of his way to emphasize that mere involvement by a judge in charitable work for an organization that had an interest in a case would not normally form the basis for his or her automatic disqualification. Thus, he

Another prominent example, bearing the hallmark of the above-described, on which to conclude this aspect of the discussion is the English case of *Locabail (UK) Ltd v Bayfield Properties.*[102] There, the Court of Appeal adopted a contextual approach to assessing bias remarking that

> [i]t would be dangerous and futile to attempt to define or list the factors which may or may not give rise to a real danger of bias. Everything will depend on the facts, which may include the nature of the issue to be decided. *We cannot, however, conceive of circumstances in which an objection could be soundly based on the religion, ethnic or national origin, gender, age, class, means or sexual orientation of the judge.* Nor, at any rate ordinarily, could an objection be soundly based on the judge's social or educational or service or employment background or history, nor that of any member of the judge's family; or previous political associations; or membership of social or sporting or charitable bodies; or Masonic associations; or previous judicial decisions; or extra curricular utterances (whether in textbooks, lectures, speeches, articles, interviews, reports or responses to consultation papers) . . . . By contrast, a real danger of bias might well be thought to arise if there were personal friendship or animosity between the judge and any member of the public involved in the ease; or if the judge were closely acquainted with any member of the public involved in the case, particularly if the credibility of that individual could be significant in the decision of the case; or if, in a case where the credibility of any individual were an issue to be decided by the judge, he had in a previous case rejected the evidence of that person in such outspoken terms as to throw doubt upon his ability to approach such person's evidence with an open mind on any later occasion; or if on any question at issue in the proceedings before him the judge had expressed views, particularly in the course of the hearing, in such extreme and unbalanced terms as to throw doubt on his ability to try the issue with an objective judicial mind; or if, for any other reason, there were real ground for doubting the ability of the judge to ignore

---

stated: 'Only in cases where a judge is taking an active role as trustee or director of a charity which is closely allied to and acting with a party to the litigation should a judge normally be concerned either to recuse himself or disclose the position to the parties' . . . ." See Bryden, above note 88.

102 [2000] QB 451 (CA), online: www.uniset.ca/lloydata/css/2000QB451.html [*Locabail*]. For a detailed exposition of the law of disqualification in the United Kingdom, see Bryden, above note 88 at 563: "In England, most non-financial situations will be assessed using the 'real danger of bias' test in a manner that may not be fundamentally different than the approach a Canadian court would take using the 'reasonable apprehension of bias' test."

> extraneous considerations, prejudices and predilections and bring an objective judgment to bear on the issues before him.[103]

For our purposes, as concerns over misinformed, miscompiled, frivolous, or even malicious accusations directed at members of the judiciary in the Internet age proliferate, the above-described standpoint and above-drawn distinction between appropriate and unsuitable activities or characteristics can provide us with a broader perspective. It can serve to inform our perceptions of the reasonableness of further restricting judicial expression and association in light of search engines and permit us to assess the "apprehension of bias" contextually and in a manner that is proportional to the imperatives of the technology age, in keeping with a desire to maintain a vibrant, multicultural judiciary of varied backgrounds and interests.

---

103 *Locabail*, *ibid* at para 25 [emphasis added].

CHAPTER 7

Social Networking and Cyber Research Undermining the Jury System

A. INTRODUCTION

"[I]f the jury system is to survive as the system for a fair trial . . . the misuse of the Internet by jurors must stop," cautioned the Lord Chief Justice, Lord Judge, the most senior judge in England and Wales.[1] In one instance, a juror in Manchester — in a flagrant breach of court rules and common sense — posted the details of a rape trial on her account (via her mobile phone). She proceeded to survey her friends on the site, asking: "Did he do it?"[2] The task of stopping jurors from tweeting or placing posts on sites such as Facebook is daunting.

Presumably rebuking the laxity characterizing most jurors' — and indeed, many courts' — lenient attitude towards social networking and other related "mishaps," oft dismissed as an inevitable trend derivative of progress, the same judge refreshingly added:

> We cannot accept that the use of the internet, or rather its misuse, should be acknowledged and treated as an ineradicable fact of life, or that a Nelsonian blind eye should be turned to it or the possibility that it is happening. If it is not addressed, the misuse of the internet represents a threat to the jury system which depends, and rightly depends, on

---

1 "Jurors 'Should Be Prosecuted for Tweeting from Courts and Googling Defendants', Warns Top Judge" *The Daily Mail* (20 November 2010), online: http://bit.ly/doS1fT ["Jurors Should Be Prosecuted"].

2 Guy Patrick, "Juror's 'Is He Guilty?' Posts on Facebook" *The Sun* (26 August 2010), online: www.thesun.co.uk/sol/homepage/news/3111826/Woman-juror-discussed-trial-on-Facebook.html?OTC-RSS&ATTR=News.

> evidence provided in court which the defendant can hear and if necessary challenge.[3]

It would appear that courts are increasingly of this view as they take greater notice of the severity of juror social networking and cyber research. Accordingly, in the United States, a number of jury verdicts were reversed precisely by reason of social media use by jurors during trial. Thus, for instance, in the Maryland case of *Wardlaw v State*,[4] notwithstanding the judge's explicit instructions not to engage in any independent research, a juror cyber searched the term "oppositional defiant disorder," which a key witness was supposedly diagnosed with. More specifically, and to assess the witness's credibility, she googled whether lying was a symptom related thereto. Although the trial judge (presumably following the more traditional approach of dismissing such behaviour as mere indiscretions) rejected Wardlaw's calls for a mistrial, instructing the jury to simply rely only on the evidence presented in court, the appellate court unanimously overturned, holding that such Internet research constituted grounds for a mistrial.

The court opined:

> [T]he juror's internet research of ODD [oppositional defiant disorder], and her subsequent reporting of her finding, rightly or wrongly, that lying is associated with the disorder, constituted *egregious misconduct* . . . . Given the fact that his misconduct came to light while the jury was still deliberating, and was presumptively prejudicial to either the State or appellant, it was incumbent upon the trial court to *voir dire* the jurors to determine whether they could still render an impartial verdict based solely on the evidence presented at trial . . . .
>
> In this case, the trial court did not *voir dire* the jury, but instead gave a curative instruction admonishing the jury not to conduct outside research and reminding them that they were to render a verdict based only on the evidence presented at trial. It was error for the court to do so, because a specific inquiry into the thought processes of the jury was the only method of ascertaining whether the information about ODD, acquired through the juror's internet research, improperly and irreparably influenced the jury's deliberative process to the prejudice of appellant or the State.[5]

---

3 "Jurors Should Be Prosecuted," above note 1.

4 185 Md App 440 (Md Ct Special App 8 May 2009).

5 *Ibid*, slip op at 10–11 [emphasis added].

In yet another Maryland case, *Allan Jake Clark v State of Maryland*,[6] a different panel of the same court again reversed the lower court in a similar matter. *Allan Jake Clark* was a murder case where one of the jurors conducted independent Wikipedia research. The trial judge had denied the defence's motion for a mistrial after a court bailiff fell upon printouts of Wikipedia articles in the jury room. The searches concerned the terms "livor mortis" and "algor mortis," which related to the issue of how the time and place of death can be determined by looking at how blood settles in a corpse. The appeals court held that an "adverse influence on a single juror compromises the impartiality of the entire jury panel."[7]

Similar things have happened in other US cases. In an intricate drug case, *US v Frank Hernandez*,[8] a federal district court judge in Florida declared a mistrial after a juror confessed to the judge that his peers were engaged in independent cyber research.[9] In a Colorado murder case, there were independent juror cyber searches on the effects of the drug Paxil, "which the defendant had apparently used prior to allegedly murdering her step-grandson." The Appeals Court ordered a new trial, citing the reliability issues related to such questionable endeavours.[10] In this manner, and harkening back to Chapter 2, the perils associated with juror cyber research are not unlike those related to judicial Internet searches. Emphasizing the lack of trustworthiness of such sources as the main impetus for its decision, the court warned that

> [a]lthough the Internet has made information more accessible for the average person, the information obtained thereby may be misleading, taken out of context, outdated, or simply inaccurate . . . . *In view of the problems and dangers associated with the unsupervised use of the Internet, trial courts should emphasize that jurors should not consult the*

---

6 No 0953/08 (Md Ct Special App 3 December 2009) (unreported).

7 Quoted in Andrea F Siegel, "Judges Confounded by Jury's Access to Cyberspace: Panelists Can Do Their Own Research on Web, Confer outside Courthouse" *The Baltimore Sun* (13 December 2009), online: http://articles.baltimoresun.com/2009-12-13/news/bal-md.ar.tmi13dec13_1_deliberations-period-florida-drug-case-jurors.

8 Crim No 07-60027 (SD Fla, mistrial declared 10 March 2009).

9 See Deirdra Funcheon, "Jurors and Prosecutors Sink a Federal Case against Internet Pharmacies" *Broward/Palm Beach New Times* (23 April 2009), online: www.browardpalmbeach.com/2009-04-23/news/jurors-and-prosecutors-sink-a-federal-case-against-internet-pharmacies.

10 *People v Wadle*, 77 P3d 764 (Colo App 2003) [*Wadle*], aff'd on other grounds 97 P3d 932 (Colo 2004).

> *Internet, or any other extraneous materials, at any time during the trial, including during deliberations.*[11]

Again, the issues raised with respect to judicial independent research (in Chapter 2) have similar resonance where juries are involved. Not unlike its Maryland, Florida (Federal District), and Colorado counterparts respectively, New Jersey's Court of Appeals[12] was of the view that if one juror conducted independent cyber research, it served to *taint* the entire jury, even if and when the juror in question was discovered and eventually replaced by an alternate, as was the case in this manslaughter trial.

Once more, the Appellate Division reversed the convictions, ruling that "a mistrial should have been declared. Failure to do so constitutes reversible error. The error requires a new trial."[13] Cyber sources can, of course, be undependable, thus potentially wreaking havoc with jury deliberations, as in a 2004 Rhode Island first-degree murder case. That case ended in a mistrial "because a juror used the Internet during deliberations to research the definitions of manslaughter, murder and self-defense. The definitions found by the juror were from California and therefore could differ from those applicable to the Rhode Island case."[14]

Not only might information uncovered online be plainly wrong, as illustrated above, it might also house nuances proper to online culture, indiscernible to many jurors.[15]

B. BEYOND CYBER SEARCHES

With particular respect to social networking (including but not limited to tweeting, blogging, and Facebook), a death row inmate was recently granted a new trial when it was discovered that one of his jurors had

---

11 *Wadle, ibid* at 771 [emphasis added].

12 *New Jersey v Scott*, 2009 NJ Super Unpub LEXIS 1901 (NJ App Div 20 July 2009), certification denied, 2009 NJ LEXIS 1370 (NJ 9 November 2009).

13 *Ibid*, slip op at para 52.

14 Daniel A Ross, "Juror Abuse of the Internet" *New York Law Journal* (8 September 2009). See also Talia Buford, "New Juror Policy Accounts for New Technology" *The Providence Journal* (17 May 2009).

15 For cyber culture generally, see Ian A Kerr, "Mind Your Metaphors: An Examination of the Inefficacy Argument as a Reason against Regulating On-line Conduct" in Lester Pourciau, ed, *Ethics and Electronic Information in the 21st Century* (West Lafayette: Purdue University Press, 1999) at 231.

tweeted throughout the trial.[16] With regard to the harm sustained, opined the Arkansas Supreme Court: "the prejudice results from the fact that the juror admitted to the misconduct, which proves that he failed to follow the court's instructions, and it is the failure to follow the law that prejudiced Appellant."[17]

So, too, a building materials company (Stoam Holdings) in Arkansas appealed a $12.6 million verdict, arguing that a juror's tweets (Twitter messages) sent before and after the trial displayed bias against them. As *ABC News* reported: "According to court papers, Jonathan Pollard, the juror, posted a message about what he was doing that day that read: 'Oh, nothing really, I just gave away TWELVE MILLION DOLLARS of somebody else's money.' Another read: 'Oh and nobody buy Stoam. Its bad mojo and they'll probably cease to Exist, now that their wallet is 12m lighter.'"[18]

The same week, *The New York Times* reported[19] that "defense lawyers in the federal corruption trial of a former Pennsylvania state senator, Vincent J. Fumo, demanded before the verdict that the judge declare a mistrial because a juror posted updates on the case on Twitter and Facebook. The juror had even told his readers that a "big announcement" was coming on Monday."[20] Fumo was subsequently found guilty and his lawyer's appeal on the basis of the impugned Internet postings was dismissed, notwithstanding the Lord Justice's flagrant critique and stern warnings respecting the severity of such breaches and their impact on the justice system and fairness of process.

---

16 Matt Cantor, "Death Row Inmate Gets New Trial Because of Twitter" *Newser* (9 December 2011), online: www.newser.com/story/135072/death-row-inmate-erickson-dimas-martinez-gets-new-trial-because-of-twitter.html.

17 *Ibid*. See also "Arkansas Death Row Inmate Spared by Juror's Tweet" *The Guardian* (9 December 2011), online: http://gu.com/p/34xkk/stw.

18 Scott Michels, "Cases Challenged over 'Tweeting' Jurors" *ABC News* (17 March 2009), online: http://abcnews.go.com/Technology/story?id=7095018&page=2. See also John Schwartz, "As Jurors Turn to Web, Mistrials Are Popping Up" *The New York Times* (17 March 2009), online: http://nyti.ms/vcBewb.

19 See Schwartz, *ibid*.

20 *Ibid*. A motion made by one of Senator Fumo's defence lawyers to declare a mistrial following tweeting activities by one of the jurors was rejected by the court: see Duchess Harris, "Courts Wrangle with Twittering by Jurors" *Litigation News* (15 July 2009), online: http://apps.americanbar.org/litigation/litigationnews/top_stories/twitter-jurors.html.

C. ALTERNATIVES TO THE MISTRIAL

Declaring a mistrial (although preferable to a casual dismissal of such incidents) seems a poor — albeit exceedingly costly[21] — remedy for breaches of online jury etiquette. It is certainly one intended to be used sparingly. It is by no means a panacea or answer to a pervasive phenomenon, which must itself be carefully addressed. The harshness of declaring a mistrial might, in turn, explain why presumably in want of other solutions many courts (as in the *Fumo* and Arkansas case) simply (even casually) dismiss the censured cyber conduct as improper,[22] which, for the reasons so fluently outlined by the Lord Justice above,[23] is most problematic.

Plainly put, the tendency to focus on *repairing* the harm caused by juror cyber searches or social networking with the blunt instrument of mistrials, rather than *preventing* these breaches *ab initio*, seems to stem from a somewhat defeatist approach to the phenomenon, rooted in a feeling of impotence in the face of technology, neatly summarized by the president of the American Society of Trial Consultants who emphatically noted: "It's really impossible to control it."[24]

But social networking in this vein is no different than any other forms of communication and must be treated with the same severity and drive. The technological changes that have occurred in the last few decades are, indeed, significant, but they do not necessarily undermine the paradigm that has defined the legal framework underlying jury research and outside communications to date. They simply require stricter monitoring and enforcement, coupled with a culture that discourages rather than downplays the severity of such transgressions or that dismisses transgressions as "inevitable" because they are the fruit of ever-daunting, ever-mighty technology. Therefore, rather than entirely reworking paradigms (a risky endeavour with technology advancing at a rapid pace), courts might con-

---

21 Brian Grow, "As Jurors Go Online, U.S. Trials Go Off Track" *Reuters* (8 December 2010), online: www.reuters.com/article/2010/12/08/internet-jurors-idUSN0816547120101208. See also Eric P Robinson, "Courts in Colorado, Maryland, New Jersey, Florida Declare Mistrials after Juror Internet Research" *Digital Media Law Project* (25 January 2010), online: www.citmedialaw.org/blog/2010/courts-colorado-maryland-new-jersey-florida-declare-mistrials-after-juror-internet-researc.

22 Harris, above note 20.

23 See above note 1 and accompanying text.

24 Douglas L Keene, president of the American Society of Trial Consultants, cited in Schwartz, above note 18.

sider stricter, more explicit instructions coupled with and followed by harsh punishment when such instructions fail.

A prominent example that gained publicity worldwide and may serve to spearhead (or at least encourage) a more proactive/preventive approach to inappropriate Internet use by jurors comes to us from the United Kingdom. Most probably with an eye towards deterring such conduct and emphasizing its seriousness, a British juror was found in contempt of court and jailed for contacting a defendant via Facebook and conducting a cyber search on another defendant while the jury was still deliberating.[25]

Perhaps the spectre of jail time (for an otherwise law-abiding citizen, such as the above-mentioned middle-aged mother of three) will serve to impress upon future jurors the gravity of the sort of prohibited communication that has thus far been trivialized. It may have more impact on jurors than declaring a mistrial ever could, and it would avoid the many other drawbacks for the justice system and taxpayers that are associated with mistrials.

Indeed and paradoxically, although daunting and seemingly unstoppable at first glance, cyber communications may, in fact, better lend themselves to regulation than their predecessors (telephone, verbal, and written exchanges) because with the latter, only parties to the communication, often friends and family, were aware of the breach and had the power to disclose. As Jack King, director of communications and public affairs at the (US) National Association of Criminal Defense Attorneys, explains: "The difference I see now: When they're using social media, they're getting caught because it's out there to actually find and see . . . . Perhaps that's a silver lining."[26]

To reiterate, the vulnerability of social networking and the like lies in its very transparency: in the very public and accessible character of its communications. In the past, the only way for a fallen juror's indiscretions to be exposed was if a spouse or friend "sold out" the juror; today, these same outbursts are readily readable by a wise attorney who tracks down

25 "It's important that the integrity of our justice system and the integrity of our jury system is maintained and preserved and seen to be so": Michael Holden, "Juror Jailed for Facebook Contempt" *Reuters* (16 June 2011), online: http://ca.reuters.com/article/technologyNews/idCATRE75F22X20110616. See also Jill Lawless, "Juror Faces Jail for Facebook Chat with Defendant" *Yahoo! News* (14 June 2011), online: news.yahoo.com/juror-faces-jail-facebook-chat-defendant-153835996.html.

26 Jonathan Berr, "Why Facebook, Twitters and Jurors Don't Mix" *Daily Finance* (12 September 2010), online: www.dailyfinance.com/2010/09/12/why-facebook-twitter-and-jurors-dont-mix.

such matters regularly. (For example, consider a juror telling her husband "this guy's fried" versus that same comment as a tweet or post.) Courts and attorneys therefore might consider harnessing that transparency towards upholding the integrity of trial and interests of their clients.

D. INSTRUCTIONS AND INJUNCTIONS

In light of the apparent futility of traditional instructions, a number of US states recently changed their standard jury directions in both civil and criminal cases. Thus, for instance, in Florida the new language warns jurors against doing Internet research or using "electronic devices or computers to talk about this case, including tweeting, texting, blogging, emailing, posting information on a website or chat room, or any other means at all."[27] Connecticut instructs jurors to avoid "Internet maps or Google Earth" and "not communicate to anyone any information about the case . . . by any means including text messages, email, Internet chat rooms, blogs and social networking websites like Facebook, Myspace, YouTube, or Twitter."[28] In the state of New York, jurors are instructed to avoid "text messages, email, internet chat rooms, blogs or social websites, such as Facebook, My Space or Twitter."[29]

Another example of modified instructions comes from Oregon (Multnomah County), where judges take pains to stress what seems obvious: namely, that Twitter is a form of communication and is therefore proscribed. The instructions provide as follows: "Do not discuss this case during the trial with anyone, including any of the attorneys, parties, witnesses, your friends, or members of your family . . . . 'No discussion' also

27 Supreme Court of Florida, "In Re: Standard Jury Instructions in Criminal Cases — Report No 2010-01 and Standard Jury Instructions in Civil Cases — Report No 2010-01, No SC10-51" (21 October 2010) at 6, online: www.floridasupremecourt.org/decisions/2010/sc10-51.pdf.

28 State of Connecticut Judicial Branch, "Criminal Jury Instructions" (23 September 2013), online: www.jud.ct.gov/JI/Criminal/Part1/1.2-10.htm; State of Connecticut Judicial Branch, "Civil Jury Instructions" (11 October 2013), online: www.jud.ct.gov/JI/Civil/Part1/1.1-1.htm.

29 John W Clark, Andrea Wierzchowski, & Chelsea Luker, "Social Networking and the Contemporary Juror" (2011) 47:1 *Criminal Law Bulletin* 83 at 91 [Clark et al], quoting John G Browning, "The Online Juror" (2010) 93:6 *Judicature* 231 at 234.

means no emailing, text messaging, tweeting, blogging or any other form of communication."[30]

San Francisco courts, for their part, are in the process of implementing the distribution of standard mandatory juror questionnaires and instructions, explicitly prohibiting independent cyber research and the like: "You may not do research about any issues involved in the case. You may not blog, Tweet, or use the Internet to obtain or share information."[31]

To facilitate matters, the National Center for State Courts provides sample instructions that may be used by judges throughout the United States (and possibly even beyond). Finally and more rigorously perhaps, in response to mounting incidents of cyber use by jurors (be it for independent research or proscribed communications), the Judicial Conference of the United States "issued 'Twitter instructions' to every federal judge, to be read to jurors at the beginning of a trial and before jury deliberations begin. These recommended federal instructions prohibit the use of any electronic device or media in connection with the case, as well as any website use, such as Facebook."[32]

E. ADMONITION AND PUNISHMENT

"So folks need to lighten up"[33]
— Al Roker

Although specific instructions do represent an important step forward, the prevailing social culture, which can best be described as somewhat dismissive of even the inappropriate use of new technologies as inevitable or innocuous (as illustrated by Al Roker's comment) notwithstanding the violence to fairness of process, invites courts to consider additional steps.

---

30 National Center for State Courts, "Cell Phone Policies/Instructions for Jurors" *Jur-E Bulletin* (1 May 2009).

31 Kate Moser, "Court Lays Down Law on Jury Internet Use" *The Recorder* (9 September 2009), online: www.courts.wa.gov/content/PublicUpload/eclips/9.9.09%20law.com.pdf.

32 Kathleen Elliott Vinson, "The Blurred Boundaries of Social Networking in the Legal Field: Just 'Face' It" (2010) 41 *University of Memphis Law Review* 355 at 410.

33 TV weatherman Al Roker's comments in response to his tweeting his jury experience. Corky Siemaszko, "Al Roker Gets Ripped for Snapping Court Pix & Tweeting during Jury Duty" *NY Daily News* (28 May 2009), online: www.nydailynews.com/entertainment/tv-movies/al-roker-ripped-snapping-court-pix-tweeting-jury-duty-article-1.374749.

Consequently, having jurors sign a declaration committing to refrain from inappropriate Internet use and imposing day fines as sanction for those who do not comply is another useful measure, increasingly gaining traction in the United States and abroad.[34] Originating in Europe, day fines are meant to dissuade and punish inappropriate behaviour in court by foreseeing admonition proportionate to the severity of the offence and intended to have a similar economic resonance on individuals of dissimilar means, convicted of the same offence. Thus, for instance, in the United States (in Michigan) one juror, Hadley Jons, was removed and admonished for posting a biased comment about the case on Facebook. She was fined $250 and ordered to write a five-page essay on the Sixth Amendment of the Constitution.[35] As fate would have it (and illustrating the importance of tracking case-related cyber activity, noted below), the defence attorney's son had found the following troubling Facebook post by Jons while googling a juror prior to deliberations: "it's gonna be fun to tell the defendant they're guilty."[36] Presumably, Jons was of modest means; otherwise, a heftier fine would be required in light of the above-stated rationale relating to day fines!

To reiterate a key idea: Social networking's Achilles heel lies in its beauty, in the access that for the most part it offers, which can allow courts and attorneys to more readily uncover breaches that in past years were just as damaging but not so easily discovered.

Albeit a step in the right direction, the punishment in the Jons case appears mild in comparison to the jail time afforded the above-mentioned UK (Manchester) juror who, unlike her seemingly mean-spirited Michigan counterpart, acted in good faith, however ignorant of the effect of her actions on the fairness of trial.[37]

Clearly, the United Kingdom has gone much further than the United States in terms of punishment for juror cyber use, including not only day fines but also incarceration for contempt. Relatedly, and again in the United Kingdom, a pioneering court issued an injunction, the first of its kind, explicitly barring the sharing of information on Facebook or Twitter

---

34 Bureau of Justice Assistance, *How to Use Structured Fines (Day Fines) as an Intermediate Sanction* (November 1996) at 1 and 4, online: www.ncjrs.gov/pdffiles/156242.pdf.

35 Clark et al, above note 29 at 91.

36 Martha Neil, "Oops. Juror Calls Defendant Guilty on Facebook, before Verdict" *ABA Journal* (2 September 2010), online: www.abajournal.com/news/article/oops._juror_calls_defendant_guilty_on_facebook_though_verdict_isnt_in.

37 See above note 25 and accompanying text.

(and the like).[38] The ban is on publishing information on any "social network or media including Twitter or Facebook," as well as in other media.[39]

F. ADDITIONAL PRECAUTIONARY AND PROACTIVE MEANS

Attorneys, as previously alluded to, have their part to play in the process. With an eye towards preserving fairness of trial, lawyers should consider incorporating explicit questions on social networking and Internet use more generally whenever *voir dire* is available.[40] Taking such a proactive measure might enable trial lawyers to better root out active bloggers or social networkers, who might naturally find it more difficult — if not almost physically painful — to refrain from engaging in their usual pastime, possibly even obsession. That, in turn, would reduce the number of awkward instances where an attorney, as an officer of the court, is held to report improper cyber activity by one or more jurors to the judge.[41]

Such reporting has gained support. "In *R v Davey*,[42] Karakatsanis J commented that information discovered on the Internet in a 'readily accessible' way need not be disclosed, thereby implicitly endorsing the view that Internet searches of potential jurors are acceptable."[43] Moreover, the Law Society of Upper Canada's *Rules of Professional Conduct* support the view that it is acceptable to search the online profiles of prospective jurors. The Ontario rules specifically permit lawyers to "investigate" the suitability of prospective jurors. The commentary relating to Rule 5.5-1 reads:

> A lawyer may investigate a prospective juror to ascertain any basis for challenge provided that the lawyer does not directly or indirectly communicate with the juror or with any member of the juror's family. But a lawyer should not conduct or cause another by financial support or

---

38 Charles Arthur, "Twitter and Facebook Publication Banned for the First Time in Injunction" *The Guardian* (13 May 2011), online: http://gu.com/p/2p42h/stw.

39 *Ibid.*

40 As per David A Soley, former chair of the ABA Litigation Section's Trial Practice Committee, quoted in Harris, above note 20.

41 "'If you learn about a substantive twitter during the case, weigh carefully your obligation to report it to the judge,' says Soley. You are an officer of the court, he cautions, and '[need to] remember your reporting obligation holds true regardless of whether the post is positive or negative for your client'": Harris, *ibid.*

42 2012 SCC 75.

43 Michal Fairburn, "Social Media and the Jury: Could Technology Have Saved Tom Robinson?" (2013) 32:3 *Advocates' Journal* 7 at para 18.

otherwise, to conduct a vexatious or harassing investigation of either a member of the jury panel or a juror.[44]

It is important to note that, while Rule 5.5-1 authorizes lawyers to "investigate" prospective jurors to determine whether to challenge, it precludes lawyers from communicating directly or indirectly with any prospective jurors and their families. In light of the non-communication rule, lawyers would be well advised to understand the technology engaged as they search on the Internet. Passively searching jurors' publicly available online profiles is one thing; attempting to bypass privacy shields is quite another.

Regardless of any prior investigation, attorneys should, given the pervasiveness of the phenomenon and potential harms, take it upon themselves to reasonably monitor popular sites and conduct relevant cyber searches during trial in order to unearth any improper activity before it compromises the process. That, of course, raises questions about whether jurors might be required to disclose passwords related to their social networking activities, either *ab initio* or on reasonable suspicion of breach of duty, and the obvious privacy implications. This having been said, social media are not always adversaries to justice.

Although many courts are choosing to ban portable devices enabling such features from the courtroom, "the Federal Court in Australia has decided that as with other media, individual judges will be able to decide on a case by case basis if they will allow live Twitter coverage from within their courtrooms."[45]

Another approach, although not a panacea, offers one way to balance the benefits of technology while maintaining fairness and the appearance of propriety. A suggested interim measure is to institute the sorts of filters used for exams on personal computers (laptops) in law schools (and similar institutions),[46] which allow individuals to keep their devices, all while preventing access to sites (such as Twitter or Facebook) deemed most problematic in this context.

---

44 Online: www.lsuc.on.ca/uploadedFiles/RulesofProfessionalConduct.pdf.

45 Jennifer Van Grove, "Who Needs Cameras? Judges Allow Twitter in the Courtroom" *Mashable* (19 October 2009), online: http://mashable.com/2009/10/19/twitter-australia-courts.

46 Called "blocked" laptop exams. See online, for example: www.law.umich.edu/currentstudents/registration/exams/Pages/laptopExamInformation.aspx#blocked.

Conclusion
A Final Word

The illusion of accuracy that is fostered by Internet resources, both in terms of judicial out-of-court expression and of independent research (by judges and jurors) *inter alia*, seems to underlie many of the hardships associated therewith. Approaching the networked environment with cautious openness rather than with trepidation or unbridled enthusiasm is a simple, but helpful stance. Reflection is required in order to ensure that the benefits of technology are harnessed towards the better administration of justice, rather than subverted for undermining public confidence or further curtailing necessary judicial activities. The Internet age — with its promises and hurdles — cannot bypass the judiciary.

Too often, it has become almost instinctual to seek out "new and improved" standards, but this approach is not the most useful. Although advances in science and technology do at times cry out for rethinking outdated constructs, reverting to existing frameworks — informed, but not necessarily transformed by technological change and enlightened by comparative inquiry and proportionality — is more apropos. For we are no longer dealing with an irreducible conflict between hopelessly opposed entities — privacy and access (as discussed in Chapter 3) or the "political judge" versus the "neutral," or removed, judge (as discussed in Chapters 5 and 6). Instead, the duty to protect privacy can — and must — be construed as part of courts' responsibility to maintain access to justice *and* prevent disinformation in their new capacity as "publishers." So, too, might the traditional duty of reserve be balanced against the judge's responsibility not to be cut off from society in the digital age.

Privacy more generally is no longer about the right to be left alone. In its place, in this Web-dependent age, privacy might ultimately be *about* the very access to justice we seek to protect and its integrity. As alluded to above, unbridled postings (about litigants or judges themselves) create the illusion of "access." Although third parties unrelated to the proceedings can easily collect the most intimate details concerning the litigants, witnesses, and others, participants are left unprotected notwithstanding the court's duty towards them. Not surprisingly then, sacrificing participants' right to dignity and privacy in the justice process for the illusion of transparency, coupled with a significant loss of judicial control over how and what information is disseminated online, eventually risks fostering an unwillingness to participate in the justice process. Thus, paradoxically, the very access to justice that the digital revolution meant to enhance is undermined.

Comparative analysis, as former Israeli chief justice Aharon Barak observes, is an "important source of inspiration, one that enriches legal thinking, makes law more creative, and strengthens the ties and foundations of different legal systems."[1]

The civil legal method's conception of privacy as personality rights, with their countervailing duties, appears commensurable with privacy management in an age of rapid technological advances. Consider the personality rights paradigm used at a high level of abstraction. Loss of meaningful control over the integrity of information rather than freedom from observation constitutes the primary privacy harm, as illustrated by the German example and its focus on "informational self-determination." Instead of opening the dreaded floodgates, however, this seemingly broad and dignity-centric conception is pragmatically tempered by a profound attachment to the notion of duties alongside rights, fostering empowerment and responsibility.

Perhaps this glimpse into civilian thinking can eventually lead to an alternative, cross-cultural (hybrid) approach to conceptualizing privacy in the digital context. In other words, while the old notion of aloneness or seclusion is passé, privacy as the inherent right and duty to control one's identity — and privacy harm as the loss of that autonomy — is very much alive (be one a judge or a litigant).

Privacy, it follows, becomes a matter of affirmative rather than negative rights. In other words, it can be conceived as the right to engage in individual self-definition and self-invention rather than seclusion or the freedom from surveillance. To adopt civilian parlance (with rights as corollaries of duties), it is also the responsibility not to unnecessarily

---

1 Adam Liptak, "U.S. Supreme Court's Global Influence Is Waning" *The New York Times* (17 September 2008), online: http://nyti.ms/1OnQD65.

compromise one's own information in the naive hope that it will not be misused.

With an eye towards eventually crafting a transsystemically viable framework, clarifying what we mean by "privacy" is crucial to courts and litigants. In light of the enduring, potentially devastating ramifications of privacy blunders, judges dependent on the public trust and litigants themselves share a profound interest in rethinking the basic concepts that populate the current privacy framework(s). If nothing else, continental thinking, as the preceding suggests, can help advance that discussion.

That having been said, it is worth reiterating the modest idea that the potential of technology should be set in critical context mindful of existing principled frameworks. This approach constitutes an effort to bring some direction to the discussion on the Internet's effect on courts and judicial ethics. It seeks to foster awareness of the effect of technology use on judging, to identify and guard against some of the risks associated with technological changes, and to nurture a process of reflection thereupon. Once these issues are identified and characterized, it will, of course, be possible to devise strategies aimed at reducing the difficulties in question.

Appendix

May 22, 2009
MEMORANDUM
To: Chief Judges, United States Courts
From: James C. Duff
RE: INTERNET MATERIALS IN JUDICIAL OPINIONS AND ORDERS **(ACTION REQUIRED)**

At its March 2009 session, the Judicial Conference approved a policy that "all Internet materials cited in final opinions be considered for preservation" and that "[e]ach judge . . . should retain the discretion to decide whether the specific cited resource should be captured and preserved." The Conference directed Administrative Office (AO) staff to work with the Court Administration and Case Management Committee to develop guidelines to assist judges in determining whether and how to use citations to Internet sites, preserve cited materials, and use hyperlinks in their opinions and orders. That guidance is attached.[1]

Judges are citing to and using Internet-based information in their opinions with increasing frequency. Unlike printed authority, Internet

1 These guidelines were based on recommendations made to the Committee on Court Administration and Case Management by an ad hoc working group of circuit librarians who had experimented with capturing and preserving Internet resources cited in circuit judges' opinions. The group made its recommendations with the input of other AO advisory groups.

information is often not maintained at a permanent location, and a cited web page can be changed or deleted at any time. Obviously, this has significant implications for the reliability of citations in court opinions. To address this issue, the attached guidelines suggest practices for judges and their staffs regarding the use and preservation of cited Internet data. The guidelines suggest that if a web page is cited, chambers staff could preserve the citation by downloading a copy of the site's page and filing it as an attachment to the judicial opinion in the CM/ECF system. The attachment, like the opinion, would be retrievable on a non-fee basis through PACER.

Another concern is the use of hyperlinks to commercial databases (such as Westlaw or LexisNexis) in court opinions. Use of these links in opinions could create an inappropriate appearance that a judge endorses a particular vendor or service provider. The Judicial Conference recommends that judges either eliminate such hyperlinks or include a disclaimer in their opinions. A sample disclaimer is included in the attached guidelines.

We encourage your court to consider these guidelines in developing any local policies. Also, one year from the date of this memorandum, you will be asked to inform the Court Administration and Case Management Committee of your court's progress so that we may reexamine the process and ensure that these concerns are being addressed appropriately. We will provide you with a reminder when the reporting time is near.

If you have any questions, please contact Mark Miskovsky or Jane MacCracken of the Court Administration Policy Staff at (202) 502-1560.

Attachment

....

GUIDELINES ON CITING TO, CAPTURING, AND MAINTAINING INTERNET RESOURCES IN JUDICIAL OPINIONS/USING HYPERLINKS IN JUDICIAL OPINIONS

1. REVIEWING WHETHER TO CITE TO INTERNET RESOURCES IN JUDICIAL OPINIONS

In determining whether to cite to Internet resources in their opinions, judges should consider the following:

- Especially in situations where the cited material cannot be found in an authoritative print resource or the Internet site or information itself is the subject of the opinion, citation to an Internet address or URL[2] in a footnote or in a textual citation may be necessary.

- Some litigants, particularly those who are *pro se*, may not have access to electronic resources. Judges should be mindful of this when considering whether to cite Internet sources.
- The material should be stable and likely to remain accessible using the citation the judge employed when originally visiting the site.
- Judges should apply the same evaluation criteria to the Internet sources they cite in their opinions as they would apply to more traditional media:
  (1) Accuracy—the factual correctness and completeness of the information.
    - Is there a second reliable source that gives the same information?
    - Is it a peer-reviewed source?
    - Does the publisher use editors and fact checkers?
    - Is the citation made to original and official source documents?
  (2) Scope of coverage—the extent to which the source examines a topic.
    - Does the source cover a particular period of time, geographic region, or other aspects of a topic?
    - Does the source provide information about its scope?
  (3) Objectivity—the absence of bias with respect to interpretation or analysis of facts.
    - Is the source trying to persuade you?
    - Who sponsors or publishes the information?
    - What can you discover about their intentions?
  (4) Timeliness—the information is current at the time of publication.
    - Does the source provide a date for this specific webpage or entry, as opposed to a general site revision date?
  (5) Authority—the reliability of the source of information.
    - Can you determine the name of the author and publisher?
    - Is the author a recognized expert on the topic?
    - What is the publisher's reputation?
  (6) Verifiability—the ability to confirm the facts or information.
    - Is there a second reliable source (especially when using resources such as administrative regulations or statutes)?
    - Does the material cite to its sources of information?

---

2 The URL or "Uniform Resource Locator" is a format for the address of an Internet document; this address is used by a browser in locating the relevant document on the Internet.

- Judges are encouraged to seek assistance from their librarians in finding the best resource to cite to, including finding the most authoritative and stable Internet-based source to rely upon and/or alternatives to Internet versions of resources, if they exist. Where there is a readily accessible and reliable print version of the cited resource, it may not be necessary to cite to the Internet version.
- As with citation to any other resource, applicable rules of citation, for instance, Rule 18.2 of ***The Bluebook: A Uniform System of Citation*** (18th ed. 2005), should be followed.
- URLs should be carefully reproduced and then confirmed. Cutting and pasting the citations from a browser's address window will help to ensure accuracy. Be aware, however, that some links are automatically inserted when you cut and paste. One way to avoid this is to use the "paste special" option in your word processing software; in addition, you may need to change the automatic formatting so that a live hyperlink is not created when a URL is pasted into the document.

2. EVALUATING WHETHER TO CAPTURE CITED INTERNET RESOURCES

When determining whether to capture and preserve Internet resources cited in opinions, judges should consider the following:

- **If a cited Internet resource is fundamental to the reasoning of the opinion and refers to a legal authority or precedent that cannot be obtained in any other format (such as a published print resource), it is recommended that it be captured and preserved and attached as part of the opinion.**
- If there is particular reason to expect that the cited Internet resource will be removed from the website or altered, it is recommended that it be captured and preserved.
- Where there is a readily accessible and reliable print version of the cited Internet resource, it may not be necessary to capture the Internet version.
- If an Internet resource is cited simply for the purposes of background or illustration, it may not be necessary to capture the cited resource.
- Where the court chooses not to capture or preserve a cited Internet resource, it may want to provide a disclaimer alerting readers that, by citing to an Internet resource, the judiciary does not exercise any responsibility over the content of the Internet resource or the current viability of the URL provided.

3. CAPTURING CITED INTERNET RESOURCES

When capturing and preserving Internet resources cited in opinions, judges should consider the following:

- If it is determined that an Internet resource to be cited in an opinion is to be captured, it should be downloaded and preserved as closely as possible to the time it is viewed by chambers, to ensure that the exact version of the Internet resource that was relied upon by the judge will be preserved.
- It is recommended that the downloaded webpage or document be converted into PDF format. (See instructions on page 5 describing the process for capturing a webpage and converting it to a PDF document.)
- It is suggested that the captured resource include some notation of the date it was viewed and the case to which it relates. One method to accomplish this is to insert a "watermark" indicating the case in which the resource is to be cited and the date the resource was viewed. (See instructions on page 5 describing the process for inserting a watermark into a PDF document.)
- **It is recommended that courts utilize CM/ECF to maintain the captured Internet materials together with the opinion.** The specifics of the actual process by which the Internet resources are integrated into CM/ECF are to be determined by local court policy and operational procedures.
- Public access to the captured materials may need to be limited to the extent cited materials are protected by copyright law; if necessary, prior to publication on PACER, appropriate measures, such as delay in posting, obtaining permission or license, or other special treatment may be taken. If copyrighted materials are cited and captured, any copyright notice appearing on the materials should also be captured.
- Courts also may want to require counsel to capture and attach Internet resources cited in motions or briefs filed with the court, to ensure that the information relied upon by counsel is readily available to the judge.

4. INSERTING WORKING HYPERLINKS IN OPINIONS

When considering whether to include working hyperlinks in opinions, judges should consider the following:

- Generally, judges should avoid including working hyperlinks that lead directly to a commercial vendor's fee-based version of a cited resource.

- If the court or judge determines, as a matter of policy, to include working hyperlinks leading directly to a commercial fee-based Internet service, appropriate disclaimer language should be provided. The disclaimer should alert readers that, by including working commercial hyperlinks in the opinion, the judiciary does not endorse the product or organization at the destination, exercise any responsibility over the content at the destination, guarantee that the hyperlink is currently working or that the hyperlink is to the same content as that relied upon by the court, or receive any remuneration or special consideration when a reader pays the commercial vendor to access the information. Sample disclaimer language reads as follows:

  > The court accepts no responsibility for, and does not endorse, any product, organization, or content at any hyperlinked site, or at any site to which that site might be linked. The court accepts no responsibility for the availability or functionality of any hyperlink. Thus, the fact that a hyperlink ceases to work or directs the user to some other site does not affect the opinion of the court.

- Where an opinion cites to another federal court opinion, courts can include a working hyperlink to the CM/ECF or PACER version, if currently available within CM/ECF or PACER.

5. INSTRUCTIONS FOR CONVERTING A WEBPAGE TO PDF AND CREATING A WATERMARK[3]

(1) When at the page you want to archive, right click and select "Convert to Adobe PDF."
(2) When the conversion is complete, the webpage will open in Adobe Acrobat as a PDF.
(3) Select "Document" then select "Add Watermark and Background." This page will open:

[screen capture omitted]

Working from this page, you will do the following:

1. Under "Type" select "Add a Watermark."
2. Under "Source," type in the box what you want the watermark to say. We recommend: "Last viewed by [Judge/Law clerk] on [DATE]."

---

3 Created by Michelle Ayers, Third Circuit Library, 2008.

3. Under "Position" and "Appearance," change "rotation" to 25% and "opacity" to 25%.
4. Click OK. You should then see your watermark.
5. Save the PDF to the appropriate file.

Table of Cases

Index

About the Author

Karen Eltis is a law professor specializing in Internet law and policy (privacy and data security), comparative law, and democratic governance. She is a tenured professor at the Faculty of Law of the University of Ottawa, Canada (*Section de droit civil*), the former co-director of the Centre for Law, Technology and Society, and director of the Human Rights Centre. Professor Eltis is also an associate adjunct professor and visiting scholar at Columbia Law School in New York, where she focuses on the impact of new technologies on constitutional rights. She served as senior advisor to the National Judicial Institute where her focus was bijuralism, technology, and ethics. Fluent in French, English, Hebrew, Romanian, and Spanish, Professor Eltis holds law degrees from McGill University, the Hebrew University of Jerusalem, and Columbia Law School (Harlan Fiske Stone Scholar). She clerked for Chief Justice Aharon Barak of the Supreme Court of Israel. Prior to joining the faculty at the University of Ottawa, Professor Eltis was a litigation associate in New York City, practising in the area of international dispute resolution.

FSC
www.fsc.org
MIX
Papier | Fördert
gute Waldnutzung
FSC® C083411

Kolibri 360 GmbH
Ferdinand-Jühlke-Straße 7
99095 Erfurt, Deutschland
produktsicherheit@kolibri360.de